A M E R I C A N
HOMELESSNESS

A Reference Handbook

Third Edition

Other Titles in ABC-CLIO's
Contemporary
World Issues
Series

Books in the Contemporary World Issues series address vital issues in today's society such as genetic engineering, pollution, and biodiversity. Written by professional writers, scholars, and nonacademic experts, these books are authoritative, clearly written, up-to-date, and objective. They provide a good starting point for research by high school and college students, scholars, and general readers as well as by legislators, businesspeople, activists, and others.

Each book, carefully organized and easy to use, contains an overview of the subject, a detailed chronology, biographical sketches, facts and data and/or documents and other primary-source material, a directory of organizations and agencies, annotated lists of print and nonprint resources, and an index.

Readers of books in the Contemporary World Issues series will find the information they need in order to have a better understanding of the social, political, environmental, and economic issues facing the world today.

AMERICAN HOMELESSNESS

A Reference Handbook

Third Edition

Mary Ellen Hombs

**CONTEMPORARY
WORLD ISSUES**

ABC-CLIO

Santa Barbara, California   Denver, Colorado   Oxford, England

Library of Congress Cataloging-in-Publication Data
Hombs, Mary Ellen.
   American homelessness: A Reference Handbook / Mary Ellen
Hombs.—3rd ed.
      p.   cm.
   Includes index.
   ISBN 1-57607-247-9 (hardcover : alk. paper)
   1. Homelessness—United States—Handbooks, manuals, etc.
I. Title.
HV4505.H647   2001
362.5'0973—dc21

                                                    2001002779

06   05   04   03   02   10 9 8 7 6 5 4 3 2

This book is also available on the World Wide Web as an e-book. Visit abc-clio.com for details.

ABC-CLIO, Inc.
130 Cremona Drive, P.O. Box 1911
Santa Barbara, California 93116-1911

This book is printed on acid-free paper ∞.
Manufactured in the United States of America.

Contents

Preface

The problem of homelessness in the United States has grown dramatically since it first became very visible during the 1980s, and responses to it have changed. Most people once gleaned their knowledge about homelessness from media reports during winter months and holiday periods. Later, increasing numbers of Americans began to see homeless people in their daily travel between home and work or school. Now we are accustomed to finding the indications of homelessness around us in public places, whether it is seeing a person carrying their belongings or pushing a shopping cart, or someone asking for money on the street or holding a sign asking for help. We sometimes read about fundraising events for local shelters and soup kitchens. But, on the whole, we find less media coverage than ever before. Often coverage focuses on negative events, such as a shelter attempting to open in the face of neighbors' opposition or a public incident involving a homeless person with mental illness. There is also less high-profile public advocacy than in the 1980s. What once seemed to be an emergency in our country now appears to be such an ongoing problem that many younger people have never known a time when homelessness of this scale did not exist.

Although the problem has become more commonplace, it seems difficult to solve, and ordinary citizens and policymakers question what actions they should take in response to it. For example, individuals question whether they should give money to apparently homeless people because they have doubts about whether it helps the person, and many communities have passed laws to control "aggressive" public requests for money. Advocates question whether a problem caused when a person loses their place to live is solved by a cot in a shelter, yet housing prices in many areas have steadily climbed out of reach of even moderate income people and production of subsidized housing is at an all time low. Policymakers question whether people should be entitled to ongoing services without work or some personal investment being expected in return, and welfare programs nationally have been drastically overhauled during the last eight years with just that aim. Others suggest that homeless people should find jobs like other people, but research shows that many homeless people have jobs and cannot afford housing.

It is indisputable that homelessness has become deeply rooted in the United States over the last twenty years. During that time, a massive federal effort has been passed in legislation and funded with ever greater sums of tax dollars. A 1999 federal report found over 40,000 programs serving homeless people. Beginning in the late 1990s, a surge of economic growth brought unprecedented prosperity to the United States—and unprecedented levels of homelessness. In New York City in early 2001, the number of homeless people was reported to be at its highest level since the late 1980s. In Massachusetts in 2001, adult shelters entered their third year of overflow occupancy. The annual survey of the U.S. Conference of Mayors reported an average 15 percent increase nationally in demand for shelter, the largest increase since 1990.

More policymakers than ever before understand that effective solutions to homelessness require the examination of many interrelated factors and systems, including the housing and labor markets, the health care system (including the systems for mental health and substance abuse treatment), the foster care and juvenile justice systems, the federal, state, and local corrections systems, and welfare programs. But for ordinary citizens and policymakers alike, this seems like an overwhelming task. And it is one that removes from our sight, our thinking, and from the public debate a moral dimension to the dialogue, any reminder of the actual suffering of the men, women, and children who are experiencing homelessness.

In December 1993, a dramatic event occurred in Washington, D.C., that underscored this individual human reality meeting the world of policy and programs, showing just how close homelessness is to our everyday lives. A woman who had been chronically mentally ill and in and out of homelessness was found dead one morning in a bus shelter where she had been sleeping. The bus shelter was located outside the U.S. Department of Housing and Urban Development (HUD), the federal agency charged with administering the largest federal homeless programs. HUD secretary Henry Cisneros, who had recently said that ending homelessness would be his top priority, declared the woman's death a wake-up call for Americans to do more and to prove people were not tired of trying to solve the problem.

Cisneros ordered emergency spending for the winter months and told his employees to assist any homeless person they saw, including bringing homeless people into the HUD building for shelter. For many people, the individual toll of homelessness was recalled with an urgency that had been missing from the public dialogue. The emergency programs Cisneros funded within a few weeks of that event have shown many successes and have become established services in their communities. And homelessness has continued to grow. Cisneros himself felt this frustration, and when he left office in 1996, he characterized efforts to reduce homelessness as being like "bailing a leaking boat." The numbers of homeless people and federal programs have continued to grow ever since, supported by record federal appropriations.

The deep roots of homelessness are reflected not only in the dimensions of the problem itself but in the resources that have evolved to deal with it. Not only are there now many service and advocacy organizations across the nation, but virtually every state has a homeless organization addressing state policy. We know a good deal more about homelessness from research, and our information resources have developed along with the growth of electronic communications. Specialized newsletters and databases are available. National organizations have formed. We can visit web sites to learn about homelessness in other countries. We can read what homeless people have to say about their experiences.

The problem of homelessness shows no sign of ending. It is frustrating and challenging, but we can understand some key facts about it, and we can examine successes in addressing it. This book offers resources to do that, as well as the tools to locate current information. It is no longer possible to list all of the resources available, because they have proliferated so rapidly and in so many directions. Homelessness has been with us for so long that some resources, events, and data are outdated.

Chapter 1 provides an introduction to the fundamentals of the problem of homelessness. Who is homeless and why? How many people are homeless, and what do we know about them? Chapter 2 looks at important events in the contemporary development of the problem. Chapter 3 profiles some key individuals who have had a significant impact on public awareness, responses to homelessness, or research.

Chapter 4 presents some of the available factual material about homelessness and poverty, including information on public programs and use of services. Chapter 5 includes excerpts and material from published documents and reports that reflect the range of issues and policy questions on homelessness. Chapter 6 summarizes significant federal legislation on homelessness, including the McKinney-Vento Act and other key international documents. Chapter 7 provides a summary of how the law has been used in response to homelessness in the United States and internationally. It examines both the role of litigation and the use of international agreements.

Chapter 8 provides a directory of organizations in the United States and other countries that are working on issues of homelessness. Chapter 9 offers references to some of the key printed materials on homelessness and related issues, as well as government reports and resources, and highlights video resources, computer databases, and the increasing number of electronic resources. A glossary at the end of the book provides useful terms for understanding the range of issues and programs that people need to consider to gain a full understanding of homelessness.

This book provides a tool for understanding homelessness. Some readers may admire or question the efforts they read about, or agree or disagree with the theories presented, but it is important to remember that the problem of homelessness is the problem of individuals—men, women, and children who must consider every day, as best they can, where to sleep that night, where to get a meal, where to get out of the weather, and where to sit down for a moment. Whatever understanding comes from reading this book should be translated into a commitment to ending homelessness and setting aright the lives of those who experience it.

There are those among us who have made it their work to respond to homelessness—to explain it, to address it, to question it. Many of us have worked far longer than we ever expected and have seen less progress than we anticipated from our efforts. I have had the privilege of knowing and working with most of the individuals whose work is presented in this book. I know the depth of their personal commitment to preventing and ending homelessness. I thank them for their work and their partnership in the challenge of advocating for those who are our poorest neighbors.

1

Introduction

How does homelessness persist and even grow in the United States even though more is being done to address the problem and at the same time the prospering U.S. economy is driving unemployment to record lows? A 1996 national survey sponsored by twelve federal government agencies found about 40,000 food, shelter, and service programs for homeless people in the United States (Burt et al. 1999). Unemployment in late 2000 stood at 3.9 percent, its lowest level since 1969, and wages for the lowest-paid workers began to increase after a period of steady decline (CBPP 2000). How has such a paradoxical situation drawn less and less public attention in the nation? This book provides an overview of key materials that will help the reader explore these questions.[1]

Homelessness as a growing problem is not confined to the United States. The second part of this chapter and subsequent chapters also provide insights into homelessness in Western Europe, Canada, and Australia. Europe presents the unique characteristic of being a multitiered system in which policy is made both in the nations and increasingly within the European Union (EU).

In the United States, we typically know little of the governing systems, social welfare policies, or key issues of other countries. As the European countries evolve a more borderless society and economy, what problems are they confronting in addressing domestic homelessness, as well as the influx of immigrant populations? What role do their social systems and housing markets play in addressing homelessness? The role of these systems may be especially key during the emergence of a common European economic market with shared social policies. This development itself may mirror the tiered federal-state system of the United States, where some states have historically been more involved than others in budgeting state funds to address homelessness, while also seeking and using federal resources.

Recent Developments in the United States

In October of 2000, a presidential election year in the United States, record levels of funding were appropriated by the 106th Congress for federal homeless programs operated by the U.S. Department of Housing and Urban Development (HUD). Included in the HUD budget bill were two provisions that offer clues to the state of the homelessness problem more than twenty years after it emerged in its modern form in the United States and thirteen years after federal programs were first put into place to address homelessness. One provision established a temporary and separate funding mechanism for the continued funding of existing permanent housing programs for formerly homeless people with disabilities. A second provision allowed the secretary of HUD to withhold homeless assistance funds from state and local governments that apply for them, when those government entities do not have in place the means to prevent the homelessness of individuals already in their care or custody in other public institutions, such as hospitals and prisons (P.L. 106-377, 2000). This last provision signifies a new measure to address a form of homelessness that results when a person who has been hospitalized or incarcerated is ready to leave the public institution in which they have been living, but has no place to go in the community. The practice of sending or discharging individuals into the community when they no longer need to be in an institution is called deinstitutionalization. The preparation of that person for their eventual release is called discharge or aftercare planning.

For example, the person may have no family to go to, or may have lost their home while they were in the hospital. If the individual just received treatment for mental or physical illness, the lack of a stable, safe place to live may cause a relapse of their illness. If the person has been incarcerated, the lack of a home or a job may cause them to commit a crime. If the person is eighteen years old and has been released from foster care, he or she may not have the skills to get a job or the money to rent an apartment.

Who is responsible to see that the person has a stable place to go when they leave these situations? Do publicly funded institutions have a responsibility to provide reintegration resources, such as transitional programs, in the community rather than creating homelessness by sending individuals in these situations to homeless shelters?

Each of these three steps taken by Congress—the appropriation of record amounts of funding, the future underwriting of housing for formerly homeless people, and the direction to the states not to seek federal funding to solve a situation of homelessness for which they might be responsible—came at a time when levels of homelessness among men, women, and children across the nation were reaching new records. According to the U.S. Conference of Mayors' Status Report on Hunger and Homelessness in America's Cities 2000, requests for shelter had grown at the highest rate since 1990, with an average of a 15 percent increase in requests for shelter. A total of 80 percent of the survey cities reported increases in shelter demand.

These congressional changes also came during a year and an era when stock markets climbed to records never imagined, during a period of unparalleled national economic prosperity and lowered poverty rates. According to figures based on a report from the Center on Budget and Policy Priorities (CBPP), the number of Americans living in poverty declined to its lowest point in more than twenty years, dropping to 11.8 percent of the population. Furthermore, "rates for people 65 and over, African-Americans, people living in the South, and families headed by single women fell to all-time lows. Among non-Hispanic whites and Hispanics, poverty rates fell to levels statistically equal to the previous all-time lows for these groups. . . . The new Census data, which cover income as well as poverty status, also show that median household income reached a new high in 1999. . . . The Census data show that the reduction in poverty in 1999 was concentrated in the nation's cities, with 81 percent of the drop in poverty between 1998 and 1999 occurring in the cities, as distinguished from suburbs and non-metropolitan areas. The number of poor people nationally fell by 2.2 million, from 34.5 million to 32.3 million. Some 118 million of this 2.2 million drop occurred in the cities" (CBPP 2000).

And finally, these changes came four years after the passage of major federal welfare reform legislation, which resulted in welfare rolls dropping by more than 50 percent (Pear 2000).

How does homelessness persist and increase in the United States in these economic conditions? A leading analyst of homelessness in the United States has demonstrated that the key factors affecting homelessness include a variety of interacting elements that center on income and housing:

- income, including social policies regarding benefits and people with disabilities
- unemployment and the job market
- availability of social and fiscal capital, levels of homeownership and renting
- the availability and cost of housing, including fiscal and monetary policy, interest rates, tax policy, the housing market, and government policy regarding low-cost housing (Burt 1992)

So, after years of the homelessness problem in the United States and analyses of it, do we know of any solutions? If homeless people are first and foremost people who lack housing, why, as one author has phrased it, is the "bottom of the housing distribution on the street, rather than at [an old lodginghouse]?" (O'Flaherty 1998). Many argue that we do know the solution to the problem—an ambitious expansion of available housing for this population—but we have not acted to provide the resources necessary (National Alliance to End Homelessness 2000). Although access to housing and a source of income have been shown to offer the key antidotes to homelessness, a range of public systems of care, treatment, and custody (mental health, substance abuse, child welfare, prison) has also been found to play critical roles in promoting stability and self-sufficiency and preventing homelessness. Beginning in the early 1980s, the problem of homelessness received increasing attention across the country; the sheer visibility of contemporary homelessness is perhaps its most identifiable attribute. Whether it is the sight of a person begging on the corner, a family living in a car, the countless homeless people in the streets and subways of big cities, or the ragged men and women silhouetted against the local monuments, striking images of this utmost poverty are inescapable for most Americans. Ultimately replacing the heavy media coverage of the mid-1980s were more intermittent and less sympathetic stories purporting to reveal the "truth" about homelessness. These stories included the reported incidence of drug use, prevalence of

HIV/AIDS, and lack of interest in employment among homeless people, as well as the exploitation of available resources (such as stories about people entering shelters in order to receive permanent housing). Gone—except for the traditional Thanksgiving and Christmas press coverage—were the stories asserting that "homeless people are just like us except they've had a few bad breaks."

Throughout the years, a pair of debates have continued. First, are there homeless and very poor people who are simply victims of bad luck and deserve our help and support, and are there also people whose own personal behavior—whether alcohol- or drug-related, whether because of laziness or lack of thrift—could be rectified by their own efforts and contribute to their more stable, more "normal" future? In other words, aren't some of the poor deserving of help, and some not? Second, what are the true dimensions of the homelessness problem?

News coverage and other articles actually began to increase in 1993, due to several factors. Shortly after U.S. Secretary of Housing and Urban Development Henry Cisneros declared homelessness to be his agency's top priority, a homeless woman died at a bus stop outside the agency. Just a few months later came the release of the federal plan on homelessness, prepared as a result of President Clinton's 1993 Executive Order; news of the report was carried around the nation (Interagency Council on the Homeless 1994). During the same period, more and more communities passed new laws or undertook enforcement campaigns of existing laws to regulate the behavior of homeless people in public spaces by prohibiting acts such as sleeping, storing belongings, or distributing food. These actions also brought new and increased press coverage, though seldom of a sympathetic nature.

If some truth is to be known about homelessness at this point, it is this rather complex realization: From coast to coast, communities of all sizes discovered within their own borders a new version of a problem many Americans previously associated only with the Depression years or with certain stereotypes. Homelessness now describes a more recent version of very poor people, one that involves single adults, families with children, and homeless youth (Burt et al. 1999).

Homelessness itself has not been new for more than twenty years. What is new is the size and scope of the problem, as well as the questions of how it has come about, whom it affects, and what our individual and collective attitudes and responses toward it are. In the 1980s, homelessness appeared to have reached epidemic proportions in this country. As the number of people affected continued to increase, service providers and public officials alike recognized that the problem is complex, touching on many issues of poverty such as public assistance, wage levels, and housing costs. Nor are these issues neatly confined to our borders any longer, as larger economic shifts are driven by global influences.

The nation faces a significant challenge: People continue to be pushed to the streets, programs are demonstrated to be effective in moving them from homelessness, and more people continue to join the ranks of the homeless. Reports show that homelessness is growing around the nation—in communities large and small—and families with children represent a rapidly expanding segment of that population, as do racial and ethnic minorities, who are disproportionately poor (Burt et al. 1999).

What Is Homelessness?

What are we talking about when we talk about homelessness? Are homeless people just those we see on our streets, begging or sleeping in parks? What about people in emergency shelters? What if an individual has a nearby relative and chooses not to stay with that person? Is someone homeless when friends or family offer temporary accommodations on a sofa? Or is that person at risk of becoming homeless if this arrangement fails? When we say a person is homeless, do we really mean he or she is houseless? Does homelessness mean more than the absence of shelter in its most fundamental form?

This question has been the focus of much discussion in the United States. There is no single, generally accepted definition of homelessness, although it should be apparent that the choice of definition has significant influence when estimating the size of the problem of homelessness. However, in many settings, the definition created in the 1987 federal McKinney Act is used as a standard.

> A homeless individual (1) lacks a fixed, regular, and adequate nighttime residence and (2) has a primary nighttime residence that is (a) a supervised, publicly or privately operated shelter designed to provide tem-

porary living accommodations (including welfare hotels, congregate shelters, and transitional housing for the mentally ill), (b) an institution that provides a temporary residence for individuals intended to be institutionalized, and (c) a public or private place not designed for, or ordinarily used as, a regular sleeping accommodation for human beings. (P.L.100-77 1987)

As noted by more than one analyst, this definition focuses on a housing oriented definition of homelessness, one that defines homelessness by "where you slept last night" (O'Flaherty 1998). Although many housed people derive at least a part of their identity from how they spend their waking hours—usually in compensated work—the possibility of employment or unemployment as a defining characteristic for homeless people is not a component of this definition. A recent national survey found that 44 percent of those homeless people interviewed had done paid work during the previous month (Burt et al. 1999). In the five years since federal welfare reform was signed into law, emphasizing employment over public assistance, employment levels among single, never-married women rose to 65 percent (Pear 2000).

Further, a definition based on shelter use overlooks the reality that shelter is not the only service used by homeless people, and not all shelters can or do admit anyone who comes to their doors. Thus, those in shelters or on the streets will constitute only a portion of those who may be homeless. What about those homeless people who use food programs, such as soup kitchens? As described by one national expert on the enumeration problem, "A lot of people avoid shelters . . . but they will eat" (Gugliotta 1994).

How Many People Are Homeless?

What are the dimensions of the problem of homelessness in the United States? From the difficulty revealed in arriving at a definition of homelessness, it should be apparent that there is no single adequate way to arrive at an estimate of the size of the population. There has been enormous controversy over numbers since homelessness began to burgeon in the early 1980s. Figures offered range from a low of 250,000 people to at least 3 million. The 250,000 figure was first asserted in the 1984 study released by the

U.S. Department of Housing and Urban Development (HUD). Assistant Secretary of Community Planning and Development S. Anna Kondratas was one of the chief public defenders of this figure, which was criticized as low by homeless advocates. The advocacy organizations, which included the Community for Creative Non-Violence and the National Coalition for the Homeless, however, continued to state that they believed that 3 million people are homeless.[2] Subsequent research, which reflected shelter use over multi-year periods, established relatively high percentages of homelessness.

Substantial problems of methodology exist in trying to count homeless people, not the least of which is that many homeless people work very hard to obscure their homelessness by dress, appearance, and daily schedule. They try to make their homelessness invisible to those who might not otherwise recognize it. Still others achieve invisibility by sleeping in abandoned buildings, in cars parked behind shopping malls, or in tents in the woods. As revealed by the definitional problem, the homelessness of many others is hidden by precarious housing arrangements with friends or families, circumstances that can be quickly ended.

As described in one summary of the problem: "Street counts have always been the Achilles heel of homeless studies. Finding people who don't want to be found, talking to people who don't want to talk, and searching for people who don't want to be found can make outdoor census taking haphazard at best" (Gugliotta 1994). Street and shelter counts frequently have been undertaken as one-night, or "point in time," counts, an approach that has inherent limits. Point in time counts do not include turnover, or use of beds or services over time, by several people in the course of a year. The Washington, D.C.-based Urban Institute conducted one such study in 1987, and it is given credibility by many observers. That study found that as many as 600,000 people were homeless during a one-week period in March 1987 (Burt and Cohen 1989).

A 1994 study in which 1,500 people were asked in a telephone survey about prior homeless experiences revealed high numbers. Bruce Link, a psychiatric epidemiologist at New York's Columbia University School of Public Health found that over 13.5 million Americans had been homeless at some point. These people had stayed in shelters, abandoned buildings, and depots or on the streets. Another 12.5 million had stayed with friends or family (Link et al. 1995).

New Insights From U.S. Research

The common idea about people who are homeless is that not much is known about them, that they are anonymous and alone. Data showing that many of the homeless are single men, who have never married and who may have physical, mental, and/or addiction problems, helps support the notion that these must be people separated from the mainstream and thus destined to remain homeless.

In the United States, much public policy for homeless adults (not families) has been based on stereotypes of these individuals as unreachable, isolated, and untreatable. However, the research of Dr. Dennis Culhane of the University of Pennsylvania during the 1990s employed a "hospital model" of length of stay in shelter beds to reveal that the population is made up of three distinct groups (Culhane and Kuhn 1998).

- The largest group (80 percent) is transitional, staying only a brief time in shelters and never returning. These individuals are helped by access to permanent housing and income through jobs. Their homelessness shows that safety net programs have failed to prevent their homelessness.
- A second group (10 percent) does stay and also returns. Their homeless cycle is responsive to assistance that effectively transitions them to self-sufficiency through more structured programs.
- The third group, for whom most policy is made, is the chronically homeless (10 percent). Their stays in shelters are virtually unbroken, their levels of disability from mental illness and substance abuse are deeper, and their almost permanent residence in emergency programs absorbs 50 percent of available funds. They are excellent candidates for supportive housing programs that combine appropriate services with housing subsidies.

Thus, according to this research, the largest portion of shelter beds—fully 80 percent—are occupied by individuals who stay only a short time and never return. Culhane found that bed turnover in most shelters was from four to seven times annually, putting into context the point in time model as an underestimate of homelessness during the course of a year. Policy and funding, however, have been shaped by the idea that the chronic population—which accounts for only 10 percent of shelter users—constitutes the majority profile.

Who Is Homeless?

Until the beginning of the 1980s, the prevailing stereotype of a homeless person was that of a middle-aged, white, urban, male alcoholic—a transient who either wandered the country (as a vagrant, tramp, or hobo) or inhabited downtown skid row areas characterized by low-cost hotels, rooming houses, and bars. Most of all, this person was viewed as shiftless for not living a responsible life with a job and a family. He was also considered blameworthy for whatever poverty, misery, or suffering that accompanied this voluntarily chosen lifestyle.

Traditionally, the only services available to this homeless person were church-based services, those of the mission establishments, such as the Salvation Army and the Gospel Mission, which offered overnight sleeping space and meals in exchange for a small fee and a sincere desire to rehabilitate one's life by attending mandatory sermons and renouncing alcohol.

No longer does this description of homeless people or homeless services hold true. As the causes of homelessness have broadened and become more tied to fundamental economic changes in our nation, homelessness has become both a symptom of chronic poverty and an event that cuts across traditional defenses of income, education, and geography. The population of the streets has been democratized correspondingly.

The most recent, large-scale, national study of homelessness found the following profile, described in more detail in Chapter 4.

- Members of homeless families make up 34 percent of homeless service users, and 84 percent of these are female. This includes 38 percent white non-Hispanic, 43 percent black non-Hispanic, 15 percent Hispanic, 3 percent Native American, and 1 percent other races. Some 26 percent are ages 17 to 24, 74 percent are ages 25 to 54, and less than 0.5 percent are ages 55 and older. 41 percent have never married.
- Single people make up 85 percent of homeless clients, and 77 percent are male. This includes 41 percent white

non-Hispanic, 40 percent black non-Hispanic, 10 percent Hispanic, 8 percent Native American, and 1 percent other races. People between the ages of 17 to 24 represent 10 percent of this group, 81 percent are ages 25 to 54, and 9 percent are ages 55 and older. In this group, 50 percent have never married.

- Of all homeless people, 40 percent went one or more days in the last 30 days without anything to eat. Within the prior month, 66 percent reported a mental health, drug, or alcohol problem. 55 percent have no medical insurance, and 46 percent report having chronic health conditions, such as arthritis, high blood pressure, diabetes, or cancer.
- A total of 44 percent of homeless people reported that they did paid work during the prior month, while 37 percent received food stamps. Of homeless families with children, 52 percent received Aid to Families with Dependent Children (AFDC).[3] 11 percent received Supplemental Security Income (SSI), and 30 percent received Medicaid.
- While 42 percent said their greatest need was a job to end their homelessness, 38 percent said they needed housing, and 30 percent said they needed housing assistance, such as money to apply to their rent, utilities, etc.

What Causes Homelessness?

Why do people continue to become homeless? Who are the new people refilling the beds in emergency shelters? Recent research shows that homeless people are often frequent users of systems of care that are funded by public dollars. They come from youth services, foster care, state hospitals, for-profit managed care hospitals, state and county correctional facilities, substance abuse programs, and Supplemental Security Income (SSI) a federal income support program for people with disabilities. Sometimes tens of thousands of dollars have been spent on their care before they end up in shelters.

Several major contributing causes have been identified by researchers examining the growth of homelessness. One of the leading analysts of homelessness in the nation found that the key variables leading to increased homelessness in urban areas are:

- the unemployment rate and the employment market
- population change
- percentage of one-person households, indicating possible social isolation
- absence of General Assistance benefits
- cost of living
- failure of benefits to keep pace with cost of living (Burt 1992)

Lack of a continuum of community-based care

Although the deinstitutionalization of mental patients was widely viewed as the primary cause of homelessness in the early 1980s, deinstitutionalization itself was not to blame. The rationale behind releasing mental patients from long-term hospital care when they did not require such a setting was a good one. This rationale was underscored in a 1999 Supreme Court decision supporting greater community integration for persons with disabilities (*Olmstead* v *L. C. ex rel. Zimring* 1999). What resulted in the 1980s, however, was the careless depopulation of state institutions without the necessary community-support facilities, housing, and services that would allow former patients to live securely in the community. When combined with tightened readmission standards at the same hospitals, the wave of vulnerable dischargees was characterized by one psychiatrist as akin to being "dumped amid the broken promises" (Torrey 1988).

General agreement exists as to the national prevalence of serious mental illness, including schizophrenia and manic depression, among homeless people. Experts state that there are twice as many mentally ill homeless persons as there are institutionalized patients. Increasing numbers of incarcerated people suffer from mental illness; many of them were homeless when jailed and will be homeless upon their release. As long as insufficient provisions are made for released patients, and adequate housing is unavailable in the community, the plight of the mentally ill homeless will be dismal (Torrey 1988).

Inappropriate discharge planning

The impact of a lack of community-based care extends to the need for post-acute residential facilities for homeless persons in recovery from alcohol and drug abuse, for ex-offenders, and youths turning eighteen and aging out of foster care, as well as for people who suffer from mental illness. These resources are sometimes referred to as "stepdown," or transitional, resources. Homelessness of all these groups has been documented as people emerge from public care or custody into shelters, with their homelessness resulting from inappropriate discharge and after-care planning and the inadequacy of community placements. These community placements include both short-term placements and permanent housing units, which are in short supply because of a lack of funds and continuing community opposition to racial and socioeconomic residential integration for those leaving public care or custody (MHSA 2000).

In 2000, a sweeping statewide review of the discharge policies and practices of public agencies that resulted in homelessness was undertaken by the state of Massachusetts. The product was a comprehensive report on the coordination of such policies across systems including corrections, foster care, managed care, psychiatric facilities, and more. In addition, Republican Governor A. Paul Cellucci gave an unprecedented speech on the state's responsibility to close this door to increasing homelessness (Commonwealth of Massachusetts 2000). Few policy speeches on homelessness have been made recently by chief executives in government, fewer still on such an emerging topic of policy. The visibility of discharge planning as a policy issue had helped fuel a reconceptualization of the role of prevention. Traditionally, homelessness prevention efforts have focused on keeping people housed by offering assistance for rent, mortgage, and utility payments. Discharge planning supports the notion of preventing the movement into homelessness of individuals for whom other systems bear responsibility. For instance, in the legal case *Brad H.* v. *City of New York*, the Appellate Division of the New York State Supreme Court's decision, on October 31, 2000, required New York City to provide discharge planning for jail inmates who have a mental illness and are prone to become homeless and to recidivate.

Working but not making enough

Even in the booming economy, the ranks of the homeless poor include working people, because housing costs are rising beyond the reach of low wages. When coupled with the rising costs of housing, it is not difficult to see why many shelters are populated with workers who have nowhere else to live. Reports from major cities bear out the urgency of employment issues for homeless people. In a 1996 national study, 44 percent of homeless people surveyed reported that they did paid work during the prior month (Burt et al. 1999).

Fewer safety-net programs and less available housing

The benefits programs that once would have constituted a final protection for people from becoming homeless have been greatly eroded. Programs designed to help people out of poverty or to ease its misery have been cut or have failed to keep up with the cost of living. For people who have income problems, the search for housing is compounded because the availability of low-cost housing can make the difference between chronic hardship and outright homelessness. During the 1980s there was a radical reversal of the federal government's forty-year commitment to provide low-income housing. The dire consequence of this reversal is that assisted housing availability does not begin to meet demand.

According to one report, "nowhere in the United States—in no state, metropolitan area, county or New England town—is the minimum wage adequate to afford the Fair Market Rent for a 2 bedroom unit. Moreover, in only 3 of the 3,646 counties and New England towns analyzed in this report can a household with an income at 30% of the area median income afford the FMR for a 2 bedroom unit"(NLIHC 2000).

Unsubsidized low-rent housing in the private sector is also in crisis. Between 1970 and 1982, many cities lost from 50 to 85 percent of their single-room-occupancy (SRO) rooms. The General Accounting Office (GAO) estimated that 1. 1 million of these units were lost between 1970 and 1982 (Schwartz, Ferlauto, and Hoffman 1988).

The Response to Homelessness

Homelessness is a complex problem, one that cannot be solved quickly given the many factors and systems involved in addressing it. The material in this book demonstrates the fundamental need for housing to solve the most pressing of the problems facing homeless people, as well as the need for all the health care, income, and social supports that can move people away from crisis and into stability.

European Homelessness

Homelessness as a growing problem is not confined to the United States. The second part of this essay and subsequent sections of the book also provide insights into homelessness in Western Europe, Canada, and Australia. Europe presents the unique characteristic of being a multitiered system in which policymaking is done in the individual nations and, increasingly, within the European Union (EU). This book concentrates on a few countries in Europe and some of the emerging issues in the EU. Europe also has seen more activity focused on the establishment of a right or entitlement of all persons to housing.

Within the United States, we typically know little of the governing systems, social welfare policies, or key issues of other countries. As the European countries evolve a more borderless society and economy in the EU, what problems are they confronting in addressing domestic homelessness, as well as the influx of immigrant populations? What role do their social systems and housing markets play in addressing homelessness? The role of these systems may be especially key during the emergence of a common European economic market with shared social policies. This development itself may mirror the tiered federal-state system of the United States, where some states have historically been more involved than others in budgeting state funds to address homelessness, while also seeking and using federal resources.

Homelessness in Europe seldom breaks into the U.S. press, unless the occasion involves the plight of a homeless person in an extreme weather event. The press might choose a story based on whether the idea of homeless people near the Eiffel Tower or the Vatican or another European landmark makes the story as striking as the sight of homeless people near the White House or the Washington Monument once did in the United States. The problem of homelessness in Europe does not receive the same attention there that U.S. homelessness has received in the United States. According to one government body,

> The homeless may not appear as a concern of the European institutions. There was no specific reference to them in the White Paper on European social policy . . .
> It is agreed in all EU countries that homelessness is unworthy of generally prosperous countries. It is also

agreed in all these countries that it is a sort of distillation of social and urban problems. The homeless are the most visible representatives of exclusion, which in its various forms is continuing to spread throughout Europe . . .

Since the late 1980s the number of people living under such conditions has become alarming. Although an objective increase in homelessness is borne out by the increasing local pressure on official or voluntary-sector services, little is actually known about the real scale of the problem: by the same token, hard data on the homeless themselves is hard to come by. Significant progress has however been achieved thanks to recent research efforts (Committee of the Regions 1999).

To the casual reader, the emphasis of the European discussion of homelessness is on the problem as a form of social exclusion, emphasising that a solution lies in access to housing for those who are "sleeping rough." There is also a heavy emphasis on joblessness as a key factor in homelessness. Understanding the differences in the United States labor market and the European one is helpful. According to one analyst:

First, during recessions American unemployment quite often increases substantially, even more so than European unemployment. This is the case, for example, during the recessions of 1974–76 and 1980–82. It is less so during the recession of 1991–93. However, during the upturn of economic activity, the American unemployment always declines to its pre-recession level. As a result, the long term trend in the American unemployment rate is flat. In contrast, although the European unemployment rate typically increases less than the American one during the recession, it never declines to its pre-recession level. As a result, the long term trend is upwards. This ratchet effect is quite worrisome. It appears that each time Europe is hit by a shock (say, a recession) unemployment goes up, while when the economy improves unemployment stays put or goes down only partially. Thus, temporary disturbances like recessions have permanent effects on European unemployment. This feature is totally absent from the U.S. data . . . The ratchet effect in the European unemployment is particularly striking during the 1990s. We see that European unemployment increased by close to 40% during the decade. This increase occurred essentially during two years, i.e., from 1991 to 1993 when unemployment went from 8% to 11%. After that, it pretty much remained unchanged despite a recovery of economic activity. (De Grauwe 1998)

Relative to U.S. discussions of homelessness where there is often a heavy focus on the presence of disabilities among the homeless population, there is little mention in Europe of the role of chronic disability (including physical disability, mental illness, and substance abuse) and continuity in public systems of care, treatment, and custody (including child welfare, hospitals, prisons, and treatment facilities).

But the problem is prevalent and in the public eye nonetheless. The EU Committee of the Regions found, in its 1999 opinion on homelessness, that their visibility has been increasing in public areas over the last two decades and that "extreme forms of poverty are unanimously judged to be unacceptable in a society of plenty. The position and living conditions of homeless people are everywhere viewed as an affront to human rights" (Committee of the Regions 1999). This identification of homelessness as a human rights issue is a clearly distinguishing factor between the U.S. discussion and international discussions of homelessness in general. Non-U.S. countries in general look to both international law and human rights accords—ratified by most nations besides the United States—to define this standard.

But when the discussion turns to remedies, the European analysis is very reminiscent of the U.S. trend toward criminalization and removal of persons in public places:

The problem of homelessness goes to the very heart of the socio-economic and cultural make-up of each European country. It is handled locally, giving rise to reactions which invariably run the gamut from repression to solidarity. While official action on the homeless does receive broad public backing in the various countries, at the same time it has to come to terms with a degree of ambiguity in popular sentiment, with local people calling for the homeless to be either taken in or dispatched elsewhere. (Committee of the Regions 1999)

Defining Homelessness in Europe

If a key concept in describing the problem of homelessness is to arrive at a common definition for research and policy purposes, then European nations are hindered by having no common legal or research definition. The EU's efforts at "harmonizing" policies of different nations into more cohesive, common, and less different approaches does not have this fundamental ground on which to build its efforts. Although there is recognition that homeless people are not a homogenous population, there is also recognition that the public and policy response to various homeless subpopulations can differ greatly (Committee of the Regions 1999).

Similarly to the U.S. discussion, "very different aspects (lack of housing, the public spectacle of social abandonment, begging, vagrancy, extreme forms of poverty, changes in market trends and housing policy, etc.), are brought together under a single heading" (Committee of the Regions 1999).

Who Is Homeless?

Despite the definitional development still under way, a few key characteristics about homeless people can be identified, according to the EU. These include:

- extreme poverty
- high proportion of single males
- growing numbers of women and young people
- high levels of alcohol or drug consumption
- generally poor state of health, particularly mental health
- growing number of homeless non-nationals, either from elsewhere in the EU or from North Africa, Sub-Saharan Africa, and Eastern Europe (Committee of the Regions 1999)

How Many People are Homeless?

Without agreement on definitions, arriving at an estimate of the European homeless population is just as difficult as it has been in the United States. Nevertheless, EU members have contributed some estimates based on reports from service providers and some government data (see Table 1.1). According to FEANTSA, the leading organization of providers, "Approximately 1.1 million European citizens pass through agencies for the homeless every day. Over a one-year period, this figure rises to 1.8 million." Again, FEANTSA estimates almost 18 million EU citizens live in very low-grade accommodation or "unconventional" housing, i.e., in premises not intended as dwelling-places (FEANTSA 2000). National estimates of annual and daily averages of individuals using services are given in Table 1.1.

Addressing Homelessness in Europe

Given the dimensions of homelessness in Europe, what has been done to address it? Several of the chapters that follow demonstrate that, just as in the United States, several nongovernmental organizations act as advocacy voices in Europe as a whole and in the major countries of the region as well. In addition, they and others act as gateways to a larger network of service and shelter providers offering assistance to homeless people. Clearly there are research communities and governmental bodies examining

TABLE 1.1
European Estimates of Homelessness by Country

Country	For an Average Day, or for the Day Surveyed	For a One-Year Period
Austria	6,100	8,400
Belgium	4,000	5,500
Denmark	2,947	4,000
Finland	4,000	5,500
France	250,000	346,000
Germany	490,700	876,450
Greece	5,500	7,700
Ireland	2,667	3,700
Italy	56,000	78,000
Luxembourg	194	200
Netherlands	7,000	12,000
Portugal	3,000	4,000
Spain	8,000	11,000
Sweden	9,903	14,000
United Kingdom	283,000	460,000

Source: FEANTSA 2000.

policy and resource questions as well. As described by the Committee of the Regions of the EU,

> Numerous studies report the political and social changes which have gone furthest to swell the ranks of the homeless. They include new forms of poverty, the advance of insecurity and long-term unemployment, the problem of mental illness, the closing down of institutionalized mental hospitals, drug and alcohol consumption, the increasing number of single-parent families, welfare cutbacks in some countries, counterproductive increases in others, and difficulties in access to housing.
>
> Depending on the point of view adopted by the various social actors, homelessness is first and foremost a question of housing, of employment, demographics, mental illness, drug or alcohol abuse, domestic violence, cuts in—or excessive growth of—social budgets, the relative breakdown in family ties, or a spin-off of rising or changing poverty.
>
> There are two major schools of thought on how to explain homelessness. The focus can be on analysing structural phenomena (unemployment, changes in the housing market, etc.); or it can be on the more personal reasons which lead to an individual becoming homeless (emotional trauma, illness, initial social disadvantage, etc.). (Committee of the Regions 1999)

In some respects, the description reads much like one that could be found in the United States, but the similarities do not extend very far. The efforts at regionalism brought on by the EU do not exactly mirror relations between the various states in the United States as they address homelessness, since the issues between and among countries are effectively transnational in nature at a time when nations are adjusting to a regional consciousness in Europe. Further, as described briefly in the next section, the underlying body of EU law and authority, coupled with international law, as mentioned earlier, provides a basis for a different level of response to homelessness than exists in the United States currently.

Progress on the Right to Housing

All the member states of the EU have ratified international documents on the right to housing. As a result, each recognizes adequate housing—whether in the form of shelter or housing—as a basic right of human beings. Following the international Habitat II conference in 1996, Europe has moved to a more recognizable European version of this right, including incorporating it into individual national constitutions. For instance, Belgium, Finland, the Netherlands, Portugal, Spain, and Sweden have added this right to their constitutions. The United Kingdom and Ireland do not recognize the right to housing but have required local authorities to house specific categories of people, and authorities in Denmark must provide accommodation (Committee of the Regions 1999).

In late 2000 it is an unfortunate truth that contemporary homelessness has come and stayed in communities across the United States and across Europe. This book offers a portrait of a complex problem that has come to many nations in larger scale and lasting presence than was ever expected in the early 1980s. The material included here offers somewhat of a historical context where that is helpful or explanatory, but it tries to provide a look at useful resources, promising developments, provocative research, and the lessons that can be learned across borders about similarities as well as differences regarding the causes of homelessness and its solutions.

References

Burt, Martha R., and Barbara Cohen. *America's Homeless: Numbers, Characteristics, and the Programs That Serve Them.* Washington, DC, The Urban Institute Press, 1989.

Burt, Martha, Laudan Aron, Toby Douglas, Jesse Valente, Edgar Lee, and Britta Iwen. *Homelessness: Programs and the People They Serve. Findings of the National Survey of Homeless Assistance Providers and Clients (NSHAPC).* Washington, DC: The Urban Institute, 1999.

Center on Budget and Policy Priorities, "Poverty Rate Hits Lowest Level since 1979 as Unemployment Reaches a 30-Year Low." Press release, Washington, DC: Center on Budget and Policy Priorities, 10 October 2000.

Committee of the Regions, *OPINION on Housing and the Homeless.* Brussels. 17 June 1999. The Committee of the Regions of the European Union was established by the Maastricht Treaty in 1993, and brings together 222 members who represent local, regional, and city-level public authorities in the fifteen member states of the EU.

Commonwealth of Massachusetts, Executive Office for Administration and Finance. *Moving from Serving the Homeless to Preventing Homelessness.* Policy Report No. 4, October 2000.

Culhane, Dennis, and Randall Kuhn. "Patterns and Determinants of Shelter Utilization among Single Adults in New York City and Philadelphia." *Journal of Policy Analysis and Management*, 1998.

De Grauwe, Paul. *European Unemployment: A Tale of Demand and Supply.* University of Leuven, Belgium: Center for Economic Studies, 1998.

European Federation of National Organizations Working with the Homeless (FEANTSA) *(Fédération Européenne d'Associations Nationales Travaillant avec les Sans-Abri).*

Gugliotta, Guy. "Institute Finds a Number That Adds Up, Has Meaning on the Streets," *Washington Post*, 16 May 1994.

Interagency Council on the Homeless. *Priority: Home! The Federal Plan to Break the Cycle of Homelessness.* Washington, DC: U.S. Department of Housing and Urban Development, 1994.

Link, Bruce, Jo Phelan, Michaeline Bresnahan, Ann Stueve, Robert Moore, and Ezra Susser. "Lifetime and Five-Year Prevalence of Homelessness in the United States: New Evidence on an Old Debate." *American Journal of Orthopsychiatry*, 1995.

Massachusetts Housing and Shelter Alliance (MHSA), *Four-Year Summary of Subpopulations of Homeless People.* Boston: MHSA, 2000.

National Alliance to End Homelessness. *A Plan—Not a Dream: How to End Homelessness in Ten Years.* Washington, DC: National Alliance to End Homelessness, 2000.

National Low Income Housing Coalition (NLIHC). *Out of Reach: The Growing Gap between Housing Costs and Income of Poor People in the United States.* Washington, DC: National Low Income Housing Coalition, 2000.

O'Flaherty, Brendan. *Making Room: The Economics of Homelessness.* Cambridge, MA: Harvard University Press, 1998, 4, 10.

Olmstead v. *L. C. ex rel. Zimring*, 119 S. Ct. 2176 (1999).

Pear, Robert. "Far More Single Mothers Are Taking Jobs." *New York Times*, 5 November 2000. Burt, Martha R. *Over the Edge: The Growth of Homelessness in the 1980s.* Washington, DC: The Urban Institute Press, 1992.

P.L. 100-77, Stewart B. McKinney Homeless Assistance Act (now McKinney-Vento Act).

P.L. 106-377, Department of Veterans Affairs and Housing and Urban Development, and Independent Agencies Appropriations Act, 2000.

Schwartz, David C., Richard C. Ferlauto, and Daniel N. Hoffman. *A New Housing Policy: Recapturing the American Dream.* Philadelphia: Temple University Press, 1988, 204.

Torrey, E. Fuller. *Nowhere to Go.* New York: Harper & Row, 1988, 3.

Notes

1. Portions of this introductory material were previously published as "Federal Policy for the Homeless" in volume I of the *Stanford Law and Policy Review* of Stanford Law School. They are used here by agreement with the Board of Trustees of Leland Stanford Junior University.

2. In September 1989, however, Kondratas stated during her Senate confirmation hearings that she endorsed the 650,000 figure offered in the National Academy of Science's 1988 report, *Homelessness, Health and Human Needs.*

3. In 1996, when the survey was conducted, AFDC was still operating.

2

Chronology

1976   **June**. Habitat I, the first United Nations (UN)–sponsored Conference on Human Settlements, is held in Vancouver, B.C., in 1976. It involves government representatives from 132 nations and results in the adoption of the Vancouver Declaration on Human Settlements and the creation of the UN Centre on Human Settlements, a specialized United Nations agency devoted to housing concerns. The Vancouver Declaration's sixty-four-point plan of action emphasizes that planning and development, infrastructure and services, environment, transportation, and public participation in decisionmaking are fundamental to adequate housing. The Vancouver document also reflects the view that adequate housing intersects with and is dependent upon the fulfillment of other human rights, in particular, the right to freedom of movement, the right to freely choose one's place of residence, the right to be free from social and racial discrimination, and the right of individuals and communities to participate directly in decisions affecting their lives.

December. The Community for Creative Non-Violence (CCNV), a local advocacy organization, begins a local campaign to offer shelter to all who need it in Washington, D.C.

1978   **November**. CCNV starts two-week occupation of the National Visitors Center (Union Station) as a shelter

1978
(cont.)

for homeless people in Washington, D.C., to dramatize the number of people in need in the city.

1979

October. *Callahan* v. *Carey* lawsuit is filed in New York City by Wall Street attorney Robert M. Hayes to establish a right to shelter for homeless men.

1980

April. CCNV burns census forms to protest inadequate measures for counting homeless people in the 1980 national census.

May. *Williams* v. *Barry* lawsuit is filed in Washington, D.C., to prevent the closing, with only forty-eight hours' notice, of city-run shelters for men.

July. Coalition for the Homeless is formed in New York City as a result of public activities in response to the removal of homeless people from the area around Madison Square Garden, site of the Democratic National Convention.

September. *A Forced March to Nowhere*, an initial CCNV survey of homelessness and services around the nation, is presented to the House District Committee hearing on urban problems.

1981

February. Demonstrators block Pennsylvania Avenue in response to the diminished provisions for poor people announced in the first Reagan administration budget the previous evening.

March. *Private Lives/Public Spaces* is released in New York City, after researchers Kim Hopper and Ellen Baxter complete a lengthy survey of homeless people in that city.

July. In Boston, a group of Franciscan friars begins serving coffee and sandwiches on the sidewalk in front of their workers' chapel in downtown, starting the city's first outdoor breadline since before the days of Lyndon Johnson's Great Society. The first week, the brown-robed friars hand out sandwiches and hot, black coffee daily to 40 or so of the city's down-and-out people. By January of the following year, they will serve 120.

August. Consent decree is signed in *Callahan* v. *Carey* lawsuit, providing overnight shelter for single homeless men in New York City, as well as court-ordered standards for the operation and expansion of shelters for men.

October. The Massachusetts Coalition for the Homeless is formed.

November. Building commences on the "Reaganville" demonstration tent encampment in Lafayette Park across from the White House, by members of CCNV, who serve a traditional Thanksgiving meal in the park; the protest is meant as a reminder of the "Hooverville" homeless settlements of the Great Depression. Demonstrators are arrested, but tents remain until spring.

December. A memorial service for the nation's homeless people is held in Lafayette Park, in Washington, D.C.; service is attended by hundreds of advocates for the homeless from around the country, who plant over 400 crosses bearing the names and dates of death for homeless people.

1982   **March**. Crosses are removed from Lafayette Park by homeless advocates, who carry them to Capitol Hill and present one to each member of Congress.

April. National Coalition for the Homeless is formed.

May. *Klosterman* v. *Carey* is filed, seeking housing for former state psychiatric patients who are homeless.

December. *Homelessness in America: A Forced March to Nowhere*, by Mary Ellen Hombs and Mitch Snyder, is released as a national survey of homelessness and the responses to homelessness in cities around the nation. Also included is an examination of Reagan administration policies. The book is released in conjunction with congressional hearings on the same day.

1983   **January**. The People's State of the Union event occurs when sixty-three homeless people, shelter providers, and civil rights and peace movement leaders occupy the Capitol rotunda in order to provide an alternative voice to the traditional presidential speech, and are arrested. They demand food, shelter, and jobs for the poor. Later that month, the Emergency Jobs Appropriations Act of 1983 is passed in Congress, providing $100 million for emergency food and shelter.

1983
(*cont.*)

September. A campaign for the right to overnight shelter is begun in Washington, D.C.; the goal is a ballot initiative on the November 1984 presidential ballot.
October. *Hodge* v. *Ginsberg* is filed and becomes a successful West Virginia case to establish a right to shelter.

1984

January. Federal City College shelter for men opens at the site of the old Securities and Exchange Commission building in downtown Washington, D.C. The second congressional hearings on homelessness in America are held in the basement of the homeless shelter.
February. *Maticka* v. *Atlantic City* lawsuit is filed in New Jersey to establish a right to shelter.
May. A congressional hearing is held on the HUD report on homelessness; the report is widely criticized by advocates for the assertion that only 250,000 people are homeless.
June. Supreme Court rules in *CCNV* v. *Clark* case stemming from the 1981 encampment in Lafayette Park; the Court rules against the right of homeless people to demonstrate by sleeping in the park.
November. Initiative #17, the D.C. Right to Overnight Shelter law, is passed by 72 percent of the city's voters.

1986

May. Hands Across America occurs, as millions of Americans join hands to form a human chain across the country to raise funds for hungry and homeless people.
November. Mitch Snyder and homeless advocate Michael Stoops of Portland, Oregon, move to the U.S. Capitol grounds to live while they work for passage of the $500 million legislation to aid homeless people.

1987

January. HR 558, Urgent Relief for the Homeless, is introduced by the House leadership.
1987. The International Year of Shelter for the Homeless begins. The United Nations General Assembly develops and adopts the Global Strategy for Shelter to the Year 2000.
July. HR 558, now the Stewart B. McKinney Homeless Assistance Act, is signed by President Reagan.

1988   **February**. Ten thousand homeless people, their sup-
porters, and civil rights leaders march in Atlanta just
prior to the Super Tuesday presidential primaries.
December. Ten thousand march in New York City for
action to house homeless people.

1989   **January**. Two hundred homeless people and activists
meet for two days in Atlanta to form a national agenda
to end homelessness and provide affordable housing.
February. President George Bush calls for full funding of the McKinney homeless assistance programs in
his first budget message to Congress.
October. HOUSING NOW!, a historic and broad-
based coalition to end homelessness and secure affordable housing, brings hundreds of thousands of
marchers to Washington, D.C.
December. A federal district court judge in Washington, D.C., rules that the federal government must
make available thousands of vacant federal buildings
for homeless people during the coming winter. The
judge finds that the federal government has made
"pitifully few" properties available as required under
the McKinney Act and orders a strict schedule for
compliance.

1990   **March**. The U.S. Census conducts S Night, a count of
selected components of the homeless population. The
count and its procedures are controversial among advocates and service providers.
July. Mitch Snyder, regarded as the most visible and
controversial advocate for homeless people, commits
suicide in the CCNV shelter in Washington, D.C.
Thousands of people from all walks of life attend his
funeral.

1991   **November**. The National Coalition for the Homeless
releases a report, *Heroes Today, Homeless Tomorrow?* examining the growing problems faced by homeless
veterans.

1992   **March**. The Federal Task Force on Homelessness and
Severe Mental Illness releases its report, *Outcasts on*

1992 *(cont.)*	*Main Street.* The report calls for more appropriate and integrated services and housing for those in need, estimated at 200,000 persons.

March. Michigan Governor John Engler moves to eliminate his state's General Assistance program, a form of income assistance received primarily by single poor people. Other states, including Massachusetts, follow suit.

March. Arkansas Governor Bill Clinton, running for president, promises to "end welfare as we know it" if elected.

October. President George Bush signs into law a new program aimed at homeless people in rural areas and a new demonstration program called Safe Havens, to reach seriously mentally ill homeless people who are unwilling or unable to participate in other programs. New laws also require service providers to create employment opportunities for homeless people and to include homeless people on boards of service-providing organizations.

November. On Veterans' Day, President George Bush signs P.L. 102-590, the Comprehensive Services for Homeless Veterans Act. The new law makes grants and services available to programs serving homeless veterans.

1993	**November**. House Republicans announce their welfare reform plan. It has 160 cosponsors and supporters state that it will save $20 billion over the next five years. It limits all major welfare programs, including income support and food stamps, and requires work in exchange for assistance.

1994	**January**. The Clinton administration's Working Group on Welfare Reform, Family Support, and Independence finishes a draft proposal that will put a two-year limit on welfare benefits.

The *Boston Globe* reports that Japan is also experiencing a growing homeless population, with jobless, homeless Japanese living in cardboard boxes in train tunnels and wearing shabby rags, as pitiful as any to be found on the streets of Boston or New York.

April. The Clinton administration submits a budget request to Congress that seeks $60 billion in housing funds for the next two years. The request proposes raising homeless assistance funding to $2.2 billion.

The *New York Times* reports that a memo prepared for President Clinton suggests that use of the two-year time limit for welfare reform could lead to increased homelessness.

May. The Clinton administration releases *Priority: HOME! The Federal Plan to Break the Cycle of Homelessness*. The report is the result of work done under Clinton's Executive Order issued in 1993. The report sets a goal of reducing homelessness by one-third during the Clinton administration.

August. A federal judge overturns a Baltimore law against aggressive panhandling, ruling that the law unfairly singles out street beggars from other people who aggressively solicit money.

September. Elliot Liebow, sixty-nine, the anthropologist and sociologist who wrote about homeless women, dies.

December. The U.S. Conference of Mayors issues its annual report on hunger and homelessness. The report states that hunger and homelessness in the nation continue to rise despite increases in assistance.

A homeless man is shot by the U.S. Park Police in front of the White House. The police state that the man wielded a large knife at the officers.

1995   **February**. The new Republican majority in the U.S. Congress votes to cut $7.2 billion in low-income housing funds from the federal budget.

July. The Department of Housing and Urban Development awards $900 million nationwide for homeless services programs. This is the largest award in the history of the program.

Congress holds a hearing on a proposal that would encourage states to give psychiatric treatment to homeless mentally ill people against their will. The proposal is criticized by many witnesses at the hearing.

August. The *Washington Post* reports that the number of homeless people in Paris is increasing.

1995
(cont.)

Three European partner organizations create IGLOO (Intégration Globale par le LOgement et L'emplOi), a joint initiative by CECODHAS (European Liaison Committee for Social Housing), ETUC (European Trade Union Confederation), and FEANTSA (European Federation of National Organisations Working with the Homeless). IGLOO seeks to provide social support and integrated solutions for people with problems of housing, training, and employment.

October. A broad coalition of advocates issues sharp criticism of President Clinton for his support of federal welfare reform measures. The groups demand that he veto a compromise welfare bill that they call "immoral, wrong, unjust and un-American."

Visiting the United States, Pope John Paul II asks in a speech, "Is present day America becoming less sensitive, less caring toward the poor, the weak, the stranger, the needy? It must not!"

1996

January. The *Washington Post* reports on growing numbers of homeless people and deaths among the homeless population in Moscow. Also in January, the *Post* reports on how Tokyo is addressing its growing homeless problem.

February. The *Post* reports on how welfare cuts in Canada seem to have increased the number of homeless people seeking shelter in Canadian cities.

March. U.S. Department of Housing and Urban Development Secretary Henry Cisneros releases a study showing that 5.3 million households were spending more than half of their income on rent or living in severely substandard housing.

June. The Senate Armed Services Committee votes to end the Pentagon's program to help the homeless, stating that the program interferes with military operations.

The second United Nations Conference on Human Settlements (Habitat II) is held in Istanbul, Turkey. The event brings together national leaders from 171 countries, representatives of local governments, the private sector, and nongovernmental and community-based organizations. The conference has two themes: "adequate shelter for all" and "sustainable human settlements in an urbanizing world." Controversy over the right to housing is a theme throughout the conference, since the United States remains one of the few countries that has not recognized that right in numerous, prior international documents.

August. A new study of welfare mothers in Worcester, Massachusetts, is released. The study finds that 92 percent of those who were homeless and 82 percent of those who were without homes had experienced severe physical violence or sexual assaults at some time during their lives.

President Clinton signs the nation's first major overhaul of its welfare programs, ending the guarantee of cash assistance for the nation's poor. The law reduces federal responsibility for welfare programs and gives states new latitude to assist the poor through employment programs.

October. Mayor Willie Brown of San Francisco says he may not be able to solve the city's homeless problem, long regarded as a local political issue. San Francisco has an estimated 10,000–15,000 homeless people.

December. A national advocacy group on homelessness issues a report stating that the nation's fifty largest cities are more and more adopting laws aimed at discouraging homelessness and ordering police to clear homeless people out of public areas.

1997   **January**. U.S. Department of Housing and Urban Development Secretary Henry Cisneros steps down after four years in office. Cisneros expresses disappointment at not reducing homelessness during his tenure, stating that attacking the problem is "like bailing a leaking boat." He is succeeded by Assistant Secretary Andrew Cuomo, who says he'll work to improve the agency's management and efficiency while meeting the needs of the poor. Cuomo formerly operated homeless programs in New York City.

February. Food stamp cuts go into effect under the nation's new welfare reform law. About 1 million

1997
(cont.)
people are expected to be affected by the largest cut during the program's thirty-five-year history.

May. The European Parliamentary Resolution on the Social Aspects of Housing is adopted by the European Parliament.

October. The House of Representatives approves a plan to preserve the nation's largest low-income housing program from massive foreclosures that could have resulted in the eviction of poor tenants around the country.

December. The U.S. Conference of Mayors issues its annual report, stating that the growing economy and low unemployment have not dented the demand for food and shelter in the nation.

President Clinton announces that he will ask Congress to increase spending on homeless programs by 40 percent next year.

1998
October. The National Symposium of Homelessness Research is convened by the two key federal agencies addressing homelessness: the U.S. Departments of Housing and Urban Development and Health and Human Services. Over 175 researchers, policymakers, and formerly homeless people attend to discuss the latest research on homelessness.

November. Unusually cold weather kills eight homeless people in France. Shelters are crowded with others needing assistance. French leaders issue public appeals for compassion.

The European Federation of National Organisations Working with the Homeless (FEANTSA) adopts "Europe Against Exclusion: Housing for All," a policy report that presents a series of practical policy proposals to promote social inclusion and ensure access to decent housing for all citizens and residents of the European Union.

1999
January. President Clinton announces that he will seek $280 million in new funding to assist young people who must leave the foster care system when they turn age eighteen, the age when they are considered adults.

March. A bill introduced by Representative Rick Lazio (R-NY) to reorganize the McKinney Act housing programs for homeless people is sent to the Housing Subcommittee for consideration.

June. The Clinton administration, convening a White House conference on mental illness, proposes that health insurance plans provide the same level of coverage for services related to substance abuse and mental illness as they do for physical health problems.

The U.S. Supreme Court rules in the *Olmstead* v. *L. C.* case in Georgia. The Court finds that states' unjustified institutionalization of people with disabilities is prohibited discrimination under the Americans with Disabilities Act (ADA) and that the individuals should be placed in the most integrated community setting possible.

July. The Department of Justice reports in its first comprehensive study on the subject that about 16 percent of inmates in state and local jails and prisons are mentally ill. The report states that mentally ill inmates are more than twice as likely as other inmates to have been homeless before their arrest.

August. A class action lawsuit is filed in New York on behalf of mentally ill inmates in city jails and charges that the city and its medical provider routinely release patients who have received mental treatment behind bars without making any provision for their care, causing some to become homeless.

September. The new Miss America, formerly Miss Kentucky, announces that she will support the cause of homeless veterans. Heather Renee French is the twenty-four-year-old daughter of a disabled veteran.

November. New York police, carrying out Mayor Rudy Giuliani's new policy against allowing homeless people to sleep on city streets, arrest 23 people and send 127 others to shelters.

December. U.S. Department of Housing and Urban Development Secretary Andrew Cuomo announces that HUD will take over jurisdiction of federal funds for homeless programs in New York City, following allegations by New York advocates that the city's mayor,

1999
(*cont.*)

Rudy Giuliani, has deprived them of funds based on their advocacy against his "get tough" policies.

There is national attention to a warehouse fire in Worcester, Massachusetts, when six firefighters are killed in a blaze started by an overturned candle in an area where a homeless couple had been staying. The couple escapes from the fire and is later arrested. President Clinton attends the firefighters' memorial service.

The U.S. Department of Health and Human Services, Office of the Surgeon General, issues a landmark report on mental illness in the United States. Tipper Gore, wife of Vice President Al Gore, is active in homelessness and mental health issues, and states that she has undergone treatment for depression.

President Clinton announces that he will seek $690 million in new housing funds next year to help low-income families pay their rent.

2000

February. A national advocacy group on homelessness announces that its research shows that a growing number of separate and substandard schools are being established for homeless children around the country. The National Law Center on Homelessness and Poverty states that this action possibly violates a federal law that guarantees these children equal access to an education.

The *Washington Post* reports that the booming Silicon Valley economy is producing a darker side for some workers: the inability to find housing has some sleeping in shelters.

A New York judge rules that homeless people seeking shelter in New York City do not have to comply with a work requirement proposed by Mayor Rudy Giuliani.

March. The Vatican announces that it will investigate the possibility of sainthood for Catholic Worker founder Dorothy Day. Day aided homeless people in New York City beginning in the Depression and inspired the creation of numerous houses of hospitality and soup kitchens across the country and around the world.

July. The New York Supreme Court rules in the case called *Brad H.* that was brought on behalf of mentally ill inmates in the city of New York's jails. The suit had alleged that such inmates are routinely discharged from custody directly to the streets without medical or psychiatric services. The court ruled that New York City must provide for the continuing mental health care of inmates after they are released.

3

Biographical Sketches

A number of individuals have had significant influence on the course that homelessness policy and research have taken over the last two decades. Some are in the public arena in positions as policy makers and appointed officials. Some are in the public eye because of their efforts in organizing or litigation. Others are in academia or research, and their work sometimes attracts media attention. Some have been associated with initiatives or studies of importance. Although there are no famous homeless people, biographical sketches of two individuals related to public awareness and advocacy are included here to remind us of the individual human circumstances at the heart of homelessness.

Steven Banks

Steven Banks is deputy attorney-in-charge of the civil division of the Legal Aid Society in New York City and coordinating attorney of the Homeless Rights Project. He is also counsel to the Coalition for the Homeless in New York City. He has been a leading litigator on behalf of homeless people for over fifteen years. The Legal Aid Society's Homeless Rights Project provides direct legal assistance to homeless children and their families in 3,000 cases each year and serves as class counsel in the *McCain* litigation in which court orders have been in place for over ten years requiring New York City to provide safe, suitable, and adequate emergency shelter, assistance, and services to homeless families. For example, since 1986, court orders have prohibited the overnight housing of homeless children and their families in welfare offices, where they would have to sleep on floors or chairs. Banks has challenged the city's practice of moving homeless chil-

dren between overnight housing at offices and short-stay placements in commercial welfare hotels for weeks at a time as they
undergo the shelter application process. As counsel to the Coalition for the Homeless, he represents homeless single adult men
and women in the *Callahan* litigation in which court orders dating
from the early 1980s require the city to provide shelter which
meets basic standards of habitability to single adults. He received
his law degree from New York University.

Ellen Bassuk

Ellen Bassuk is associate professor of psychiatry at Harvard Medical School. She is cofounder and president of the Better Homes
Fund, a nonprofit organization started in 1988 by *Better Homes
and Gardens* magazine to help homeless families by developing
and helping to implement preventive and comprehensive policies and programs. Dr. Bassuk has published many articles,
monographs, and books and has undertaken key research about
homeless families and children. She is the principal investigator
of a longitudinal study, investigating the risks of family homelessness and its impact on children. Dr. Bassuk received her B.A.
from Brandeis University, her M.D. from Tufts Medical School,
and completed a residency in psychiatry at Beth Israel Hospital.
She has served as director of Hospital's Continuing Care Clinic
and Psychiatric Emergency Services. Dr. Bassuk was also a fellow
at the Bunting Institute, Radcliffe College, and has served as editor for the *American Journal of Orthopsychiatry.*

Martha M. Burt

Martha M. Burt is director of the Social Services Research Program at the Urban Institute in Washington, D.C. She began research on homelessness is 1983 with a study of the Federal Emergency Management Agency's work. She has written on the
means of counting homeless people and analyzed the federal
government research in the 1996 National Survey of Homeless
Assistance Providers and Clients. In 1992 she published *Over the
Edge,* analyzing the causes of homelessness in the 1980s. Her research has since focused on the impact of federal and state policy
changes affecting children and youth, on homelessness, on
hunger among the elderly, on services integration projects for at-
risk youth, and on service issues related to domestic violence. She

directed the first national probability-based study of the urban homeless in 1987. She helped plan and conduct a second study, the *National Survey of Homeless Assistance Providers and Clients,* which was published in 1999. She helped to develop and disseminate research on ways to count and describe homeless children and adults, and she has examined state policies, legislation, funding, and programs to serve homeless people. She served as a key evaluator of the effectiveness of the Emergency Food and Shelter Program funded through the Federal Emergency Management Administration, and she has worked with European researchers on homeless measurement.

Henry Cisneros

Henry G. Cisneros was secretary of the U.S. Department of Housing and Urban Development during the first term of the Clinton administration. As secretary, Cisneros announced that homelessness would be the agency's top priority. He proposed increased spending and realignment of the agency's programs for homeless people. Appointed by President Bill Clinton in January 1993, he also fought racial discrimination in public housing, helped to increase the national homeownership rate and federal assistance to the homeless, and designated the first group of empowerment zones to give tax breaks to businesses in depressed urban areas. He left the cabinet in November 1996 during an investigation of his statements to federal investigators prior to taking his cabinet post. He later acknowledged making false statements, pled guilty, and was pardoned by President Clinton as he left office. Cisneros left government to become president of Univision Communications, a Spanish-language television network. He remained in that position until August 2000, when he resigned to form American CityVista, a joint venture with one of the largest homebuilders in the United States. American CityVista will concentrate on "infill" projects, the construction of homes on available, underused land in central cities. In 1981, he was elected the first Hispanic mayor of a major U.S. city—San Antonio, Texas, the nation's tenth largest city. As a four-term mayor, serving from 1981 to 1989, he rebuilt the city's economic base. He also served as president of the National League of Cities, chairman of the National Civic League, deputy chair of the Federal Reserve Bank of Dallas, and as a board member of the Rockefeller Foundation. He received his master's degrees from Texas A&M (urban and regional planning) and Harvard University (public administration) and a doctorate in public administration from George Washington University.

Dennis P. Culhane

Dennis P. Culhane is associate professor at the School of Social Work at the University of Pennsylvania. He also holds an appointment as a senior fellow at the Leonard Davis Institute of Health Economics. His primary area of research is homelessness, including shelter use, geographic and housing market factors associated with housing instability, and the design and evaluation of homeless prevention programs. He has also studied the mental health and substance abuse service histories of homeless adults in Philadelphia. His work includes studies of the impact of homelessness on utilization of Medicaid services, public hospitals, state psychiatric hospitals, jails, prisons, and behavioral health treatment in New York City, and studies of the dynamics of public shelter use in New York and Philadelphia. He helped develop an information management system for tracking utilization of homeless services for the federal government. He also completed studies of housing and neighborhood factors related to the distribution of homeless persons' prior addresses in New York, Philadelphia, and Washington, D.C. He is leading an effort to integrate property, neighborhood, and human services data from Philadelphia into a geographic information system to support policy analysis and program planning and evaluation. He became involved in homelessness and housing issues as a shelter worker in Philadelphia in 1982. He was an organizer for the Union of the Homeless from 1986 to 1988 and served as director of technical assistance and organizing for the National Union of the Homeless from 1987 to 1988. He received his Ph.D. from Boston College in social psychology in 1990. He has been affiliated with the University of Pennsylvania since 1990.

Andrew M. Cuomo

Andrew M. Cuomo became secretary of the U.S. Department of Housing and Urban Development in 1997, after serving as assistant secretary for Housing and Community Development from 1993 to 1996 under Secretary Henry Cisneros. Cuomo came to HUD from New York City, where he headed the New York City Commission on the Homeless in 1991. The New York commission's report first defined the "continuum of care" concept later adopted by HUD. He built and operated housing for homeless people. He was the first HUD secretary to have experience in producing housing as founder of Housing Enterprise for the Less Privileged (H.E.L.P.) in 1986 and the Genesis Project, designed to develop innovative approaches to urban revitalization, community development, and tenant management. He was also a partner in the law firm of Blutrich, Falcone, and Miller and assistant district attorney in Manhattan in 1984. He served as special assistant to his father, Governor Mario M. Cuomo (D-N.Y.) and as campaign manager of the Cuomo for Governor campaign in 1982. He graduated from Fordham University in 1979 and received a law degree from Albany Law School in 1982. He is married to Kerry Kennedy Cuomo, a human rights activist and daughter of the late Robert F. Kennedy. Upon leaving office after the 2000 presidential election, he announced that he would join the New York law firm of Fried, Frank, Harris, Shriver, and Jacobson and organize a campaign to run for governor of New York State.

Maria Foscarinis

Maria Foscarinis is founder and executive director of the National Law Center on Homelessness and Poverty (NLCHP) in Washington. She has been involved in legal issues affecting homeless people since the mid-1980s, when she left the Wall Street firm of Sullivan and Cromwell to litigate full-time on behalf of homeless people. She previously worked with the National Coalition for the Homeless before starting the National Law Center in 1989. At NLCHP she has been a leading voice on issues affecting homeless children's education and the criminalization of homeless people in public places. Her efforts have increased access to educational development programs for homeless children; forced compliance with McKinney Act provisions by state administrators and federal agencies; and increased the conversions of closed military bases into shelters, job training, child care, and food program sites. She was a member of the U.S. delegation to Habitat II in Istanbul and helps lead the follow-up effort in the United States.

Representative Barney Frank

Representative Barney Frank (D-MA) is the senior democrat on the Housing and Community Opportunity Subcommittee of the

U.S. House of Representatives. He was first elected to the U.S. House of Representatives in 1980. He has been an active advocate for homeless and housing programs and for the elderly. He cosponsored the original McKinney Act and was cosponsor of the Lazio-Frank bill in Congress, which would have reorganized the homeless programs into a formula grant. He represents the Fourth Congressional District of Massachusetts. He graduated from Harvard College in 1962. In 1968, he became the chief assistant to Mayor Kevin White of Boston, a position he held for three years. He served for one year as administrative assistant to U.S. Congressman Michael J. Harrington. In 1972 Congressman Frank was elected to the Massachusetts Legislature, where he served for eight years. In 1977, he graduated from Harvard Law School.

Tipper Gore

Tipper Gore is the wife of former vice president Al Gore. She is an advocate for families, women, and children and is actively involved in issues related to mental health, education, and homelessness. She has also been the special adviser to the Interagency Council on the Homeless, which formerly was a federal body of the cabinet agencies and subsequently became part of the White House Domestic Policy Council. She partnered with the National Alliance for the Homeless to coauthor *The Way Home: Ending Homelessness in America,* a collection of photography by Mrs. Gore—who is herself an accomplished photographer—and other prominent photographers focusing on solutions to end the problem of homelessness.

Buddy Gray

Buddy Gray worked on behalf of homeless and poor people in the Over-the-Rhine neighborhood of Cincinnati from the early 1970s until his death in 1996, when he was killed in his office by a client. He developed a number of nonprofit organizations that provide emergency shelter, supportive services, and permanent housing. He frequently battled with more conservative voices in Cincinnati to protect the rights of homeless people. He worked to help homeless and formerly homeless people develop leadership roles in organizations that served them, and he focused on working with high school and college students to expose them to volunteerism and poor people in their communities. He was a close ally of the late Mitch Snyder and frequently visited Washington, D.C., to make his views known to policy makers. He was a founding board member of the National Coalition for the Homeless, which awards the "Buddy Gray Award for Homeless Activism" annually.

Robert M. Hayes

Robert M. Hayes filed the landmark New York City right to shelter case, *Callahan* v. *Carey*, in 1979, as an attorney at the Wall Street firm of Sullivan and Cromwell, where he concentrated in banking, securities, and antitrust litigation. He left the firm in 1982 and founded both the Coalition for the Homeless, oriented to New York City issues, and the National Coalition for the Homeless, a legal and policy advocacy organization with offices in Washington, D.C., and New York City. He directed major class action lawsuits, organized advocacy groups across the country, and led legislative campaigns before Congress and state legislatures. He returned to private practice in 1989 as special counsel to the New York office of O'Melveny & Myers where he concentrated on employment and labor law, as well as general corporate litigation. He is a 1974 graduate of Georgetown University and a 1977 graduate of New York University School of Law. He received a MacArthur Foundation Fellowship in 1985 and numerous awards from state and national bar associations. He was named one of the nation's ten most influential lawyers for the 1980s by *American Lawyer* magazine, and the *National Law Journal* named him among the nation's fifty leading attorneys of his generation.

Representative Rick Lazio

Representative Rick Lazio (R-NY) was elected to the U.S. House of Representatives in 1992. Lazio subsequently became chair of the Housing and Community Opportunity Subcommittee of the House of Representatives and led efforts to reform housing and community policies. In the 106th Congress, he proposed reorganization of the McKinney housing programs into a formula grant with a renewed emphasis on housing for homeless people and with the inclusion of new homelessness prevention measures regarding discharge and aftercare planning aimed at state polices. Before becoming a member of Congress, he was a prosecutor and first won elected office in 1989 as a Suffolk County legislator. With the election of the republican majority in the House of Representatives in 1994, Lazio was named deputy majority whip and later the assistant majority leader in the House of Representatives. He became chairman of the Housing Subcommittee where he sponsored legislation on public housing reform and reorganization of the homeless programs. In 2000, he ran an unsuccessful campaign for a U.S. Senate seat from New York State, losing to then First Lady Hillary Clinton. He graduated from Vassar College and American University Law School.

Philip F. Mangano

Philip F. Mangano is president of ¡ENDING HOMELESSNESS! The Roundtable on the Abolition of Homelessness, an advocacy initiative to counter the accommodation of homelessness through aggressive public policy measures designed to end homelessness in the United States. Mangano is executive director of the Massachusetts Housing and Shelter Alliance, a position he has held with that statewide advocacy organization since 1990. He has given speeches across the country comparing the struggle against homelessness to the work of the abolitionists in ending slavery. In the policy arena, he has developed the understanding of the prevention of homelessness at the "front door" of shelters by looking at the origins of people seeking shelter to identify other systems of care which may have discharged them to the shelter. Similarly, he has advanced the idea of the "back door" of homeless assistance programs as a place to link targeted housing resources to specific subpopulations of homeless people, such as working people and people with disabilities. He also serves as president of Social Action Ministries, an interfaith advocacy initiative focused on homelessness and hunger. He was director of homeless services in Cambridge, Massachusetts, from 1986 to 1990 and also worked with several local minority organizations to stimulate their involvement in addressing homelessness and building housing for homeless families. He holds a master's of Theological Studies degree from Boston Theological Institute.

Mel Martinez

Mel Martinez became the first secretary of Housing and Urban Development during the Bush administration in January 2001.

He had previously served as the chairman of Orange County, Florida, the elected chief executive of the regional government, with responsibility for the provision of services to over 860,000 people and many tourist attractions. He was first elected to a four-year term in 1998, and he began a series of initiatives emphasizing public safety, growth management, the needs of children and families, clean neighborhoods, improved transportation, and streamlining government. In 1962, at age fifteen, he left his birthplace in Cuba and was taken in by foster families until he was reunited with his family in Orlando in 1966. He graduated from the Florida State University College of Law in 1973. He practiced law in Orlando for twenty-five years.

Representative Stewart B. McKinney

Representative Stewart B. McKinney, for whom the McKinney Homeless Assistance Act was named, was a Republican member of the House of Representatives at the time of his death from AIDS in 1987. McKinney represented Connecticut's 4th District for over sixteen years. From 1983 until his death, he was the ranking Republican member of the Banking Subcommittee on Housing and Community Development, where he fought to preserve domestic programs in the 1980s. It is believed that he contracted fatal AIDS-related pneumonia from being outdoors in the cold during the demonstrations for the homeless that occurred at the U.S. Capitol during the winter of 1987, when the bill first introduced as "The Urgent Relief for the Homeless Act" was being considered.

Senator Jack Reed

Senator Jack Reed is United States Senator from Rhode Island. Elected to the Senate in 1996, he previously served three terms as a member of the U.S. House of Representatives from Rhode Island's 2nd Congressional District. He is the ranking Democrat on the Senate Subcommittee on Housing and Transportation and authored a bill for the 107th Congress that would maintain the continuum of care concept established in the federal homeless programs but add new emphasis to permanent housing and the use of other entitlements and benefits programs to help homeless people. He has been active in the House and the Senate on education, health care and campaign finance reform, international affairs, and child care. He is a graduate of the United States Military Academy at West Point where he received a Bachelor of Science degree in 1971. Following his graduation and an active duty commission in the United States Army, he attended the John F. Kennedy School of Government at Harvard University where he received a Masters of Public Policy. He was an army ranger and a paratrooper and served in the 82nd Airborne Division. He resigned from the army as a major in 1979 and went to Harvard Law School, where he graduated in 1982. He was elected to the Rhode Island State Senate in 1984 and served for three terms. In 1990, he was elected to the U.S. House of Representatives. He is also a member of the Senate Armed Services Committee and the Health, Education, Labor, and Pensions Committee. He is the senior Democratic member of the Joint Economic Committee.

Nan Roman

Nan Roman is president of the National Alliance to End Homelessness (NAEH). She was previously vice president of Policy and Programs with the Alliance, where she has worked since 1987. She has helped build the organization into a leading voice on homelessness in Washington, D.C. The Alliance is a national advocacy and capacity building organization with more than 2,000 nonprofit and public sector members. Nan oversees all program and policy activities, including congressional and federal agency advocacy, training, technical assistance, and research. She was part of the U.S. delegation to Habitat II in Istanbul. She has received the Miss America Woman of Achievement Award, which is awarded annually to a woman who has demonstrated zeal, devotion, and contribution to an issue of benefit to American society. In 2000 she unveiled a ten-year Alliance plan to end homelessness around which NAEH hopes to organize support for new programs. She has been active in antipoverty and community organizing activity at the local and national levels for over twenty years.

Rebecca Smith

Rebecca Smith, a homeless woman, froze to death in a box on a New York City street corner in 1982. Her death received extensive press coverage after it was discovered that the sixty-one-year-old woman, hospitalized repeatedly for schizophrenia, had been vis-

Biographical Sketches **49**

ited by at least fifty people who sought to give her food and shelter during the last weeks of her life. Smith, a mother and once valedictorian of her college class, was declared an "endangered adult" under the city's protective services law; she died before the order could take effect and remove her from the street.

Mitch Snyder

Mitch Snyder was a member and highly visible spokesperson for the Community for Creative Non-Violence (CCNV) in Washington, D.C., which he joined in 1973 in order to open a small residence for homeless people who would otherwise be held in jail because they lacked a fixed address. He had recently been released from federal prison, where he had met and studied with many antiwar activists who influenced his thinking about social justice. He was born in Brooklyn, New York, and quit school as a teenager. Snyder committed numerous acts of nonviolent civil disobedience, fasted publicly, and lived on the streets for extended periods of time to draw attention to the needs of homeless people. He engaged the interest and participation of many policy makers and celebrities who joined in and supported some of the more visible protests against homelessness, including the landmark HOUSING NOW! march in Washington, D.C., in 1989. He led the campaign for Initiative 17, a 1984 D.C. ballot measure that was passed with a 72 percent vote in support of providing shelter for all in need. He led the 1986–1987 campaign to develop and pass comprehensive federal legislation to help homeless people. As part of this effort, he slept outside the U.S. Capitol from the time the bill was introduced until its ultimate passage as the Stewart B. McKinney Homeless Assistance Act. Advocates, providers, and homeless people joined the effort by traveling to Washington and sleeping outside the Capitol at night and visiting members of Congress during the day. He coauthored *Homelessness in America: A Forced March to Nowhere* with Mary Ellen Hombs. He was well known as an organizer and activist, as well as a speaker on poverty and homelessness. He committed suicide in 1990.

Representative Bruce Vento

Representative Bruce Vento was a twelve-term democratic member of the U.S. House of Representatives from St. Paul, Minnesota. He died in October 2000 of a rare type of cancer caused by inhaling asbestos fibers. He had worked as a young man as a state-paid laborer in several St. Paul–area facilities that he believed exposed him to asbestos fibers. He served on the Housing and Community Opportunity Subcommittee, where he helped lead congressional efforts to assist homeless people by establishing the emergency shelter grants program and sponsoring legislation on homeless programs throughout the 1980s and 1990s. Upon his death, the McKinney Act, named for his late colleague Stewart McKinney, was renamed the McKinney-Vento Act in his honor. Vento was born in St. Paul and attended the University of Minnesota and Wisconsin State University. He was a science and social studies teacher before being elected to a seat in the state legislature in 1970. He was elected to the House of Representatives in 1976.

4

Facts and Statistics

This chapter looks at key research results that help define homelessness in several countries, including both the United States and England. The material in this chapter first provides a look at recent statistics about homelessness in the United States, including facts about homeless people and programs concerning the homeless. The chapter concludes with information about homelessness in England.

Defining Who Is Homeless

How do we define homelessness? Who is homeless? These important questions determine who is eligible for assistance from some shelters, service programs, and housing programs. *Priority: HOME! The Federal Plan to Break the Cycle of Homelessness*, published by the federal Interagency Council on the Homeless in March 1994, states:

In the Stewart B. McKinney Homeless Assistance Act of 1987, the legislation that created a series of targeted homeless assistance programs, the federal government defined *homeless* to mean:

(1) An individual who lacks a fixed, regular, and adequate night-time residence; and
(2) An individual who has a primary nighttime residency that is:
    (i) A supervised publicly or privately operated shelter designed to provide temporary living accommodations (including welfare hotels,

51

congregate shelters, and transitional housing for
the mentally ill);
(ii)   An institution that provides a temporary residence
for individuals intended to be institutionalized; or
(iii) A public or private place not designed for, or
ordinarily used as, a regular sleeping
accommodation for human beings.
(3) This term does not include any individual imprisoned
or otherwise detained under an act of Congress or a
state law.

People who are at imminent risk of losing their housing, because they are being evicted from private dwelling units or are
being discharged from institutions and have nowhere else to go, are
usually considered to be homeless for program eligibility purposes.

Key Characteristics of
the Homeless Population

*The National Survey of Homeless Assistance Providers and Clients
(NSHAPC)* was conducted in 1996 to provide information to federal agencies responsible for administering homeless assistance
programs and to other interested parties involved in homeless assistance programs and the people who use them. This important
national survey provided new information about homelessness
in the United States.

The survey was funded by twelve federal agencies under
the auspices of the Interagency Council on the Homeless, a working group of the White House Domestic Policy Council. The U.S.
Bureau of the Census collected the data, and the Urban Institute
in Washington, D.C., analyzed it.

The Bureau of the Census conducted the study. NSHAPC
selected a sample of seventy-six geographical areas to represent the entire United States, including the twenty-eight largest
metropolitan statistical areas, twenty-four small and medium-
sized areas randomly selected; and twenty-four groups of rural
counties randomly selected. Using telephone interviews and a
mail survey, the study identified and gathered information
about sixteen types of homeless assistance programs, including
emergency shelters, transitional programs, permanent housing
programs for formerly homeless people, food pantries, soup

kitchens, physical and mental health care programs, alcohol and drug programs, outreach and drop-in programs, and migrant labor camps.

A client survey of homeless people was also conducted. Users of these programs (clients) were randomly selected and interviewed to learn about their characteristics, situations, and needs.

Some key results of the survey are summarized here. The complete report of the survey is available at *www.urban.org*. Detailed data are available from *www.hud.gov*.

Homeless families

The national survey found that 34 percent of homeless service users are members of homeless families. Key characteristics of parents in homeless families include:

- 84 percent are female and 16 percent are male,
- 38 percent are white non-Hispanic, 43 percent are black non-Hispanic, 15 percent are Hispanic, 3 percent are Native American, and 1 percent are other races,
- 26 percent are ages 17 to 24, 74 percent are ages 25 to 54, and less than 0.5 percent are ages 55 and older,
- 41 percent have never married, 23 percent are married, 23 percent are separated,
- 13 percent are divorced, and none are widowed,
- 53 percent have less than a high school education, 21 percent have completed high school, and 27 percent have some education beyond high school.

Single homeless adults

The survey also interviewed single homeless adults. The key characteristics of this group included:

- 85 percent of homeless clients of programs are single,
- 77 percent are male and 23 percent are female,
- 41 percent are white non-Hispanic, 40 percent are black non-Hispanic, 10 percent are Hispanic, 8 percent are Native American, and 1 percent are other races,
- 10 percent are ages 17 to 24, 81 percent are ages 25 to 54, and 9 percent are ages 55 and older,
- 50 percent have never married, 7 percent are married, 14 percent are separated,

- 26 percent are divorced, and 4 percent are widowed,
- 37 percent have less than a high school education, 36 percent have completed high school, and 28 percent have some education beyond high school.

Hunger among homeless people

The survey found that:

- 28 percent say they sometimes or often do not get enough to eat, while only 12 percent of poor American adults say this is true,
- 20 percent eat one meal a day or less,
- 39 percent say that in the last thirty days they were hungry but could not afford to eat,
- 40 percent went one or more days in the last thirty days without anything to eat.

Alcohol, drugs, mental health

The survey asked whether homeless people had used alcohol or drugs or suffered mental problems.

Within the prior month,

- 38 percent reported alcohol use problems,
- 26 percent reported drug use problems,
- 39 percent reported mental health problems,
- 66 percent reported one or more of these problems.

Physical health problems

The survey asked about the health insurance status and medical problems of homeless people.

- 55 percent have no medical insurance.
- 46 percent report having chronic health conditions, such as arthritis, high blood pressure, diabetes, or cancer.
- 26 percent report having acute infectious conditions, such as a cough, cold, bronchitis, pneumonia, tuberculosis, or sexually transmitted diseases other than AIDS.
- 8 percent report having acute noninfectious conditions, such as skin ulcers, lice, or scabies.
- 3 percent report having HIV/AIDS.
- 3 percent report having tuberculosis.

Victimization or violence

The survey asked about the crimes homeless people have experienced while they have been on the streets or in shelters.

- 38 percent say someone stole from them.
- 22 percent have been physically assaulted.
- 7 percent have been sexually assaulted.

Income and employment

- Single homeless clients reported a mean income of $348 during the prior month.
- This is only 51 percent of the 1996 federal poverty level of $680/month for one person.
- Family households reported a mean income of $475 during the last thirty days. This is only 46 percent of the 1996 federal poverty level of $1,023/month for a family of three.
- 44 percent of homeless people reported that they did paid work during the prior month.
- 20 percent worked in a job lasting or expected to last at least three months.
- 25 percent worked at a temporary or day labor job.
- 2 percent earned money by peddling or selling personal belongings.
- 21 percent received income from family members or friends, including:
  9 percent from parents.
  2 percent from a spouse.
  5 percent from other relatives.
  12 percent from friends, including boyfriends and girlfriends.
  1 percent from child support.
  8 percent report income from more than one type of family member or friend.

Benefits and entitlements

- 37 percent received food stamps.
- 52 percent of homeless households with children receive Aid to Families with Dependent Children (AFDC). (In 1996, when the survey was conducted, AFDC was still operating.)

- 11 percent received Supplemental Security Income (SSI).
- 9 percent received General Assistance or another state or local cash assistance benefit.
- 6 percent of homeless veterans received veteran-related disability payments.
- 2 percent received veteran-related pensions.
- 30 percent receive Medicaid.
- 7 percent received medical care from the Department of Veterans Affairs.
- 8 percent reported income from panhandling.

Services homeless people want

- 42 percent said they most needed a job to end their homelessness.
- 38 percent needed housing.
- 30 percent needed housing assistance (rent assistance, utilities, etc.)
- 19 percent needed transportation.
- 18 percent needed clothing.
- 17 percent needed food.

Providers of homeless services

- 85 percent of programs are operated by nonprofit agencies.
- 51 percent of programs are operated by secular organizations.
- 34 percent of programs are provided by religious organizations.
- 14 percent are provided by government agencies.
- For-profit companies provide 1 percent.

Kinds of programs offered

- 60 percent of housing programs are operated by secular nonprofits.
- 55 percent of food programs are operated by religious agencies.
- 5 percent of food programs are provided by government.
- 51 percent of health programs are operated by government.

Funding for homeless assistance

- 51 percent of food programs receive no government funds.
- 55 percent of health programs receive only government funds.
- 25 percent of housing programs for homeless people receive only government funds.
- 23 percent receive only private funds.

Location of homeless people

Homeless people were found in every type of community.

- 71 percent are in central cities.
- 21 percent are in the suburbs.
- 9 percent are in rural areas.
  For poor people in the United States in general, these figures are 31, 46, and 23 percent, respectively.
- 29 percent of homeless families and 46 percent of single homeless clients live in a town other than where they first became homeless.

Major reasons for going to another town were the presence of relatives or friends, the possibility of work, and the availability of shelters and other services.

Where homeless people stay

- 31 percent slept on the streets or in similar nonshelter places (transportation depots, commercial spaces, cars or other vehicles, abandoned buildings, outdoor locations) within the prior week.
- 66 percent used an emergency shelter, transitional housing program, or similar program offering vouchers for emergency accommodation within the prior week.
- 36 percent used soup kitchens within the last week.
- 10 percent used other homeless assistance programs (e.g., drop-in centers, food pantries, outreach programs, mobile food programs) within the prior week.

Experiences of homelessness

- 49 percent of homeless people were in their first episode of homelessness.

- 34 percent have been homeless three or more times.
- 37 percent of single homeless people had been homeless three times or more, while only 23 percent of families had been homeless that frequently.
- 28 percent of homeless people had their current episode last three months or less.
- 30 percent had their current episode last more than two years.
- 49 percent of homeless families had been homeless for three months or less, compared to 23 percent of single homeless people.
- 34 percent of single homeless people had been homeless for more than two years, compared to only 13 percent of families.

Homeless people and their children

- 60 percent of homeless women had minor children.
- 65 percent of these women lived with at least one of their children.
- 41 percent of homeless men had minor children.
- 7 percent of the men lived with at least one of their children.

Of the children,

- 53 percent were male and 47 percent were female.
- 20 percent were ages 0 to 2, 22 percent were ages 3 to 5, 20 percent were ages 6 to 8, 33 percent were between the ages of 9 and 17, and age was not given for 5 percent.
- 51 percent of the children were in households receiving AFDC (this survey was pre–welfare reform).
- 70 percent were in households receiving food stamps.
- 12 percent were in households receiving SSI.
- 73 percent received Medicaid.

Homeless veterans

- 23 percent of those interviewed were veterans. About 13 percent of all American adults were veterans in 1996.
- 98 percent of the homeless veterans were men.
- 33 percent of male homeless clients are veterans. 31 percent of American men in 1996 were veterans.

- 21 percent served before the Vietnam era.
- 47 percent served during the Vietnam era (between August 1964 and April 1975).
- 57 percent served since the Vietnam era (after April 1975).
- 33 percent of the male veterans in the study were stationed in a war zone.
- 28 percent were exposed to combat.

Childhood experiences of homeless people

- 27 percent of homeless clients lived in foster care, a group home, or other institutional setting.
- 25 percent reported childhood physical or sexual abuse.
- 21 percent reported childhood experiences of homelessness.
- 33 percent reported running away from home.
- 22 percent reported being forced to leave home.

Available homeless programs

This survey estimated that there were about 40,000 homeless assistance programs in the United States, offered at about 21,000 locations. These include:

- 9,000 food pantries
- 3,500 soup kitchens
- 5,700 emergency shelters
- 4,400 transitional
- 3,300 outreach programs

49 percent of all homeless assistance programs are located in central cities, 32 percent in rural areas, and 19 percent in suburban areas.

Comparisons to prior research

The Urban Institute analyzed the data from the 1996 survey. The Urban Institute also conducted a similar national survey in 1987. The following statistics show how the data compare.

- Homeless shelter and soup kitchen clients located in central cities in 1996 are less likely to be white (39 versus 46 percent) and more likely to be black (46 versus 41 percent).

- They are more likely to have completed high school—39 versus 32 percent, and to have some education beyond high school—27 versus 20 percent.
- More have never married (51 versus 45 percent).
- They are more likely to get government benefits:
  - AFDC among homeless families with children—58 percent in 1996 versus 33 percent in 1987;
  - food stamps among all homeless—38 versus 18 percent; and
  - SSI among all homeless—13 versus 4 percent.
- They have higher average monthly incomes per capita after adjusting for inflation ($267 in 1996 versus $189 in 1987), but are still very poor.
- No differences were found in the percentage experiencing inpatient treatment for alcohol or drug abuse or for mental health problems.

Cities Report Growing Homelessness

Each December, the U.S. Conference of Mayors issues a report on hunger and homelessness in the nation's cities. The mayors' 2000 report found the following from its survey cities:

- requests for emergency shelter for homeless families increased by 17 percent;
- 80 percent of cities experienced an increase;
- in 50 percent of the cities, it was found that the length of time people are homeless had increased;
- the number of family emergency beds in the survey cities increased by 26 percent from the previous year; and
- the number of transitional beds increased by an average of 38 percent.

How Much Homelessness Is There in the United States?

Priority: HOME! The Federal Plan to Break the Cycle of Homelessness was published by the U.S. government in 1994. The following excerpt describes why it is important to count homeless people over an extended period of time in a community, rather than to undertake a count on a one-day or a one-night basis, to discover the dimensions of the problem.

The Scale of Contemporary Homelessness

Accurately measuring the scope and magnitude of "residential instability"—with homelessness as its most extreme manifestation—has proven controversial. The debate has ranged from which definition of homelessness is most appropriate to the limitations of or biases in various research methods used to estimate the size of the homeless population. Our understanding has evolved as data collection techniques have advanced from single-day or one-week counts to computerized annual (or longer time frame) unduplicated counts. Strikingly, when researchers turn to charting the use of shelters over time, a picture of widespread vulnerability to homelessness emerges. The changes discussed in this Plan have had a profound impact on the ability of people, especially poor people, to maintain stable housing.

Point-in-time Estimates

Early methodologies for taking the measure of homelessness depended upon one-time counts in shelters, soup kitchens, other service sites, and street settings. Such counts are referred to as "point prevalence" counts, since they capture only those people who are homeless at a specific point in time. One such widely cited figure for a national point-in-time estimate was generated by an Urban Institute study. Researchers found that as many as 600,000 people were homeless during a seven-day period in March 1987.

These narrow frame pictures were, until recently, the most comprehensive we had. However, such "snapshot" counts and the descriptions of homeless people based upon them can be highly misleading if they are taken to imply that the homeless population is a static one. In fact, as recent analyses have shown, large numbers of people flow through shelters over time.

Estimates Over Time

Studies completed only in the last year have used sophisticated local administrative record keeping systems to yield new insights into the dynamics of homelessness by measuring turnover in shelters. These new studies suggest that the number of individuals and families who experience at least one episode of homelessness during longer intervals (typically one to five years) may exceed the best estimates of single-shot street and shelter counts by a factor of ten or more.

A recent study of shelter systems in New York City and Philadelphia documents the large turnover of persons using shelters. For example, in New York, a single shelter bed accommodates four different persons each year. The one-day and one-, three-, and five-year counts of persons in shelters were 23,000, 86,000, 162,000, and 240,000 persons, respectively. The turnover in the Philadelphia shelters is even more dramatic, with each bed accommodating six persons per year. The one-day, and one- and three-year counts were 2,500, 15,000 and 43,000 persons, respectively. Analysis of annual counts in other cities such as Columbus, Ohio, and St. Paul, Minneapolis, and in the state of Rhode Island reveal similar patterns of turnover. The New York City analysis found that the number of homeless persons using public shelters over periods of three and five years amounted to 2.2 and 3.3 percent of the city's population, respectively. Further confirmation of the magnitude of recent homelessness in New York is provided by the 1991 *Housing and Vacancy Report* for that city. Among housed residents in New York in early 1991, 176,000—or 3 percent of the total—had experienced at least one bout of homelessness in the previous five years. (For purposes of the study, persons were considered to have experienced homelessness if they came to that dwelling unit during the last five years "from a temporary residence such as a friend's or relative's home, shelter, transitional center, or hotel." At the time of the study, 14 percent of those who reported prior homelessness were living in doubled-up situations. For Philadelphia, the percentage of persons using shelters over 3 years was three percent of that city's population.

The results of local studies of shelter turnover converge with those of a recent national study. A nationwide telephone survey of more than 1,500 (currently housed) adult Americans found that over 3 percent of those interviewed had been homeless at some point between 1985 and 1990. In this sample, the confidence interval of the estimate ranged from 2.3 percent to 4.4 percent of the adult population.

Thus, based on these samples, the number of adults experiencing homelessness was between 4 and 8 million at some point in the latter half of the 1980s. As the Link study was performed by a telephone survey, it did not reach or include people currently homeless and households without telephones. If these adjustments were made, the estimate would likely be higher. The study did not report in any way the cause or reason for the person's homelessness.

When the number of children is added, the range for the total population is 4.95 million to 9.32 million, with a midpoint of approximately 7 million. The number of children is estimated at 15 percent of the total homeless population and this number is applied to the adult population estimates.

But even these estimates of the number of persons experiencing homelessness do not take into account the large number of extremely vulnerable persons who are on the edge of homelessness. There are approximately 2 million families on public housing waiting lists and an additional 1 million awaiting Section 8 vouchers. There are also those who are involuntarily doubled up with friends and relatives, and those who are paying more than 50 percent of their income for rent.

The clear point is that recent studies confirm that the number of persons who have experienced homelessness is very large and greater than previously known or acknowledged. This supports several basic thrusts of this report. To make real inroads into reducing homelessness we need to make real progress in reducing poverty and providing adequate affordable housing for those who are on the edge of homelessness. And we need to steep up our efforts to prevent homelessness of those who are living on the edge. (Interagency Council on the Homeless 1994)

Shelter Use as a Factor in Understanding Homelessness

Until the early 1990s, there was little credible research to back up the common images of homeless people. In 1991, Dr. Dennis Culhane of the University of Pennsylvania published research based on his studies of homeless shelters in New York City and Philadelphia. Culhane's research brought a new dimension to the understanding of homelessness in the United States. Instead of relying on the so-called point in time study used in many communities in the form of an annual one-night count of those on the streets or in shelters, Culhane applied a "hospital model" to the shelter system. He looked at the length of time individuals used shelters and how often they returned to use the shelters again. From this study, Culhane concluded that the population of single homeless people was actually made up of three distinct groups of shelter users (see Table 4.1).

Culhane concluded that the "episodically homeless" are among the "hard to serve" population, going in and out of the shelter system. This group uses emergency shelters, corrections facilities, detoxification facilities, and hospitals. They are costly to institutions, and their homelessness shows that other institutions are failing. Culhane proposed that this is an appropriate population for transitional programs.

He concluded that the "chronically homeless" population is the one that consumes most resources in the system but that it is a stable, not an emergency, population. Emergency shelter is basically home for this population, which makes them good candidates for supportive housing. Unlike their previous image that made them appear to be the largest part of the homeless population, Culhane found that the chronically homeless are a finite population.

The third population, the "transitionally homeless," is a population that stays briefly, leaves, and doesn't return. Culhane concluded that this group shows that emergency shelters work for the majority of this population and that the absence of high rates of disability shows that their homelessness could be prevented.

Barriers Faced by Homeless People in Using Programs

In July 2000, the U.S. General Accounting Office (GAO) released the results of its research on how homeless people use mainstream or nonhomeless programs. The report examined: (1) why homeless people cannot always access or effectively use federal mainstream programs; and (2) how the federal government can improve homeless people's access to, and use of, these programs.

The key findings of the report include the following.

- Homeless people are often unable to access and use federal mainstream programs because of the inherent conditions of homelessness as well as the structure and operations of the programs themselves.

TABLE 4.1
Length of Stay in Shelter and Characteristics of Shelter Users

	Transitional	Episodic	Chronic
Shelter stays/3 yrs.	1.4	5	1–2
Number of days/3 yrs.	About 60	About 260	About 800
Percent of users	80 percent	10 percent	10 percent
Percent of days	35 percent	20 percent	50 percent
Substance abuse	14 percent	30 percent	40 percent
Mental health	Less than 10 percent		30 percent
Age	36 percent under age 30, 8 percent over age 50	35 percent under age 30, 65 over age 50	23 percent under age 30, 14 percent over age 50

Source: Randall Kuhn and Denis P. Culhane. *Applying Cluster Analysis to Test a Typology of Homelessness by Patterns of Shelter Utilization: Results from the Analysis of Administrative Data. American Journal of Community Psychology,* 1998.

- Although all low-income populations face barriers to applying for, retaining, and using the services provided by mainstream programs, these barriers are compounded by the inherent conditions of homelessness, such as transience, instability, and a lack of basic resources.
- The underlying structure and operations of federal mainstream programs are often not conducive to ensuring that the special needs of homeless people are met.
- Federal programs do not always include service providers with expertise and experience in addressing the needs of homeless people.
- These providers may not be organized or equipped to serve homeless people, may not be knowledgeable about their special needs, or may not have the sensitivity or experience to treat homeless clients with respect.
- The federal government's system for providing assistance to low-income people is highly fragmented, which, among other things, can make it difficult to develop an integrated approach to helping homeless people, who often have multiple needs.
- Alleviating these barriers would require the federal government to address a number of long-standing and complex issues.

The expert panel that GAO convened discussed a variety of strategies the federal government could pursue to improve homeless people's access to, and use of, mainstream federal programs.

These included: (a) improving the integration and coordination of federal programs; (b) making the process of applying for federal assistance easier; (c) improving outreach to homeless people; (d) ensuring an appropriate system of incentives for serving homeless people; and (e) holding mainstream programs more accountable for serving homeless people.

Most of these issues are not new, and federal agencies have tried to address them for years with varied degrees of success.

Panel members noted that federal agencies could do more to incorporate into mainstream programs the various lessons learned from McKinney Act programs and demonstration projects targeted at homeless people.

These demonstration projects have developed effective approaches to serving homeless people.

Some of their recommendations included:

- reducing the fragmentation of programs at the federal level to improve access to mainstream programs for homeless people and facilitating the coordination of programs at the state and community levels;
- reducing federal funding restrictions in order to facilitate providing integrated care for people with multiple needs at the community level;
- synchronizing federal funding cycles and consolidating funding of similar federal programs to make it easier for communities to coordinate their own programs and planning efforts;
- incorporating the best practices in coordination and integration that have been developed from the McKinney Act's targeted programs for the homeless and from several federally funded demonstration projects;
- simplifying the application processes for federal programs would facilitate homeless people's ability to access these programs;
- using a core application form that gathers the basic information required for most federal programs, so as to reduce the need for applicants to provide the same information to multiple programs;
- developing a database that would provide comprehensive information on all federal mainstream programs and benefits available to low-income people, including those who are homeless;
- granting presumptive eligibility on the basis of homelessness for some federal programs, and granting provisional eligibility on the basis of homelessness while permanent eligibility is being established for other programs;
- extending greater outreach to homeless people is needed to ensure that they have access to federal programs;
- sending mainstream program staff to places where homeless people congregate, such as shelters and soup kitchens, so that they can encourage eligible

individuals to apply for programs and assist them with the application process;

- disseminating information about federal programs more widely through more visual and creative methods; and
- developing flexible pools of funds that providers of services to homeless people can use to engage homeless individuals, particularly those living on the street, and encourage them to reconnect with the community and take advantage of services available to them.

GAO panelists stated that there is a need to create a system of incentives that encourages federal mainstream service providers to better serve homeless people. The incentives included:

- setting aside earmarked (targeted) funds or other kinds of financial incentives to help ensure that the states and communities use block grant dollars to serve homeless people adequately;
- encouraging localities to adjust performance measures for job training programs of the Workforce Investment Act so that they do not create disincentives for serving homeless people;
- tracking the numbers and outcomes of homeless people served through federally funded programs is an essential first step toward developing a system of accountability;
- developing a set of minimum standards for how block grant funds should address the needs of the homeless population that would help ensure that states and communities are held accountable for serving homeless people while still preserving the flexibility inherent in a block grant; and
- requiring recipients of some federal funds to address in their planning documents how they will serve the homeless population. (GAO/RCED 2000)

Homeless Veterans

Homeless veterans are widely reported to make up about 30 percent of the homeless adult population. The federal government spent about $630 million on programs for homeless veterans during the period 1987–1997, according to the U.S. General Accounting Office. The following excerpt is from a GAO report on these programs.

Pursuant to a congressional request, GAO reviewed the effectiveness of efforts to assist homeless veterans, focusing on: (1) describing the Department of Veterans Affairs (VA) homeless programs; (2) determining what VA knows about the effectiveness of its homeless programs; and (3) examining promising approaches aimed at different groups of homeless veterans.

GAO noted that: (1) VA's homeless assistance and treatment programs address diverse needs of homeless veterans by providing services such as case management, employment assistance, and transitional housing; (2) VA also provides medical, mental health, substance abuse, and social services to homeless veterans through its hospitals, outpatient clinics, and other health care facilities; (3) because of resource constraints and legislative mandates, VA expanded its homeless veterans efforts by better aligning itself with other federal departments, state and local government agencies, and community-based organizations; (4) the goal of this effort is to develop a continuum of care for the homeless—that is, to identify or create options for addressing the full array of housing, health, and service needs of this population; (5) VA has little information about the effectiveness of its homeless programs; (6) VA has relied on the Northeast Program Evaluation Center (NEPEC) to gather and report information about its homeless programs; (7) each of VA's homeless program sites routinely submits extensive data, mostly related to client characteristics and operations at individual program sites; (8) these data are used primarily to provide program managers with information about service delivery and are of limited use in assessing program effectiveness; (9) to evaluate effectiveness, information must be gathered about intended program results; (10) the outcome measures that NEPEC uses focus on housing, employment, and changes in substance abuse and mental health at the time veterans are discharged from VA's homeless programs; (11) little is known about whether veterans served by VA's homeless programs remain housed or employed, or whether they instead relapse into homelessness; (12) many questions about how to treat homelessness remain unanswered; and (13) experts agree, however, that a comprehensive continuum of care for the homeless—such as that which VA is striving to achieve—should include a range of housing and service alternatives, with specific approaches at any one site reflecting local needs and local resources. (GAO/HEHS 1999)

Youth Homelessness

One aspect of homelessness that dates back to the growth of the population in the mid-1980s is that which results from the emergence of young adults from public systems of care, such as the foster care system. In 1995, the National Alliance to End Homelessness published a report that examined the relationship of homelessness and foster care to determine whether the former foster care population was overrepresented among the adult homeless population. The following summarizes the study.

In order to examine this issue, the project used four sources of information: (1) existing research on the connection between foster care and homelessness; (2) data collected from organizations that serve homeless people and gather information on their clients' foster care history; (3) data obtained directly from a sample of homeless people; and (4) case studies of people who are or were homeless and who have a foster care history.

The principal findings of this study are as follows.

- There is an overrepresentation of people with a foster care history in the homeless population.
- Homeless people with a foster care history are more likely than other people to have their own children in foster care.
- Very frequently, people who are homeless had multiple placements as children: some were in foster care, but others were unofficial placements in the homes of family or friends.

In addition, there were certain demographic factors that were revealed by the research.

- Those people with a foster care history tend to become homeless at an earlier age than those who do not have a foster care history.
- Homeless people who are white are somewhat more likely to have a foster care history than homeless people who are Hispanic or African American.
- Childhood placement in foster care can correlate with a substantial increase in the length of a person's homeless experience.

The research did not find that (nor did it examine if) foster care directly caused homelessness. To the contrary, most children who experience foster care do not become homeless as adults. Rather, the indication was that foster care has an impact on personal risk factors that may eventually result in homelessness.

The foster care system often fails to help children deal with the problems that result from circumstances that caused them to be removed from their homes (these circumstances include physical or sexual abuse; parents with alcohol or substance abuse illness; family dissolution; etc.). Foster care can also fail to help children deal with problems that arise from foster care placements in abusive homes or facilities. Among the findings were the following.

- Alcohol and other substance abuse illnesses and mental illness play a significant role in the relationship between foster care and homelessness.
- Young people emancipated from foster care often lack the independent living skills that would allow them to establish a household.
- People who have experienced extensive foster care, particularly multiple placements, extended group home placements, or foster care in combination with multiple unofficial placements, may become better acculturated to institutionalized living than to living on their own.
- Young people who are emancipated from foster care and become homeless tend to lack the support

networks that other people can rely upon in times of crisis.

- Children who are moved from home to home over an extended period of time (foster care and/or unofficial placements) learn to deal with problems by leaving them behind.

It is clear from this study that what happens to children has a lifelong impact on them. When you see a homeless adult, it is quite possible that they are homeless because of people and systems that failed them as children. In order to eliminate any contribution foster care may make to homelessness, the National Alliance to End Homelessness makes the following recommendations.

- A better job must be done in supporting and strengthening families (particularly those in crisis) in order to keep children out of the foster care system.
- Once children are in the foster care system, extraordinary measures should be taken to move them quickly into a permanent living situation (family reunification or adoption), taking all necessary steps to avoid multiple placements.
- If children have experienced multiple placements, a much more directed effort should be made to help them gain the skills and other resources necessary to move to successful independence.
- The service and housing needs of homeless parents with a foster care history should be met so that their stability is promoted and their own children are not placed in foster care.
- Extraordinary steps should be taken to avoid placing children in foster care solely because of their parents' homelessness. Other measures (such as housing, employment and/or training, and services) should be taken, first. (National Alliance to End Homelessness)

Emerging Homeless Populations and Homelessness Prevention

As homelessness in the United States has continued to grow, there has been concern that additional feeders into homelessness are developing. Some increased homelessness in the last several years has been linked to reform of public assistance programs, starting with the decrease in General Assistance or General Relief income assistance programs frequently targeted to single people. Over half of all states cut or eliminated their programs in the early 1990s, affecting more than half a million recipients. Reform of the AFDC program in the late 1990s also saw more people turn to shelters for help.

But the growth in homelessness may be over and above these factors, as demonstrated by research from one statewide homelessness advocacy organization. Data collected by the Massachusetts Housing and Shelter Alliance (MHSA) has demonstrated that increasing numbers of ex-offenders, young adults, and persons discharged from psychiatric treatment in the Medicaid managed care system are entering adult shelters. According to MHSA's data collected over a period of four years:

- 18 to 24-year-olds in adult shelters more than doubled between 1998 and 2000;
- over 75 percent of new shelter guests coming from psychiatric treatment are emerging from the managed care system;
- over 1,000 people annually enter shelters from a detoxification facility for drugs or alcohol;
- 900–1,000 people annually enter shelters from a jail or prison.

Each of these subpopulations has been traced to a public system responsible for care, treatment, or custody of individuals. MHSA's findings have been directed at redefining the prevention of homelessness to include efforts to provide more adequate and appropriate discharge planning for individuals leaving these systems with no home to go to (MHSA 2000).

Reducing the Costs of Homelessness

Some of the prior data presented in this chapter show the scale of homelessness and the scope of federal spending to address it. Some researchers have documented both the costs associated with homelessness and the savings that result when people move out of homelessness and into stable living situations, especially into housing with supportive services. A few examples of data are presented here.

Hospitalization Costs Associated with Homelessness in New York City

A 1992–1993 study compared the length of stay of homeless and low-income patients in New York's public hospitals. Of a total of nearly 19,000 homeless admissions, the study found that:

- homeless patients stayed an average of 4.1 days—or 36 percent—longer than low-income patients with homes and cost an average of $2,414 more per admission;
- psychiatric patients accounted for 57 percent of extra hospital days among the homeless;
- one-third of homeless psychiatric patients averaged stays of eighty-four days conservatively; an extra cost per admission was $17,500; and
- nearly half of homeless medical hospitalizations were for conditions related to living conditions and therefore preventable (respiratory disorders, skin infections, parasites/infections, and trauma).

The study estimates that the total preventable costs associated with homeless patients for the New York City public hospital system are $100 million per year (Salit 1998).

Health Service Use and Related Costs among Homeless Veterans

A national survey of more than 9,000 veterans hospitalized in acute mental health care units of veterans' hospitals in 1995 found that nearly 35 percent were homeless upon admission; and the cost of care for a homeless veteran was $3,196 higher than for one with a home (Rosenbeck).

Supportive Housing and Its Impact on Health Issues for Homeless People

Research done between 1996 and 2000 on more than 250 people living at the Canon Kip Community House and the Lyric Hotel in

California looks at how the formerly homeless tenants used emergency rooms and inpatient care before and after they were placed in housing. The study found that 81 percent, or 204, remained housed for at least one year and that they experienced a 58 percent decrease in emergency room visits, a 57 percent drop in the number of inpatient days, and a 100 percent drop in use of residential mental health facilities (Corporation for Supportive Housing 2000).

Housing for the Homeless Mentally Ill

A 1994 federal report examined the provision of flexible support services combined with permanent housing for homeless people with severe mental illness. The study found:

- a housing retention/success rate of 83.5 percent;
- a decrease in inpatient hospitalization at the study's San Diego site, where inpatient days were reduced by 49 percent;
- a reduction in inpatient costs at the Baltimore site, where costs dropped by 52 percent;
- a reduction in annual per person inpatient costs at the Boston site, where costs were reduced by $3,800;
- a decrease in emergency room visits by 50 percent;
- a decrease in incarcerations by 50 percent; and
- a decrease in symptoms of schizophrenia and depression. (U.S. Department of Health and Human Services, 1994)

In New York City, the 1990 New York/New York Agreement, House the Homeless Mentally Ill, is a city/state program that provides housing and services for 5,225 individuals who resided in hospitals, shelters, and on the streets. As of September 30, 1997, program data show that a total of 8,370 individuals had been housed through this agreement. In addition, the NY/NY Agreement had a nearly 80 percent retention rate, with 10 percent moving on to independent settings (New York City HRA/OHMHS 1999).

The Poverty Line

The poverty line is the federal government's official measure of what it takes to support a household. The U.S. Department of

Health and Human Services releases a new set of income standards each year, and the figures for different size households determine eligibility for many assistance programs. The standards set by the poverty line also determine the federal government's official estimates of how many people are living in poverty (see Table 4.2).

Housing Affordability Problems

The high cost of housing in many areas contributes to homelessness. What does housing affordability have to do with homelessness? Persons on fixed incomes, including those on welfare benefits, may have a difficult time affording housing. Those receiving public assistance already live below the poverty line, and any unexpected expense can cause them to face homelessness. Furthermore, persons who are already homelessness may have difficulty finding permanent housing they can afford, so they might be homeless longer.

Following are some facts about housing affordability problems facing poor people. According to the National Low Income Housing Coalition (NLIHC):

- the eight most costly states in the United States in regard to housing costs, when costs for two-bedroom units at 30 percent of income are considered, are as follows: New Jersey, District of Columbia, Hawaii,

TABLE 4.2
2001 HHS Poverty Guidelines

Size of Family Unit	48 States and D.C.	Alaska	Hawaii
1	$8,590	$10,730	$9,890
2	11,610	14,510	13,360
3	14,630	18,290	16,830
4	17,650	22,070	20,300
5	20,670	25,850	23,770
6	23,690	29,630	27,240
7	26,710	33,410	30,710
8	29,730	37,190	34,180
For each additional person, add $3,020 (48 states); $3,780 (Alaska); $3,470 (Hawaii)			

Source: Federal Register, Vol. 65, No. 31, 15 February 2000, pp. 7555–7557.

Massachusetts, New York, Connecticut, California, Alaska, and New Hampshire.
- the most costly urban areas for two-bedroom units at 30 percent of income are: San Francisco, California; San Jose, California; Stamford-Norwalk, Connecticut; Nassau-Suffolk, New York; Westchester County, New York; Santa Cruz–Watsonville, California; Oakland, California; Orange County, California; Boston, Massachusetts, and southern New Hampshire. (National Low Income Housing Coalition 2000)

Facts about Homelessness in Europe

Following is research information about homelessness in England and Scotland. This information is drawn from a series of fact sheets prepared by Shelter, Britain's largest homeless services and advocacy organization. Shelter maintains about sixty housing aid centers and Shelterline, a twenty-four-hour free national housing advice hot line.

Homelessness in London

- 41,070 households were officially recognized in 1999 as homeless in the London region by local authorities. Shelter estimates that this represents about 98,600 individuals.

Of those officially recognized as homeless:

- 27,220 households were accepted as homeless in priority need;
- 1,470 households were found to be intentionally homeless; and
- 12,380 households were found to be homeless but not in priority need. (Department of the Environment, Transportation, and the Regions 1999/2000)

Temporary accommodation

At the end of December 1999 a total of 36,330 homeless households were lodged in temporary accommodations by local authorities.
Of these households in temporary accommodation:

- 6,360 households were living in bed and breakfast (a type of shelter in the United Kingdom);
- 3,700 were living in hostels;
- 8,340 were living in local authority or housing association housing;
- 13,240 were living in private sector leased properties;
- 4,690 were living in other forms of temporary lodging; and
- 5,540 further households were registered as being homeless at home. (Department of the Environment, Transportation, and the Regions 2000)

Shelter, a national organization acting on behalf of homeless and poorly housed people, provides the following statistics about homeless people in England:

- Homelessness is the most extreme form of housing need.
- In 1999 a total of 166,760 households were found to be homeless by local authorities in England. Shelter estimates that this represents over 400,000 individuals. Of these, 104,700 were households toward whom local authorities had a duty to provide housing. They were either households with dependent children or people who were considered to be vulnerable through age, mental or physical problems, or other special reasons.

Homeless mentally ill

- In 1999 a total of 7,530 households were accepted as homeless and in priority need due to mental illness.
- These figures only present the information collected by local authorities. They do not give the whole picture of the scale of homelessness. They do not include thousands of unofficially homeless people in England, for whom local authorities have no responsibility to provide accommodation and who do not seek or get help from their council.
- The majority of single homeless people are included in this category. Although data on single homelessness is not collected for England as a whole, available information suggests that the numbers involved are substantial.

- In 1999, Shelterline received 38,000 calls from single people, 25 percent of all calls made.
- It is estimated that about 41,000 people are living in hostels and vacant buildings, and over 1,100 people are sleeping on the streets on any given night. In addition, about 78,000 couples or single parents share accommodations with others as they cannot afford to set up a home on their own.
- Some studies have suggested that as many as 50 percent of the total homeless population may have some form of mental health problems, ranging from depression to severe mental health and personality disorders.
- A study found that 36 percent of day-center users, 40 percent of soup-run users, and 28 percent of homeless single people living in hostels and bed and breakfast hotels reported mental health problems. This compared with 5 percent of the general population.
- Shelter found that 10 percent of homeless people attending an accident and emergency department (A&E) in a London hospital had mental health problems. This compared with only 3 percent of the housed attendees. Mental illness was the second reason, after accidents and injuries, for homeless people attending A&E. (Shelter 1996)
- Among older homeless people, one study found that about two-thirds reported or demonstrated having mental health problems. (Shelter 1997)
- A study among residents of two direct-access hostels that cater specifically to homeless women found that 64 percent of the women met the diagnostic criteria for schizophrenia and a further 26 percent suffered from other psychiatric disorders. They were more likely to have a history of family violence or abusive relationship with partners adversely affecting their mental health. (Marshall and Reed 1992)
- Another study (Shelter 1994) found that 33 percent of women living in hostels and bed and breakfast accommodations had mental health problems. This increased to 44 percent and 55 percent for users of day centers and soup runs, respectively. This compared with 7 percent of the overall female population that reported mental health problems.

- A report found that mental health problems among women sleeping on the streets and contacted by outreach workers were higher than in men, 30 percent and 25 percent, respectively. (Shelter 1999)

Homeless men in London

- The majority of homeless people who sleep on the street are men. Nearly 90 percent of people who slept on the streets in 1999 in London were men. (Shelter 1999)

Racial and ethnic minorities

- About 50 percent of those accepted as homeless in London are from minority ethnic groups (Shelter 1999). Minority ethnic groups represent about 15 percent of all households in London. The number of minority ethnic populations living in the United Kingdom has increased since the end of World War II. Today, the growth in the minority ethnic groups is mainly due to children born in the United Kingdom, rather than through immigration. These children constitute half of the minority ethnic population living in the United Kingdom. Minority ethnic groups now total around 3.4 million people, representing 6 percent of the household population in Great Britain.
- Minority ethnic groups are overrepresented among the long-term unemployed. Youth unemployment is consistently high across all groups. (ONS 1998)

Women from racial and ethnic minorities

- In the first half of 1997/98 over 1,400 women from minority ethnic groups received help from Shelter's Housing Advice service in London.
- Around 77 percent were homeless or potentially homeless and 4 percent were fleeing domestic violence.
- Some reports suggest that these women endure higher levels of homelessness, discrimination, and deprivation. According to a survey carried out in two London boroughs, women may face sexism and stigmatization in the community, especially when they

break away from abusive relationships to live independently. In many Asian cultures it is not acceptable to leave the parental or marital homes to look for accommodations on their own. (Rao 1990)

Young people

- One study reported that depression was relatively high among young homeless people compared with the general population. It found that 45 percent of soup-run users and 31 percent of day-center users under the age of twenty-five reported mental health problems. (Shelter 1994)

People with multiple needs

- Alcohol use affects as many as 50 percent of street homeless people. It is estimated that 20 percent of people who sleep on the streets use drugs, and this is more common among younger street homeless people (Social Exclusion Unit 1998). About 28 percent of street homeless people between the ages of eighteen and twenty-five have drug-related problems. (Shelter 1999)

Health problems of single people

- Recent research has suggested that homeless people living on the streets as well as hostel dwellers are up to twenty-five times more likely than the average citizen to die early. They are most likely to die from illness such as bronchitis, pneumonia, or tuberculosis (University of Bristol 1997). It is estimated that about 2 percent of street homeless people and direct access hostel users have been found to have active tuberculosis, 200 times the national TB notification rate. (Citron 1997)
- Research has shown (Bines 1994) that compared to the general population people who sleep on the street are:
    - three times more likely to suffer from chronic chest or breathing problems
    - twice as likely to experience muscle and joint problems
    - twice as likely to have digestive problems

- between two and three times more likely to
  have wounds, skin ulcers, and other skin
  complaints
- eleven times more likely to have mental health
  problems
- A Shelter research report (Shelter 1996b) showed that
  while both homeless and housed people used accident
  and emergency departments (A&E), homeless people's
  accidents and injuries were four times more likely to be
  the result of an assault. Their wounds were twice as
  likely to be infected, so that admission to hospital for
  further treatment was required.

Homeless families

- Many homeless families and vulnerable single people
  are placed in temporary accommodations while they
  wait for an offer of settled housing from the housing
  register or waiting list.
- Since 1997, councils have a duty to house priority-need
  homeless people in temporary accommodation for a
  period of two years.
- At the end of March 2000, a total of 63,470 homeless
  families were placed in temporary accommodation by
  local authorities in England. This is an increase of over
  50 percent since March 1997.

Access to health care

- Although everyone has a right to access primary
  health care services, normally via registering with a
  general practitioner, homeless people on the streets
  and those living in temporary accommodations often
  find that accessing health services is not always
  straightforward.
- A Shelter study found that 37 percent of homeless
  people are not registered with GPs. This compares with
  only 3 percent of the rest of the population who were
  not registered with a GP. (Shelter 1996b)
- One health authority in London has operated a
  notification system with a local housing department
  since 1992. The housing department notifies visiting
  nurses of homeless households in temporary and

permanent accommodations, single homeless people who register as such with the Homeless Person's Unit, and households settling in the area from abroad including asylum seekers. Notification of changes of address enables the health authority to continue contact with the households. The health authority sees improved access to health services leading to improved health, and so reducing their costs in the long term.

Use of hospital services

- A study found that 57 percent of all visits to a London hospital A&E department by homeless people could be classed as inappropriate. (Shelter 1996b)
- Another study identified that homeless people who have spent time in hospital can be discharged either back to inappropriate accommodations or even back on to the streets, with no ongoing support or care. (Shelter 1999)

Asylum seekers

- Asylum seekers come to the United Kingdom fleeing human rights abuses in their own countries. The majority of asylum seekers are homeless on arrival, many suffering from mental or physical trauma. Many are also vulnerable in other ways, such as problems with communicating in English and knowing how or where to find appropriate help.
- Under the Housing Act 1996, the majority of asylum seekers is not eligible to apply for homelessness assistance and is also denied access to the housing register.
- Under the Asylum and Immigration Act 1996, most asylum seekers also lost entitlement to the most basic benefits such as income support, housing benefit, and council tax benefit.
- At the end of May 1998 there were approximately 15,550 asylum seekers, including 5,780 families with children who were living in temporary accommodations provided by social services because

their loss of benefits and other assistance meant they would otherwise become destitute.

The Needs of Irish People

- It is estimated that one in ten people sleeping on the streets of Greater London are Irish.
- The 1991 Census estimated that people born in Ireland represent about 1.5 percent of the population in Britain. Almost 50 percent of the Irish-born population currently resides in London and Southeast England.
- Almost a quarter of day center users in London are Irish.
- Irish people make up 10 percent of users of winter shelters.
- One in four Irish advice-center users was homeless.
- Irish people are overrepresented in private rental housing.

Social exclusion

- In recent years the number of households excluded from mainstream society as a result of poverty and its consequences has increased substantially. It is estimated that the proportion of people living in households with no one working increased from 7 percent in 1979 to 18 percent in 1995–1996. Frequently, minority ethnic groups are the most affected. They tend to be concentrated in some of the most deprived and economically disadvantaged areas.
- Many Irish-born people are concentrated in the most deprived social classes. About 12 percent of Irish-born women are at the bottom end of social classes compared with 7.5 percent of English-born women. Irish-born men are twice as likely to be at the bottom end than English-born men, 11 percent and 5 percent, respectively, according to the Registrar General's Social Group. (CRE 1997)

Access to housing

- There is a shortage of good quality affordable housing in England. In the last decade gross social housing investment has decreased by 52 percent from £6,376 to

£3,092 million. Shelter estimates that over 100,000 affordable homes will need to be provided every year between 2000 and 2011 in order to meet current and newly arising housing needs.

- There is evidence that only a small number of Irish people register on waiting lists for public housing, which means the community's needs are going unrecorded. A study of single Irish women found that very few were registering and in fact were being discouraged from doing so. As a result, Irish housing associations face problems receiving nominations from some local authorities that have few single Irish people on their registers. (CARA 1995)
- Many housing providers seem not to be aware of the relative disadvantage of Irish people. In part this is because Irish people tend not to be recorded as a separate ethnic group. A nationwide survey, with a 63 percent response rate, found that only twenty-six local authorities monitored Irish people as a separate ethnic group. Of these, fourteen were in Greater London. A survey of housing associations or Registered Social Landlords found that only fifty-one of the largest eighty-eight associations monitor Irish people as a separate group. (CRE 1997)
- A local authority has a duty under the Housing Act 1996 to provide temporary accommodations for two years to a household that is homeless, in priority need, and not intentionally homeless. A household has a priority need if it contains a dependent child or pregnant woman or if he/she is vulnerable. A person has a priority need for accommodation if she or he is vulnerable as a result "of old age, mental illness or handicap, physical disability or other special reason." Those homeless people who do not fall into priority need groups, including most single people, do not qualify for accommodation from the local authority.
- It is estimated that 11 percent of people sleeping on the streets of Greater London are Irish. (Housing Services Agency 1999)
- A recent survey found that single Irish people represent about 9 percent of the residents in direct

access hostels and 10 percent of winter shelters' population. (SHIL and LBGC 1996)

- A survey of day centers in London found that 22 percent of users were Irish.
- The latest published data reported that 24 percent of users of Irish advice centers were homeless.
- In 1997–1998, 24 percent of Irish households placed by housing associations were homeless. (University of York 1999)
- Some Irish households who approach local authorities as homeless have been treated differently compared to their English counterparts. In the early 1980s, they were often issued travel warrants to return to Ireland, rather than provided with housing. In the early 1990s, a pattern emerged of Irish people being declared "intentionally homeless" because they left Ireland. Intentionally homeless families are owed no long-term housing duty. Such practices were usually unlawful, under homelessness law, and clearly discriminatory. (Shelter 2000)

Homelessness in Scotland

- During 1998–1999, 45,584 families and single people applied to their local council as being homeless. This is an all-time high of applications. The number of applications has increased by 57 percent over the last ten years.
- Shelter estimates that this amounts to over 81,000 individuals.
- The numbers of officially recorded homeless people in Scotland has increased by 57 percent in ten years.
- Every working day in Scotland, eighty children become homeless.
- The average life expectancy for a person living on the streets is forty-nine. (Shelter 2000)

References

Corporation for Supportive Housing, Evaluation of the Health, Housing, and Integrated Services Network. New York, 2000.

Interagency Council on the Homeless. *Priority: Home! The Federal Plan to Break the Cycle of Homelessness.* Washington, DC: U.S. Department of Housing and Urban Development, 1994.

Massachusetts Housing and Shelter Alliance. *Research on Emerging Homeless Subpopulations: Comparison of Emerging Subpopulations in Massachusetts Emergency Shelters, 1997–2000.* Boston, MA: 2000.

National Alliance to End Homelessness. *Web of Failure: The Relationship of Foster Care and Homelessness.* Washington, DC: National Alliance to End Homelessness, 1995.

National Low Income Housing Coalition. *Out of Reach: The Growing Gap Between Housing Costs and Income of Poor People in the United States.* Washington, DC: National Low Income Housing Coalition, September 2000.

New York City Human Resources Administration Office of Health and Mental Health Services. *Summary Placement Report of the New York-New York Agreement to House Homeless Mentally Ill Individuals.* 1999.

Rosenbeck, Robert, MD. Northeast Program Evaluation Center, VA Connecticut Health Care System.

Salit, S. A. "Hospitalization Costs Assosiated with Homelessness in New York City." *New England Journal of Medicine,* 11 June 1998.

Shelter. *Homelessness Statistics.* Department of the Environment, Transportation and the Regions, 1999/2000.

U.S. Department of Health and Human Services. *Making a Difference: Report of the McKinney Research Demonstration Program for Homeless Mentally Ill Adults.* Washington, DC: U.S. Department of Health and Human Services, 1994.

U.S. General Accounting Office (GAO). *Homelessness: Barriers to Using Mainstream Programs.* Letter Report, 6 July 2000, GAO/RCED-00-184.

U.S. General Accounting Office (GAO). *Homeless Veterans: VA Expands Partnerships, but Homeless Program Effectiveness Is Unclear.* Letter Report, 01 April 1999, GAO/HEHS-99-53.

5

Documents and Reports

This chapter provides a documentary picture of homelessness through the use of speeches, testimony, government reports and plans, and other key items that demonstrate some of the primary facets of homelessness in the United States and in several other countries. In one sense, these documents describe the problem. But most are also filled with information that focuses on the realities and the obstacles in meeting the basic human needs of homeless people.

Early Advocacy on Homelessness in the United States

Testimony Before the U.S. Congress

In December 1982, the U.S. Congress convened the first hearing on homelessness since the Great Depression. The first witnesses to testify before the Housing Subcommittee of Representative Henry B. Gonzalez were Mary Ellen Hombs and Mitch Snyder of the Washington, D.C.-based Community for Creative Non-Violence. With their testimony, they released *Homelessness in America: A Forced March to Nowhere,* a groundbreaking look at a new and growing problem. Hombs and Snyder brought with them to the witness table the cremated ashes of "John Doe," one of the many homeless people who had frozen to death in the city. This excerpt is from their testimony.

> Americans, more than many people, are severely addicted to some very dangerous myths. Yet, we can-

not address reality, or hope to change it, until we free ourselves from the fables that entrap us. Perhaps nowhere is this more true than in regard to homeless people. To see them clearly, to understand what their existence says about us personally and collectively, and to require what their needs are requires this: we must face facts as they are, peel away stereotypical prejudices and delusions, boil off foggy thinking, and listen to the voices of those who have known and seen.

We must work from a single point: this is America, 1982. Homelessness is a national problem of massive and increasing proportions, affecting at least two million people.[1] As a fabric, it is made up of the consequences of a number of elements and conditions basic to the way our nation and our society function. We do not always choose to see these clearly, but we will examine them here is as current, authentic, and nonacademic a fashion as we can. (Hombs and Snyder 1983)

U.S. Policy on Homelessness

In January 1993, President Bill Clinton named former San Antonio, Texas, mayor Henry Cisneros to be secretary of the U.S. Department of Housing and Urban Development, the federal agency with the responsibility for the homeless housing assistance programs. Secretary Cisneros walked the streets of downtown Washington, D.C., and talked with homeless people. He also made homelessness the number one priority of his agency and sought increases in funding for homeless programs.

In May 1993, President Clinton signed an Executive Order on homelessness to create a "single coordinated Federal plan for breaking the cycle of existing homelessness and preventing future homelessness." This plan was issued in March 1994 and is called *Priority: Home! The Federal Plan to Break the Cycle of Homelessness.* Excerpts from the federal plan follow; citations have been edited for brevity.

Priority: Home! The Federal Plan to Break the Cycle of Homelessness

The Face of Homelessness: No Longer a Poor Apart

It profits us nothing as a nation to wall off homelessness as a novel social problem made up of a distinctly "different" population. Nor is it something that requires separate and distinctive mechanisms of redress, isolated from mainstream programs. In fact, the more we understand about the root causes of homelessness, the greater our sense of having been here before.

To put it plainly, homelessness in the 1990s reveals as much about the unsolved social and economic problems of the 1970s as it does about more recent developments. This Plan reveals and documents that the crisis of homelessness is greater than commonly known or previously acknowledged. Researchers have found that as many as 600,000 people are homeless on any given night. Recent research reveals the startling finding that about seven million Americans experienced being homeless at least once in the latter half of the 1980s. Hence, its resolution will require tackling the enduring roots of poverty, as well as complications introduced by psychiatric disability, substance abuse, and infectious disease. That task is rendered more difficult by today's economic realities and severe budget constraints.

By the middle of the 1980s, the number of homeless people had surpassed anything seen since the Great Depression. Disability, disease, and even death were becoming regular features of life on the streets and in shelters. For the first time, women and children were occupying quarters formerly "reserved" for skid-row men. Psychiatric hospitals continued to discharge people with little hope of finding, let alone managing, housing of their own. Crack cocaine emerged as a drug of choice for those on the margins of society. A new scourge—HIV/AIDS—joined an old one—tuberculosis—to become a major affliction of the homeless poor.

Yet for all that, there remained something disconcertingly familiar about this new homelessness. What America glimpsed on the streets and in the shelters in the 1980s was the usually hidden face of poverty, dislodged from its customary habitat.

Homelessness can be understood as including two broad, sometimes overlapping, categories of problems. The first category is experienced by people living in crisis poverty. Their homelessness tends to be a transient or episodic disruption in lives that are routinely marked by hardship. For such people, recourse to shelters or other makeshift accommodations is simply another way of bridging a temporary gap in resources. Their housing troubles may be coupled with other problems as well—dismal employment prospects because of poor schooling and obsolete job skills, domestic violence, or poor parenting or household management skills—all of which require attention if rehousing efforts are to be successful. But their persistent poverty is the decisive factor that turns unforeseen crises, or even minor setbacks, into bouts of homelessness.

For those individuals who fall in the second category—homeless men and women with chronic disabilities—homelessness can appear to be a way of life. Although a minority of those who become homeless over the course of a year, it is this group that is most visible and tends to dominate the public's image of homelessness. Alcohol and other drug abuse, severe mental illness, chronic health problems or long-standing family difficulties may compound whatever employment and housing problems they have. Lacking financial resources and having exhausted whatever family support they may have had, they resort to the street. Their homelessness is more likely to persist. Disability coupled with the toll of street-living make their situation more complex than that of those who are homeless because of crisis poverty. Those with chronic disabilities require not only economic assistance, but rehabilitation and ongoing support as well.

For the most part, homelessness relief efforts remain locked in an "emergency" register. Many existing outreach, drop-in, and shelter programs address the symptoms of homelessness and little else. Although of proven promise in dealing with the disabled homeless poor, supportive housing options remain in scarce supply. Increasingly, it has become clear that efforts to remedy homelessness cannot be fully effective if they are isolated from a broader community-based strategy designed to address the problems of extreme poverty and the inadequate supply of housing affordable by the very poor. Lasting solutions to homelessness will be found only if the issue is productively addressed in ongoing debates concerning welfare reform, health-care reform, housing, community and economic development, education, and employment policy.

Causes of Homelessness

A decade of research and practical experience has confirmed that there are many varieties of contemporary homelessness. Manifold in its causes, duration, consequences, and coexisting disabilities, its steady growth in the early 1980s reflected the confluence of a number of factors.

In accounting for homelessness, it is useful to distinguish among a number of levels of causation. Understanding the structural causes of homelessness is especially important when considering preventive strategies. When fashioning measures to reach those who are currently on the street, personal problems that contribute to the prolongation of homelessness must be addressed.

If stable residence is the goal of policy, appreciating the role of risk factors is essential. Psychiatric disability, substance abuse, domestic violence and chronic illness not only add to the likelihood that someone will become homeless, but complicate the task of rehousing someone already on the street. Among generic risk factors, poverty is the common denominator, but other circumstances have also been identified that increase the likelihood of homelessness: prior episodes of homelessness; divorce or separation among men, and single parenthood among women; leaving home or "aging out" of foster care among unattached youth; a history of institutional confinement in jails, prisons, or psychiatric hospitals; and weak or overdrawn support networks of family and friends.

We must focus more attention on individual risk factors and the underlying structural causes potentiating these factors if the cycle of homelessness is to be broken.

Why These Factors Translate into Homelessness

A number of analysts have suggested that the situation of households at risk of homelessness may be likened to a game of musical chairs. Too many people are competing for too few affordable housing units. In such a game, those troubled by severe mental illness, addiction, or potentially lethal infections, as well as those simply inexperienced in the delicate balancing act that running a household in hard times requires, are at a serious disadvantage.

Under such circumstances, the changes sketched above—in kinship, government support and work—greatly complicate the task of relocating people who have been displaced from their homes. Traditionally, as noted earlier, extended households were on hand as the recourse of last resort in difficult times. Those among the poor who were without family could make do in sections of central business districts where rooms were cheap and food could be had through the efforts of local charities. Even difficult behavioral problems could be accommodated: Such people simply moved frequently, in effect spreading the burden throughout the marginal housing sector. For those still able, spot work opportunities provided a source of income.

But extended families are finding it difficult to make ends meet. The slack in cheap housing is gone. And studies suggest that what is left of the casual labor market prefers more compliant recruits.

Faced with these changes, federal homelessness policy must be both preventive and remedial in scope. It must do more than merely relocate those who are currently homeless. It must also stabilize such housing placements once made, while securing the residences of those who are precariously housed. Government must seek, in effect, to do with deliberation and planning what the private market once accomplished: make housing work again. In today's environment, to make housing work will frequently require an infusion of fiscal resources and support services. Such services should be viewed, not as "add-on" frills, but as essential enabling ingredients—on a par with debt service, insurance, or fire control measures—that are needed for some housing to be feasible at all.

Building on What We Have Learned

Over a decade has passed since homelessness began its unprecedented postwar growth. During that time, social service agencies, advocates, and researchers acquired a wealth of experience in dealing with homelessness. This collective experience has taught us that homelessness is more complex and deeply rooted than some had originally forecast. Responsible policy must seek to address both the fundamental structures of poverty and the complicating risk factors specific to homelessness.

Solving homelessness will thus mean confronting the traditional sources of impoverishment: declining wages, lost jobs, poor schooling and persistent illiteracy, racial discrimination, public entitlements outpaced by inflation, chronically disabling health and mental health problems, the scarcity of affordable housing, and the increasingly concentrated nature of poverty. It will also mean confronting relatively new social phenomena that are adding to the costs of poverty: changes in family and household structures, the decline in traditional kin-based sources of support, and the proliferation of new drugs (such as crack cocaine) and socially-stigmatized infections, i.e., HIV and tuberculosis.

Accordingly, a comprehensive approach will have to mount initiatives on a number of fronts simultaneous. Homelessness will not be solved by simply outlawing the most visible evidence of its presence on the streets. Solving homelessness will require durable means of arresting the sources of residential instability— both structural and personal—that lie at its root. For virtually every homeless person, this will mean dealing with the affordability and availability of housing. For some, restoration of family ties and attention to the skills and resources needed to manage a household may be indicated. For others, appropriate treatment of mental illnesses and/or substance abuse problems will be essential if they are to be stably housed. Accommodating the diversity and range of assistance needs among homeless persons will require the development of comprehensive, yet flexible, community-based continuums of care, much like those VA is working to develop through its Comprehensive Homeless Centers.

If we look further ahead, an even more ambitious agenda can be seen. This agenda will encompass long-term community and economic development, education, training and job opportunities, the reinstatement of support services as part of the "welfare" apparatus, and attention to such neighborhood facilities as health clinics and day care centers. But budgetary constraints require a transition to this larger agenda that fully addresses poverty and its accompanying ills. Welfare and health care reform should begin to address many of these ills. In the short run, we will need to direct resources to ensure that those who are currently homeless receive the appropriate range of services and housing as needed and that those poised on the brink of homelessness can be brought back from the edge. (Interagency Council on the Homeless 1994)

Recent Issues in U.S. Government Programs

The General Accounting Office (GAO) is the official research agency of the federal government. Upon direction from the U.S. Congress, GAO studies both general and specific questions and in 1999–2000, GAO reported in several documents the results of its research into federally funded programs to assist homeless people.

Background

A 1999 GAO study identified fifty federal programs run by eight agencies that either are specifically targeted to the homeless or are nontargeted and therefore available to poor people in general, including those who are homeless. GAO found that both the targeted and nontargeted programs provide an array of services, such as housing, health care, job training, and transportation. In some cases, programs run by more than one agency offer the same type of service. Given the multiple agencies and the large number of programs that can potentially serve the homeless, GAO believes that coordination among federal agencies and the evaluation of programs' effectiveness are essential to ensure that the programs are cost-effective. Most agencies that administer targeted programs for the homeless have identified crosscutting responsibilities related to homelessness, but few have tried the more challenging task of describing how they expect to coordinate their efforts with those of other agencies or develop common outcome measures. GAO also found that although most federal agencies have established process or output measures for the services they provide to the homeless through their targeted programs, they have not consistently developed results-oriented and outcome measures for homelessness in their plans. This testimony also describes ongoing GAO work in the following areas: (1) state and local efforts to integrate and evaluate programs for the homeless, (2) the use of grants under the supportive housing program to deliver services to the homeless, (3) programs that serve homeless veterans, and (4) barriers to obtaining services.

In March 1999, GAO officials testified before a congressional committee on the status and scope of their efforts. Following are excerpts from that testimony.

[Homelessness] has persisted in America for decades. While no one knows exactly how many people in the United States are homeless, according to the most widely accepted estimate, up to 600,000 people may be homeless on any given night. Moreover, the causes of homelessness have become more complex, and its effects are now more widespread than in the past. The homeless population no longer consists primarily of transient adult males but also includes women, families with children, the mentally ill, the unemployed, and those who are dependent on drugs or alcohol. Addressing the needs of homeless people is often a formidable challenge because many of them face a combination of personal, social, and economic problems that prevent them from maintaining permanent housing.

Recognizing that states, localities, and private organizations had been unable to respond to the crisis of homelessness in America, the Congress enacted the Stewart B. McKinney Homeless Assistance Act in 1987. The McKinney Act was the first comprehensive law designed to address the diverse needs of the homeless and was intended to provide both shelter and supportive services.[2] Over time, some McKinney Act programs have been consolidated or eliminated and some new programs have been added. Recently, several Members of the Congress . . . have become increasingly concerned about the apparent lack of impact that federal programs have had on homelessness. This concern has arisen because federal agencies seem to have made little progress in addressing the root causes of homelessness, and federal programs seldom focus on preventing homelessness. Some congressional leaders are further concerned because, in trying to solve the problems of homeless people, the federal government has created a separate system of programs designed specifically to serve the homeless that often mirror existing federal and state social service programs that serve other populations (generally called mainstream social service programs) raising questions about efficiency in the use of limited federal resources. To address some of these issues, GAO initiated a body of work in 1998 on homelessness that we would like to describe for you today. First, we will discuss the results of a recently completed review, and then we will briefly describe four additional pertinent assignments that we have started or planned.

Last month, we completed a study identifying key federal programs that could potentially serve the homeless. Homelessness: Coordination and Evaluation of Programs Are Essential . . . identifies 50 programs, administered by eight federal agencies, that either are specifically targeted to the homeless or are nontargeted and therefore available to low-income people in general, including those who are homeless. We found that both the targeted and nontargeted programs provide an array of services, such as housing, health care, job training, and transportation. In some cases, programs operated by more than one agency offer the same type of service. For example, we found that 23 programs operated by four federal agencies offer housing services, and 26 programs operated by six agencies offer food and nutrition services. We also determined that over $1. 2 billion was obligated in fiscal year 1997 for programs that specifically served the homeless and about $215 billion was obligated for programs that served low-income populations, including the homeless. Although information is not available on how much of the funding for nontargeted programs is used to assist homeless people, we estimate that a significant portion of the funding is not likely to benefit them. Given the multiple agencies and the large number of programs that can potentially serve the homeless, we believe that coordination among federal agencies and evaluations of programs' effectiveness are essential to ensure that these programs achieve their desired outcomes in a cost-effective manner. Through our review, we found that federal efforts to assist the homeless are coordinated in several ways, and many agencies have established performance measures as required by the Government Performance and Results Act of 1993. For example, coordination can take place through the Interagency Council on the Homeless, which brings representatives of federal agencies addressing homelessness together, and through compliance with the requirements of the Results Act. The Results Act requires federal agencies to identify crosscutting responsibilities, specify in their strategic plans how they will work together to avoid unnecessary duplication of effort, and develop appropriate measures for evaluating their programs' results.

We found that most agencies that administer targeted programs for the homeless have identified crosscutting responsibilities related to homelessness, but few have attempted the more challenging task of describing how they expect to coordinate their efforts with those of other agencies or develop common outcome measures. In addition, we found that while most federal agencies have established process or output measures for the services they provide to the homeless through their targeted programs, they have not consistently developed results-oriented and outcome measures for homelessness in their plans. While some agencies have developed outcome measures for their targeted programs, other agencies either plan to develop outcome measures in the future or told us that developing such measures would be too difficult. Consequently, we concluded that federal agencies have not yet taken full advantage of the Results Act and that their efforts could be strengthened through increased coordination and the development of common outcome measures for federal programs that serve the homeless.

To address the other issues raised by congressional leaders, we have started or planned work in the following areas:

State and local efforts to integrate and evaluate programs for the homeless

To provide the wide range of services that homeless people often need, local communities sometimes have to find ways to better integrate their services for the homeless with mainstream social service systems. In addition, some states are increasing their use of outcome measures to ensure that their programs do not only focus on providing services, but also on the goal of moving people out of homelessness. Our ongoing study will describe how some states and localities have tried to (1) link their homeless programs to mainstream social service systems to better serve the homeless and (2) use program outcome evaluations to better manage their programs. For this study, we identified and visited Massachusetts, Minnesota, Ohio, and Washington. According to national experts on homelessness, these states are generally recognized as having made good progress in integrating or evaluating their programs for the homeless. We believe that the examples included in our study will be useful to other communities seeking to better integrate and evaluate their own programs, as well as provide information that can be used by federal agencies attempting similar improvements at the national level.

Use of grants under the supportive housing program to provide services to the homeless

The Congress established the Supportive Housing Program as one of the nonemergency housing programs under the McKinney Act. This program recognizes that many homeless people will need supportive services, such as mental health treatment, substance abuse treatment, and employment assistance, along with housing to help them make the transition from homelessness and live as independently as possible. In fiscal year 1997, the Department of Housing and Urban Development obligated $620 million for this program. These funds were then awarded through a competitive grant process to providers of services for the homeless, nationwide; about 60 percent of the funds were used to provide supportive services. Our ongoing review of the Supportive Housing Program will provide information on the (1) types of housing and supportive services that grant applicants provide for the homeless, (2) other sources of federal and nonfederal funding that grant applicants rely on to fund supportive service programs for the homeless, and (3) the importance of the Supportive Housing Program's funds to grant applicants' programs. To provide this information, we will analyze data obtained through a nationwide survey of about 1,200 service providers who applied for Supportive Housing Program grants.

Programs that serve homeless veterans

According to the Department of Veterans Affairs (VA), veterans make up about one-third of the adult homeless population. To address the needs of homeless veterans, over the past decade VA has established a number of targeted programs, and in fiscal year 1997 it spent approximately $84 million on these programs. Our ongoing review of VA's programs for the homeless is designed to (1) describe the various programs that serve homeless veterans, (2) determine what VA knows about the effectiveness of its programs for the homeless, and (3) identify some promising approaches that serve the needs of different groups of homeless veterans.

Barriers to accessing services

We also plan to study the barriers faced by homeless people when they try to gain access to and use services provided by mainstream social service systems. As part of this review, we will determine how existing mainstream social service systems can be changed to facilitate homeless people's access to services. Making mainstream programs and services more accessible to homeless people would expand the range of programs and services available to them. [Homelessness] has been and continues to remain a formidable challenge facing our nation. Given the federal government's high level of investment and involvement in developing solutions to this problem, we believe that addressing homelessness will continue to be a priority for the Congress, federal agencies, states and localities, private organizations that serve the homeless, and the public. Consequently, work on homelessness will continue to be important for GAO, and we look forward to providing the Congress and the public with the information they need to address this issue in the future. (Czerwinski 1999)

Homelessness in Europe

The emphasis of the European homelessness literature is on emergency services for the homeless and the provision of housing as the means to address the social exclusion resulting from homelessness. European literature tends to emphasize joblessness in explaining homelessness. Relative to United States discussion, there is little mention of the role of chronic disability (including physical disability, mental illness, and substance abuse) and continuity in public systems of care, treatment, and custody (including child welfare, hospitals, prisons, and treatment facilities).

Dr. Dragana Avramov, the leading scholar on European homelessness and research coordinator of the European Observatory on Homelessness in Brussels has recently stated:

> There is no housing policy at the European level and there is no European policy on homelessness. There is no evidence that Member States [of the European Union] have consulted with each other to share models of policy and practice in their legislative approaches to homelessness. There is no evidence that the States evaluate their preventive policies and share information about effective measures to help low-income people access and maintain a home.

Yet, Member States share many unintended consequences of privatization policies and in particular those which originate in the privatization of stare function in the provision of housing for the least advantaged. (Avramov, *The Invisible Hand of the Housing Market*)

In 1998, the European Federation of National Organisations Working with the Homeless (FEANTSA) published "Europe against exclusion: HOUSING FOR ALL," which it called "a set of practical policy proposals to promote social inclusion and ensure access to decent housing for all citizens and residents of the European Union." The report was published with the support of the European Commission, with contributions from representatives of FEANTSA member organizations, correspondents of the European Observatory on Homelessness, and selected experts. The contents of the report were unanimously endorsed by the Administrative Council of FEANTSA on November 28, 1998. The report is available from FEANTSA, 1 rue Defacqz, B-1000 Brussels. www.feantsa.org.

Key elements of the report are summarized below.

Foreword

Decent housing and living conditions are the most basic needs of each individual. Gaining secure access to adequate accommodation is often a precondition for exercising many of the fundamental rights which form the foundations of all decent societies, and should be enjoyed by everyone. These include the right of access to education, the right to work, the right to social protection, the right to healthcare, the right to personal privacy and family life, as well as access to basic services such as water and electricity.

To be "homeless"—that is, without access to adequate accommodation—is probably the most serious manifestation of social exclusion. If you are homeless it is almost impossible to realise your potential as an active member of society, such as by getting a job or by raising children. Therefore, ensuring an adequate provision of decent housing is one of the basic foundations for building a society in which everyone can play an active part. In this sense, one can say that access to housing is the principal key to social inclusion.

A growing number of European Union citizens and residents are faced with serious obstacles in gaining access to decent housing at a price they can afford. The European Observatory on Homelessness (created by FEANTSA in 1991) has conducted research to assess the situation in each of the 15 Member States. Across the European Union, some 3 million people have no fixed home of their own, while a further 15 million people live in sub-standard or overcrowded accommodation.

FEANTSA—the European Federation of National Organisations Working with the Homeless—brings together more than fifty social sector bodies and service providers in all of the fifteen Member States and also in the applicant countries. Since 1989, FEANTSA has been a strong advocate for housing issues in general, and most especially the provision of decent and affordable housing, to be seriously addressed by policy-makers at all levels: local, regional, national and European.

While we are aware that housing policy is not, according to the existing Treaties, a matter of Community competence, our members are convinced that there is a need to develop European cooperation in this field, for two main reasons: 1) the housing sector in each country is affected by a wide range of European policies (including regional development, environmental protection, monetary and fiscal policies); 2) the whole housing sphere has an important contribution to make to the achievement of common objectives in a number of vitally important policy areas (such as social cohesion and the combating of exclusion, as well as employment creation and energy conservation).

This policy paper—"Europe against exclusion: HOUSING FOR ALL"—presents a series of key proposals, and sets out the main arguments in their support, with the aim of advancing the debate at European level. The proposals are based on the experiences of our members, and on the results of the research carried out by the European Observatory on Homelessness.

1. Access to housing in the European Union
1.1 Many people have no access to decent housing
The European Observatory on Homelessness (which has conducted research on homelessness in the Member States on behalf of FEANTSA since 1991) has presented a general picture

of the situation in the fifteen European Union countries. Approximately three million people have no fixed home of their own, while a further 15 million people live in sub-standard or overcrowded accommodation. Adding these figures together, we can estimate that across the European Union as a whole, one person in 20 is denied access to decent housing.

1.2 Homelessness and housing exclusion are growing

In most member states of the European Union, it would seem that the numbers of homeless people have grown during the past twenty years. A number of developments may be identified which result in increased levels of homelessness and insecure, inadequate housing for low-income groups. These changes include demographic changes, socio-economic changes, changes in social welfare provision, and changes in housing provision. Moreover, certain groups in society are especially vulnerable to housing exclusion, such as young people and those with special individual needs, as well as women and lone-parent families.

1.3 Demographic changes

More people are living alone as single adults for longer periods than in previous decades, while couples are less stable, and are more likely to separate. As life expectancy has been extended, more people are living independently for longer periods after retirement. The combination of these demographic changes means that the rate of new household formation is in many countries much higher than the rate of net population growth. In most Member States, the number of households grew by more than 15% between 1980 and 1995 (and as much as 29% in the Netherlands). The result is that the level of demand for housing units, and in particular for those that are suitable for smaller households, has grown rapidly.

1.4 Socio-economic changes

Major trends such as economic globalisation and liberalisation, industrial restructuring and new technologies have combined to bring about big reductions in the numbers of stable full-time jobs. Millions of redundant workers have been forced either to depend on social welfare benefits, or to take insecure low-paid jobs. Across the European Union as a whole, growing numbers of people are to be found living in poverty, on low or sometimes no income. Most of these people simply cannot afford to pay for adequate accommodation on the private housing market, and many are denied access to social housing.

1.5 Changes in social welfare provision

As the numbers of unemployed and low-paid workers have grown, so more individuals and families have been left with no choice but to depend on payments and services made available through systems of social welfare. Each country has a different system, but there has been a general trend in the last twenty years towards limiting the levels of social welfare benefits, which in many cases have fallen in relation to average incomes. At the same time, restrictions on the availability of welfare benefits have been tightened, so that people must increasingly meet a series of strict conditions before receiving payments.

1.6 Changes in housing provision

Across the Member States of the European Union, there has been a general decline in the provision of social housing by public bodies and nonprofit associations, as governments have reduced levels of public investment. In some countries (such as the United Kingdom and Italy) there has been a significant reduction in the supply of social housing as a result of its sale to the occupants or to private landlords. Meanwhile, the deregulation of the private rental sector has led to increases in rent levels. The trend away from public provision towards the private market has led to low-income groups becoming increasingly dependent on housing benefit payments, which are subject to wide variations in terms of availability and eligibility.

1.7 Especially vulnerable groups

Certain groups in society face a greater risk of being directly affected by housing exclusion:

- While youth unemployment is especially high in most European Union countries, young adults (16 to 25 years) often have reduced rights in terms of gaining access to welfare benefits, including payments allocated to cover housing costs. Young people who are

without parental support, for whatever reason, are
more likely to become homeless.

- For those people who face problems related to mental
health, drugs or alcohol there has been a shift away
from institutional care towards community-based
services. However, the resources allocated to these
services are often not sufficient to allow for a proper
response to the specific needs of individuals,
particularly in terms of housing provision.

- Women may find themselves at risk of becoming
homeless as a result of separation or divorce, especially
if they are seeking to escape from a violent or abusive
male partner. Meanwhile, increasing numbers of
women and children are living as lone parent families,
often with incomes that are too low to provide for
access to decent housing.

2. The Right to Housing

2.1 Housing is a basic human right

To properly tackle housing exclusion, one must start from the
recognition that housing is a basic human right, which every
man, woman and child should be entitled to exercise. Since 1948,
the Universal Declaration on Human Rights has proclaimed that:
"everyone has the right to a standard of living adequate for the
health and well-being of himself and of his family, including
food, clothing, housing and medical care and necessary social
services . . ." (Article 25.1). But rights have no meaning unless
action is also taken to turn them from words into reality. Around
the world, more than 100 states are committed to taking
appropriate steps to ensure the realisation of the right to
housing, under article 11.1 of the International Covenant on
Economic, Social and Cultural Rights (1966).

2.2 The revised European Social Charter

Since 1950, human rights have been protected by means of the
legal instruments of the Council of Europe, which currently has
40 Member States. The European Social Charter was adopted by
the Council of Europe in 1961, and the revised European Social
Charter was opened for signature in 1996. Article 31 of the
revised charter sets out three objectives for the realisation of the

right to housing: "With a view to ensuring the effective exercise of the right to housing, the Parties undertake to take measures designed: 1. to promote access to housing of an adequate standard; 2. to prevent and reduce homelessness with a view to its gradual elimination; 3. to make the price of housing accessible to those without adequate resources." Most EU Member States have still to ratify the revised social charter.

2.3 Human rights in the European Union

The Treaty on European Union, as revised by the Treaty of Amsterdam (signed in 1997) refers to "fundamental social rights as defined in the European Social Charter" (preamble), although there is no mention of the revised version of the Charter. Moreover, the European Union currently lacks any effective instruments for the protection of civil and social rights. In 1996, a committee of independent experts (the Comité des Sages) identified the need to enshrine in the EU Treaty "a basic set of fundamental civic and social rights (in the form of a bill of rights)," and to introduce "special arrangements for legal remedy in respect of fundamental rights in the form of a Union-specific appeal court." Regrettably, these proposals of the Comité des Sages have not yet been accepted by the national governments of the 15 Member States.

There must be an effective guarantee of civil and social rights for each citizen and resident of the European Union, encompassing those rights set out in the European Convention on Human Rights (1950) and in the revised European Social Charter (1996), including the right to housing.

3. Housing and Public Policy

3.1 Public investment in the housing sector

Since the early 1980s public investment in the housing sector has decreased substantially in most of the 15 Member States. In some countries (i.e., Germany, Italy and the UK) whole parts of the public rented housing stock have been privatised. Moreover, in all of the Member States the available housing stock is not adapted to current demands. In particular, there is a crucial lack of smaller flats and apartments within the stock of housing available for rent, and especially of homes which are affordable for households with a low income. The reduced availability of good-quality, low-cost housing, whether in the private rental sector or in the social (publicly funded) sector is symptomatic of the current failure to properly address the provision of housing as a central aspect of social policy in most of the Member States.

3.2 Integrated long-term solutions

Public or state intervention to tackle homelessness has tended to become focused on measures which seek to respond to housing shortages as if they were of a purely temporary nature. Such measures include increasing the supply of emergency accommodation and of temporary housing, revising the criteria for the allocation of social housing, and selective measures for the requisition of empty housing. Although such measures can play an important role, they are often implemented in a piecemeal fashion, and they are not brought together within an integrated strategy. This undermines their effectiveness, and makes it difficult to make an overall evaluation. In order to develop inclusive housing policies, it is necessary to implement a diverse range of integrated long-term solutions. These require more effective regulation and intervention to be carried out in the public interest.

3.3 Housing as an area of general interest

FEANTSA joins the European Parliament in calling for housing to be "seen as an area of general interest, underpinning all other fundamental social rights, to be taken into consideration at all levels of decision-making in the Union" (Resolution on the social aspects of housing—PE 260.284—adopted on 29 May 1997). Universal access to adequate and affordable housing (including a high degree of housing security) would require a formal recognition by Member States that housing is an area of general interest, of importance to society as a whole. This principle should be made operational by coherent policies and measures implemented at the appropriate administrative and institutional level, including the introduction of minimum objectives for alignment at European level.

The provision of adequate housing should be recognised as an essential factor of economic and social cohesion, to be taken into consideration at all levels of political decision-making. (FEANTSA 1998)

Homelessness in Great Britain

England's New Strategy on Street Homelessness

In 1999, Britain's Prime Minister Tony Blair issued a new plan for addressing the needs of the country's "rough sleepers," or people living outside. The report was entitled "Rough Sleeping: The Government's Strategy" and was issued by the country's Department of the Environment, Transport and the Regions. Blair's statement on the plan is followed by excerpts from the plan.

> On the eve of the 21st century, it is a scandal that there are still people sleeping rough on our streets. This is not a situation that we can continue to tolerate in a modern and civilised society. That is why, in a report last year by the Social Exclusion Unit, I set the tough but achievable target of reducing rough sleeping in England by at least two thirds by 2002 . . .
>
> Many of the proposals set out in this strategy will build on and refine the valuable work that has been going on for many years. But some will require radical change.
>
> The Rough Sleepers Unit has taken a long hard look at everything being done to help rough sleepers. It is clear that some things work, and others do not.
>
> In the long term, we can only make a lasting difference on the streets by stopping people from arriving there in the first place. That is why prevention is a key part of this strategy, and why more will be done to address the reasons why particular groups such as careleavers, ex-servicemen and ex-offenders are disproportionately likely to end up on the streets. The strategy also sets out support for new temporary and permanent beds, better help in finding jobs and a more focused approach to helping people off the streets. Above all, it focuses on how a real difference can be made to the lives of the most vulnerable.
>
> Too many people are still coming onto the streets. And too many people who were sleeping rough five

or ten years ago are still out there. That is why we
need a new approach, with services to help people
come in from the cold, and support to help them
rebuild their lives.

Government will provide the tools, and the
funding. But we know that this approach will only
succeed as part of a genuine partnership—between
central and local government, the voluntary sector,
statutory bodies, businesses, community groups and
rough sleepers themselves.

I believe that this strategy sets out a way forward
which can deliver our vision—a vision of a society
where no one needs to sleep in doorways, and where
rough sleeping has become a thing of the past.

Introduction

A top priority for the new Government when it came into office
in May 1997 was to offer a fresh chance to the most excluded
members of our community. And there is no doubt that among
the most vulnerable of these are the people who sleep rough
each night on our streets. In recognition of this the Prime
Minister asked the Social Exclusion Unit (SEU) to make its first
task a study of rough sleeping. The SEU report, published in July
1998 (Cm 4008), recommended the setting up of the Rough
Sleepers Unit, with the target of reducing rough sleeping in
England to as near zero as possible, and by at least two thirds, by
2002.

This strategy builds on the analysis and findings of the SEU
report, and puts into action its recommendations. It marks a step
change in the way Government tackles rough sleeping. The
strategy reflects a further six months of discussions and
consultations with a wide range of individuals and
organisations, including rough sleepers themselves. It delivers a
new joined-up approach which, building on the excellent work
that the voluntary sector, local authorities and others have
begun, aims to develop and focus efforts, to give the key
organisations new tools to do their job, and to promote a
constructive partnership approach to tackling rough sleeping
and its causes. The result will be a better deal for rough sleepers,
and better value for the taxpayer.

Background

Since 1990, Government has spent over £250 million through the Rough Sleepers Initiative alone on services to help rough sleepers off the streets. This money has funded outreach and resettlement work, around 1300 hostel places and 3,500 units of permanent accommodation. There are still, however, around 1600 people sleeping out on the streets of England on any one night. In London alone, where the majority of this money has been spent, there are some 635 people sleeping rough on any one night. A large number of these are part of a steady population of long term rough sleepers who have not been helped effectively by previous initiatives. Therefore a new, braver approach is needed: it is neither realistic nor sufficient simply to rely on increasing the number of hostel beds. We need to do more. We need to change our approach. The balance in the system must be tipped towards the most vulnerable rather than making the streets a fast track for the most able.

In the past, Government has not adequately addressed the reasons why people sleep on the streets, and how to prevent the problem occurring in the first place. Some services have in practice sustained people in a street lifestyle, rather than helping them off the streets. Moreover, daytime street culture has become an increasing problem. Some services funded through previous Rough Sleepers Initiatives, including hostels, daycentres and permanent accommodation, have not been tightly focused on rough sleepers, and places have been taken up by others, such as daytime street users and the wider population. Responsibility for services has often been fragmented between a number of different organisations—statutory and voluntary—with a wide range of objectives. We have not concentrated enough on long term and sustainable solutions, nor have we been discerning enough in offering help to those who most need it. We have not focused effectively on occupation for people. The result has often been that human beings have fallen through the intended safety net of support.

The Government has given the Rough Sleepers Unit a very clear remit to focus its energies and resources on offering help to rough sleepers, in particular those whom previous initiatives have not succeeded in helping. We believe that people should not in the 21st century have to sleep on the streets, and that the most vulnerable among them need our help, and sometimes specialist support, to give them a lasting solution.

The reasons why people sleep rough are many and complex. But we know that in broad terms that the rough sleeper population comprises:

- 75% who are over 25
- 90% who are male
- between one quarter and one third who have at some time been in local authority care
- 50% who are alcohol reliant
- 20% who are drug users
- 30–50% who have a serious mental health problem
- under 5% from ethnic minorities

This strategy recognises the complexity of need that we must respond to, and aims to offer rough sleepers options which acknowledge their atypical and frequently chaotic lifestyles. Our long-term objective is to provide services which ensure that sleeping on the streets is never the preferred option.

The key to successful delivery of the strategy will be partnership. At its most basic, this is a partnership between the taxpayer and rough sleepers themselves. But in practical terms, it means partnership between Government and those who are charged with working with rough sleepers, or who have chosen to do so: the statutory agencies, local authorities, the voluntary and volunteer sectors and the wider community such as business and the public at large.

Six Key Principles

In developing this strategy, we have had the following six key principles in mind:

Tackle the root causes of rough sleeping
We need to understand what causes people to sleep rough, and prevent it from happening.

Pursue approaches which help people off the streets, and reject those which sustain a street lifestyle
Our aim is to reduce the numbers of rough sleepers, and to do everything in our power to persuade people to come in for help.

Focus on those most in need

We want this strategy to help those whom other initiatives have failed. There is not a bottomless pool of resources, and it is crucial therefore that we target our help on those who are least able to help themselves.

Never give up on the most vulnerable

It is inevitable that some rough sleepers, especially those who have been on the streets for many years, will have difficulty in coming back in. They will need specialist help and support if they are to succeed.

Help rough sleepers to become active members of the community

We need innovative and pragmatic approaches which build self-esteem, bring on talents, and help individuals to become ready for work and occupation away from the streets.

Be realistic about what we can offer those who are capable of helping themselves

We should be using our resources to help the most vulnerable and not to provide a fast track into permanent housing for healthy and able individuals . . .

Key Proposals for Change

A. To make more bedspaces available for rough sleepers in London, with the right sort of help for those who need it most, especially the most challenging individuals who have found it very difficult to get help through previous initiatives . . .

Accommodation will be provided on 3 levels:

- direct access hostels and shelters, the first port of call for many on leaving the streets and a focus for assessment of people's needs;
- specialist hostels and special supported schemes, designed to meet specific and higher or multiple support needs; and
- permanent move on accommodation, into which people can move when they are ready to sustain a tenancy, with tenancy support if necessary.

B. To develop a focused, more targeted approach to street work, so as to give priority to helping people off the streets; to ensure clear lines of responsibility and accountability for those working with rough sleepers; and to ensure that we are not, in seeking to help, reinforcing street lifestyles rather than providing opportunities for ending them.

C. To provide services when rough sleepers need them most.

Rough sleepers are those who sleep on the streets from very late at night to the early hours i.e., from midnight to 5 or 6 a.m. It will be crucial to the success of the strategy that services in all high concentration areas are clearly aimed at helping rough sleepers to come inside. It is likely they will be more receptive to offers of help overnight. It is anticipated that all services to rough sleepers must focus effort on the most effective ways of helping people in, once inside assistance to the individual can tackle some of the underlying causes of their problems . . .

D. To help those in most need, such as those with mental illnesses, or who misuse drugs and alcohol.

It is quite clear that the complex mental and physical health needs of those on the streets are not currently being met. Addressing these needs is central to helping people to come inside, and we are committed to doing that.

For those rough sleepers with drugs, alcohol or mental health problems, or multiple needs, we will be funding 60 new permanent specialist workers to help rough sleepers at all stages during their move off the streets—from CATs and night and day centres, through to hostels and tenancy sustainment teams. We know how successful specialist workers are both in helping people day to day and in providing a bridge back into mainstream services . . .

There are people on the streets with severe and enduring mental illness. There should be no reason for someone who is severely mentally ill to be out on the streets. We will be working with the NHS Executive, social services departments and other health partners to ensure that people sleeping rough who have severe mental illness get the help and treatment they need. As a first step some members of Homeless Mentally Ill Initiative teams in London will be integrated into the contact and assessment teams.

Sometimes rough sleepers are either in dire situations or are extremely unwell and they require crisis intervention. We will, therefore, pilot an emergency special needs response team to bring together the staff, resources and powers of the statutory bodies responsible for rough sleepers with acute medical problems and mental illness on the streets. We know we are currently failing these people and that we urgently need to address their problems. We are working with local authorities and health authorities to develop the pilot team . . .

E. To ensure a continuum of care, so that there is a clear route from the streets to a settled lifestyle, with the right number of organisations and individuals involved.

The lack of focus and coordination on the streets is often mirrored in the current resettlement process. Our aim will be to streamline the services we provide for rough sleepers. A major advantage of the multidisciplinary, focused contact and assessment approach is the scope it will give for continuity of care and assessment once a rough sleeper has accepted help and come inside . . .

Some former rough sleepers moving on to permanent accommodation have special and individual support needs. Experience shows that we have not in the past got this right.

We know that many former rough sleepers in permanent housing are still using the street during the day, sustaining a street lifestyle . . .

F. To provide opportunities for meaningful occupation, to help give people the self-esteem and lifeskills needed to sustain a lifestyle away from the streets.

Years of working with rough sleepers has shown us that resettlement support alone is not enough to help people back into mainstream society. We need to find ways to help people build self-esteem, develop their skills, and reconnect into social networks away from the streets.

A key objective of all strands of provision will be to encourage rough sleepers to find daytime occupation, to help people find and sustain a settled lifestyle. Our expectation is that immediately on moving into a permanent home, a former rough sleeper will have taken up appropriate training, education, volunteering, or some form of meaningful occupation to help them adjust to their new lifestyle. We hope that many will be in employment shortly after they move into permanent accommodation and certainly within 12–18 months. We will be developing a range of schemes for providing meaningful occupation for rough sleepers at all stages after their move from the streets, both to develop life and work skills, and to avoid the loneliness and boredom that can sometimes lead them back to the streets . . .

G. To improve the incentives to come inside, both by offering provision which meets people's specific needs and by refocusing services away from those that sustain a street lifestyle.

Many of the actions flowing from the strategy will create options for rough sleepers to come inside on their terms. Therefore there will be from next April a greater incentive for long term rough sleepers to review their lifestyles and take the opportunity of a more settled life.

By the same token, the Government believes that, if their needs can be provided through one or other of the accommodation, treatment or support routes that we are funding, rough sleepers themselves have a responsibility to come in. Once we are satisfied that realistic alternatives are readily available, we—and the public at large—are entitled to expect those working on the streets to seek to persuade people to take advantage of them. This includes the police, who sometimes have not been able to use their powers because of a lack of options to move rough sleepers on to.

H. To put in place measures to prevent rough sleeping, so that new people do not see the streets as the only option. Prevention is the only means of ensuring a lasting and sustainable end to the problem of rough sleeping.

While the immediate measure of the Unit's impact will be the progress we make in reducing the numbers of people sleeping rough by 2002, our fundamental aim is to sustain that reduction and prevent vulnerable people from arriving on the streets in the first place. We are approaching this from two perspectives—firstly, working across Whitehall to put in place the measures needed to make a critical difference and, secondly, putting in place practical projects that will make an immediate difference.

For the long term, efforts must be targeted on those groups that we know are particularly vulnerable to homelessness and to rough sleeping: young people leaving care; people leaving prison; people who have experienced family breakdown; and people leaving the armed forces. There is a central role here for Government, both in what we can achieve directly, and what we can achieve through the work of others, especially local authorities. This is a crucial challenge for us all. We must ensure that those who have been in our care as children, as prisoners or as servicemen, are properly equipped for and supported towards independent living. Rising to this challenge must be a major component not only of our work to tackle rough sleeping, but also our efforts to deal with social exclusion more widely.

Work is already underway in several Government departments to meet this challenge.

The Government's Children (Leaving) Care Bill introduced in the House of Lords in November will improve the arrangements for young people living in and leaving care and is based on the proposals set out in the Department of Health's consultation paper "Me, Survive, Out There?" £375 million is being made available to local authorities over 3 years as part of the *Quality Protects* programme, one of the aims of which is to increase the support offered to care leavers and to prevent the inappropriate discharge from care of 16 and 17 year olds. This programme will be backed up by new legislation which is intended to ensure that local authorities assess and meet the needs of 16 and 17 year olds living in and leaving care, including ensuring that they are in suitable accommodation. Local authorities will also have to oversee and support the transition from care to independence up to the age of 21, and up to the age of 24 if still receiving help from the local authority with education and training.

More immediately, the Department of Health is undertaking jointly with the Rough Sleepers Unit, an audit of careleaving packages in all London boroughs. We want local authorities across the country to move quickly to improve their careleaving service, building on the current best practice. The audit, which is due to report by April 2000, will be a method of getting to grips with the authorities in London who are doing it less well and thereby helping to improve practice both in London. The good practice will be disseminated.

The Unit, in partnership with the Prison and Probation services, has commissioned a pilot project to look at what is or is not being done to help prisoners prior to release, that will reduce their likelihood of sleeping rough on release from custody. The study is taking place in three institutions—Wandsworth, Brixton and Feltham. The first interim results are due by the end of the year, but we can already see that support is not always effective and that there are examples of both good and poor practice. As a result of the project we will be urgently examining within the prison service more effective ways of providing help to prisoners at the point of release. The Prison Service is working on key performance indicators for the success of resettlement and expects to have interim targets in place by April 2001. The Benefits Agency will lay more emphasis on benefits advice for prisoners and ex-prisoners and we will be monitoring its effect . . .

And as part of their "policies for people" initiative, the Ministry of Defence are working to reduce the vulnerability of current service personnel to future homelessness and rough sleeping, through initiatives to develop better life and work skills to help them resettle following discharge. The Unit and the MoD are also investigating the role of the benevolent organisations in helping existing rough sleepers who have been in the services reconnect back into their social networks . . .

Conclusion

Rough sleeping is at the sharp end of social exclusion. It affects a relatively small number of people, but those people are often amongst the most vulnerable. We believe that by working in a real partnership across the whole community we will be able to meet our target of reducing rough sleeping in England by at least two thirds by 2002. This is a target to which the overwhelming majority of the public have given their support.

Over the years a great deal of money has been spent, many hostels have been built, and many permanent homes are now available to former rough sleepers and single homeless people. And yet there remains a small but steady number of people out on the streets every night. This must change. We cannot allow the problem to be ignored. So, working closely with our partners we must look at everything we do, scrutinising it carefully, and, where we have to, making the real and lasting changes that will ensure that we can deliver. This will not always be easy and will require courage. But, meeting our target is not just about numbers it is about making a difference to people's lives. The strategy outlines action that will help those currently out on the streets exposed to danger and ill-health, and it puts in place measures to stop new groups becoming tomorrow's rough sleepers. We must work together so that we can be proud of living in a country that does not have rough sleepers on the streets at night (Department of the Environment 1999).

Homelessness in Canada

In 1999, a group of providers, government officials, community leaders, and others released a report on how to address homelessness in Toronto, Canada. Key findings from this report, entitled *Taking Responsibility for Homelessness: An Action Plan for Toronto*, are presented below. The study found that homelessness had changed over the previous ten years.

- A "typical" homeless person is no longer a single, alcoholic, adult male. Youth and families with children are now the fastest-growing groups in the homeless and at-risk populations. Two studies commissioned by the Task Force found that:
- Almost 26,000 different individuals used hostels in Toronto in 1996, about 3,200 on any given night (the number is much higher in the winter). 170,000 different individuals used shelters over the eight years between 1988 and 1996.
- The fastest-growing groups of hostel users are youth under 18 and families with children. Families accounted for 46 percent of the people using hostels in Toronto in 1996.
- Between 30 and 35 percent of homeless people suffer from mental illness. The estimates are higher for some population groups; for example, 75 percent of homeless single women suffer from mental illness.
- 4,400 people in 1996 (17 percent of hostel users) stayed in the hostel system for a year or more. This group of "chronic hostel users" takes up about 46 percent of the beds and services.
- At least 47 percent of hostel users come from outside Toronto.
- More than 100,000 people are on the waiting list for social housing in Toronto.
- Poverty is getting worse among the applicants for social housing; more than one third of the people on the waiting list have incomes of less than $800 a month.
- The number of families on the social housing waiting list has increased greatly: more than 31,000 children are

on the waiting list. At the current rate of placement, families would have to wait 17 years to obtain housing

Increased poverty

Both the incidence and depth of poverty have increased because of changes in the structure of the labour market and because of public policy changes such as restrictions on Employment Insurance eligibility and cuts to welfare.

Lack of affordable housing

The dwindling supply of low-cost rental units and rooming houses, along with the withdrawal of support by both the federal and provincial governments for new social housing programs, have made affordable housing much harder to find.

Deinstitutionalization and lack of discharge planning

Many people who suffer from mental illness and addictions are homeless partly as a result of deinstitutionalization without adequate community support programs; in addition, their problems have been exacerbated by the inadequate discharge planning of hospitals and Jails.

Social factors

Domestic violence, physical and sexual abuse, and the alienation of individuals from family and friends have increased the incidence of homelessness.

Homelessness is the ragged edge of the social fabric. Because the problem is so complex, it requires multipronged strategies to meet the immediate needs of the homeless population in addition to long-term policies to prevent and reduce homelessness.

Jurisdictional gridlock and political impasse

Governments are squabbling over issues of responsibility. Homelessness straddles all levels of government and many departments within governments. The federal government is devolving social housing to the provinces but, in Ontario, the federal and provincial governments have not yet agreed on how devolution should take place; meanwhile, the Province has downloaded social housing to municipalities. Also, the Province argues that the federal government should take responsibility for homelessness amongAboriginals, immigrants, and refugees, but the federal government argues that urban Aboriginals and immigrant and refugee settlement issues are also a provincial responsibility. And on and on.

Dramatically increasing poverty

The latest income statistics show that average family income fell by 12.5 percent in Toronto between 1991 and 1996. The income of the 40 percent of families at the lowest end of the scale declined by more than 20 percent. The proportion of female single parents under 25 years of age across Canada who live in poverty has increased since 1995 from 83 to 91 percent. In Toronto, 106,000 low income households pay more than 50 percent of their income on rent.

Decreasing supply of low-cost rental housing

There has been a large drop in low-rent housing supply in Toronto. The number of legal rooming houses decreased from 1,200 in 1974 to fewer than 400 in 1998. Furthermore, rents for formerly low-cost apartments have risen so that low-income people can no longer afford them.

Emergency bias

The service system is biased towards emergency and survival measures. Despite a general agreement that not enough attention is devoted to preventing homelessness, no political will to change is in evidence. Managers and service providers understandably focus on stop-gap solutions to immediate crises. This crisis mentality is reflected in the annual prewinter panic to find additional, temporary shelter beds.

Inadequate community programs and supports for people with serious mental illness and addiction problems

The overrepresentation of people with severe mental illness among the homeless population is directly linked to the lack of adequate community supports. There are even fewer such supports for those people with both mental health and addiction problems, who are at a disproportionate risk for homelessness.

No capacity for coordination

We learned about many different services and activities, saw evidence of extraordinary creativity and innovation, and were impressed by the dedication of agency staff and volunteers. But we also saw a disjointed, incrementally expanding patchwork of services and programs that frustrated their efforts. The problems are the lack of any mechanism to coordinate funding from different sources, unclear roles of different services, inadequate attention to the diverse needs of different sub-groups of the homeless population, and the absence of a comprehensive service information system.

These barriers can be overcome.

To overcome the barriers to the reduction and prevention of homelessness, the Task Force recommends changes on several fronts:

A Facilitator for action on homelessness

A Facilitator, who can overcome the barriers to change without becoming enmeshed in the day-to-day management of service delivery and operations, should be appointed for a five-year term and report to the Mayor and Council. The Facilitator should establish priorities, define action plans, and track progress on implementation, producing an annual report card to communicate results to the public.

Shelter allowances

A new shelter allowance for the working poor should be introduced to address growing poverty and to prevent homelessness. The proposed shelter allowance will reduce the share that low-income people spend on housing to between 35 and 40 percent of income to enable people to keep their housing. As well, the shelter component of social assistance, which now disadvantages Toronto, should be adjusted to reflect local market conditions.

Supportive housing: At least 5,000 additional housing units with support services should be built in Toronto over the next five years, primarily to serve homeless people suffering from mental illness and/or addictions. The new units should be created in all areas of the City; additional supportive housing units should also be built throughout the rest of the province.

New affordable housing

A City-initiated development strategy is needed to increase the supply of affordable rental housing by 2,000 units a year. Our recommendations call for a layered approach, because no single mechanism on its own can bring rents down to affordable levels.

We call on governments to subsidize land costs, waive fees and charges as well as GST and PST, modify property taxes, provide rent supplements, and help with financing costs, mortgage insurance, and capital grants.

Existing affordable housing

The City should place equal emphasis on the preservation of existing housing, which provides the majority of affordable units. It should follow the principle of "no net loss" by placing controls on demolition and conversion of affordable apartments. It should legalize second suites and rooming houses in selected areas and under certain conditions. Because rehabilitation is fundamental to preserving affordable housing, the federal government should expand its residential rehabilitation funding and extend it to rooming houses and second suites.

Incentive funding

Funding can be used to encourage the shift from emergency response to prevention strategies. A percentage of all hostel budgets should be allocated to purchase services from community agencies that will provide specialized supports to prepare people to leave a hostel and to provide follow-up after leaving. Funding can also be used to improve coordination and access to health and mental health services for the homeless population. The Ministry of Health should combine its community mental health and health funding for homeless people into a Homelessness Health Fund to be administered by the City; an important criterion for funding would be the demonstration of collaboration among different agencies.

Service planning organized around different sub-groups

To address the different needs of the different sub-groups, we recommend that service planning within the City be organized around three sub-groups: youth, families, and singles. By bringing together all the services that affect a particular group, agencies would be able to plan effectively and coordinate their efforts. Within each sub-group, strategies should be developed for those at higher risk of homelessness including abused women, Aboriginals, and immigrants and refugees.

A Homeless Services Information System

As a first step towards a fully integrated information system, a Homeless Services Information System should be established to provide a comprehensive database (with a 24 hour telephone information line) on social, health, and housing services for homeless people. This information system should include a central hostels bed registry. All agencies that serve the homeless population (including hostels, drop-ins, and hospitals) should have access to this information system.

Harm reduction

Harm-reduction facilities (one for adults, one for youth) that accept the use of drugs and alcohol on site should be established to address the needs of those homeless people with addictions or concurrent disorders (mental illness and addictions) who do not use existing services. An addictions and mental health outreach team is needed to connect these people to the new facilities. We believe that the new facilities will reach the "hardest to serve" population and provide better access to treatment.

Evictions prevention strategies and individual support

We have made a number of specific recommendations aimed at preventing homelessness. These include a rent bank to help people in short-term arrears, more systematic housing help services, adequate funding for legal assistance, and one-on-one support both to help people move from shelters to stable housing and to keep people housed.

Discharge policies and practices

Institutions should establish and implement discharge protocols for people with "no fixed address." No one should be discharged from an institution directly to the street or to a hostel without prior arrangement and follow-up.

Community economic development

Community economic development (CED) refers to businesses created by community groups to help poor or employment-disadvantaged people find work and increase their economic independence. The City should invest in the newly established Productive Enterprises Fund as part of an overall strategy to break the cycle of homelessness.

Self-help

The principle of self-help should be promoted throughout the hostel, drop-in, and supportive housing systems. Homeless people should play an active role in finding solutions.

Each level of government has a role to play.

Each level of government must participate in strategies to prevent and reduce homelessness:

Federal government

The federal government has played a pivotal role in social housing development for the past 50 years. Its withdrawal from new social housing programs in 1993 has contributed to the growing shortage of affordable housing. The federal government should provide capital assistance for the construction of new affordable housing and the rehabilitation of existing affordable housing. Furthermore, because the federal government is largely responsible for Aboriginal people, immigrants, and refugees, it should fund projects to prevent and reduce homelessness within these sub-groups.

Provincial government

Homelessness is largely caused by poverty and it is the Province that is responsible for income maintenance programs. Therefore, the Province has a critical role to play in adjusting the shelter component of welfare and establishing the new proposed shelter allowance for the working poor. Moreover, because the homeless population has a high incidence of health, mental health, and addictions problems, the Province has a key role to play in funding supportive housing and treatment programs, and enhancing access to health care.

Municipal government

The City of Toronto should take the lead in planning and managing the overall system as it affects homeless people. The City should spearhead a rental housing development strategy to produce new affordable housing and to preserve existing housing. The Greater Toronto Services Board (GTSB) can help ensure that affordable housing and supports and services are distributed throughout the Greater Toronto Area, rather than being concentrated in the City of Toronto.

The costs are affordable.

The Task Force has estimated the costs of the main recommendations in the report. Because we are the Mayor's Task Force, we focused on the budget implications of the recommendations for the City of Toronto. For federal and provincial government costs, we limited our estimates to shelter allowances, supportive housing, and housing supply.

Municipal government

We estimate the additional operating costs to the City at $15.3 million a year (including Toronto's share of the pooled welfare costs) and the new capital costs at $10.9 million for the first year of implementation. Because social assistance costs are pooled throughout the Greater Toronto Area (GTA), as are the benefits, the cost of changes to the shelter component of welfare and an additional rent supplement are $13.5 million for the rest of the GTA.

Provincial government

We estimate that it will cost the Province $230 million a year to increase both the shelter component of welfare ($52 million) and introduce a new shelter allowance for working low-income singles and families ($178 million), province-wide. Capital costs for new supportive housing will cost the Province $32 million a year.

Federal government

We estimate federal capital costs for grants and additional residential rehabilitation funding at between $46 and 66 million in Toronto.

Finally, all three levels of government will give up potential revenue by providing land for affordable housing and by reducing or waiving taxes, fees, and charges to permit the creation of affordable housing.

It should be noted that the indirect and long-term savings from investing in the recommended strategies have not been quantified. These will include, for example, savings from reduced hostel use, lower welfare caseloads, and reduced demand on the health care system, not to mention an improved quality of life. While we are convinced that these savings will be considerable, especially for the municipality and the Province, time has not permitted such an analysis. That said, the financial consequences of inaction will be considerable.

We cannot afford to do nothing.

The Task Force estimated the consequences for Toronto of not taking action on homelessness. In the next five years, the City could easily lose 25,000 to 50,000 low-rent private apartment units a year as rents rise. Between 15,000 and 30,000 new households could have difficulty affording housing (in addition to the existing 106,000 households that now have an affordability problem). If family hostel use continues to double every five years, and hostel use by singles continues to rise, in five years Toronto would have to find hostel spaces for up to 6,000 people every night. Unless people give up applying for social housing, there could well be 60,000 names on the waiting list five years from now.

Homelessness can be prevented and reduced.

The Task Force acknowledges that the prevailing political climate may not seem to favour spending money on housing and support programs, as we recommend. However, our report demonstrates that the problems are solvable and that the solutions are available. On that basis we have a moral obligation to take the actions needed. (*Taking Responsibility for Homelessness* 1999)

Homelessness in Australia

In 1999, Australia's Department of Family and Community Services published the following analysis of homelessness in Australia.

A Problem of Definition

The National Evaluation draws attention to the complex nature of homelessness and the diversity in definitions.

The Council for Homeless Persons Australia (1998) refers to a homeless person as one who, is without a conventional home and lacks the economic and social supports that a home normally affords. She/he is often cut off from the support of relatives and friends, she/he has few independent resources and often has no immediate means and, in some cases, little prospect of self-support.

Others, including overseas sources, have proposed definitions which include reference to:

- no access to safe and secure shelter of a standard not damaging to health, threatening safety, and providing adequate cooking and other facilities for adequate personal hygiene
- insecurity and transient nature of shelter
- detachment from family
- vulnerability to dangers of exploitation and abuse

A particularly complex issue is the concept of homelessness for indigenous Australians, with definitions highlighting a 'spiritual' form of homelessness, in addition to those more widely used.

The official Australian definition of homelessness in the SAAP Act 1994 (Section 4) is:

For the purpose of this Act, a person is homeless if, and only if, he or she has inadequate access to safe and secure housing.

It goes on to refer to what 'inadequate access to safe and secure housing' might be, citing situations which might damage health, threaten safety, marginalise the person from amenities and the economic and social support the home normally offers, and affordability of housing.

Whatever the definitions, the homeless are not a homogenous group, having different demographic characteristics and backgrounds, different problems, and different needs.

Routes to Homelessness

Much has been written about the causes of homelessness. Burke (1994) identifies a number of direct and indirect factors, including:

- poverty
- health
- housing
- social dislocation
- domestic violence
- cultural and social values

Causal factors do not tend to operate in isolation; rather, they reinforce and complement each other. Fopp (1995) warns of the dangers of ascribing homelessness to personal characteristics, of using anecdotal evidence to draw policy and causal conclusions, and of confusing symptoms with causes.

Implementation of the Program

In 1995/96 the nation spent $8.9 billion (representing 1.8 per cent of GDP) on providing welfare services, with actual dollar funding having increased by 89 per cent since 1989/90. SAAP recurrent funding represented 2.3 per cent of this expenditure in 1995/96, having increased by around 20 per cent over the period.

In 1996/97 it is estimated that almost 101,000 homeless people received services from 1,183 SAAP agencies at a cost of $219.8 million of joint Commonwealth–State/Territory recurrent funding. This represents a program cost per client served of $2,176. The fact that half of these clients were supported for three days or less, that 15 per cent were supported for up to 13 weeks, and that 9 per cent were supported for in excess of 13 weeks, puts this figure into proper perspective.

Data available from the National Data Collection estimates that between 37 per cent and 51 per cent of the demand for SAAP services was unmet in 1996/97. When children receiving SAAP services are included, it is estimated that about 267,000 homeless people in Australia sought to enter the SAAP system, representing approximately 1.4 per cent of the nation's population.

Of the 101,000 clients accessing SAAP services in 1996/97, only 6 per cent were employed full-time or part-time, while a further 3 per cent were employed casually. Almost two-fifths were unemployed and over half were not in the labour force. In excess of four-fifths of clients were dependent on government payments as their sole source of income, while over one in ten had no income at all. Little changed on exiting SAAP services, with over four-fifths of clients having no change in their before and after income status, and 7 per cent having no income both before and after exiting.

In 1996/97 SAAP agencies provided case management plans for half their clients. It was estimated almost one-fifth of clients were in the high need category. However, almost three-quarters of clients exiting SAAP moved into housing that could be classified as independent, which was an improvement on the figure of 55 per cent on entry. Some 43 per cent of clients on exiting SAAP were living in the private rental housing market. This could be masking a lack of public sector exit points.

On the basis of this and related information it is the conclusion of the National Evaluation Team that SAAP funds are being directed towards assisting genuinely needy homeless people who are severely disadvantaged and at risk.

Lessons from International Experiences

The National Evaluation Team conducted an extensive literature search on the nature of homelessness, policy responses and innovative programs in the United States and the European Union, with an additional emphasis on the United Kingdom.

The United States approaches focus attention on integration of programs, the development of strategies for dealing with causes rather than symptoms, and the desirability of identifying models of best practice. A number of nationally coordinated policies and programs exist, with the Clinton administration creating in 1994 a single coordinated federal plan, *Priority: Home! The Federal Plan to Break the Cycle of Homelessness.* This is an ambitious long-term community and economic development, education, training and job opportunities program, linking the welfare apparatus to neighbourhood effort and local facilities.

The European Federation of National Organisations Working with the Homeless has consultative status at the Council of Europe to promote the work of nongovernment organisations in providing services to the homeless. *The IGLOO Program,* under the auspices of The European Federation of National Organisations Working with the Homeless, is a participative initiative seeking to provide opportunities to disadvantaged persons by tackling issues of social exclusion. Since 1993 it has fostered an integrated approach to providing support through housing, vocational training and job initiatives.

The *National Assistance Act 1948, the Housing (Homeless Persons) Act of 1977,* and the *Housing Act of 1996* represent the legislative responses to housing and homelessness in the United Kingdom. Housing for the homeless is provided by local authorities which make available rental housing to certain categories of homeless persons. Housing associations and not-for-profit organisations also provide housing for the homeless, as do some cooperatives.

Both the *National Homeless Advice Scheme* and the *Rough Sleepers Initiative* are whole-of-government approaches to the issue of homelessness in the United Kingdom.

A recent initiative is the use of *foyers* in the United Kingdom and parts of the European Union as a dual-purpose response to the problems of youth homelessness and unemployment by providing a supported accommodation service with direct links to employment opportunities. By 1995, 20 foyers were operating 1,755 bed spaces for young people in the United Kingdom. Evaluations of the foyer approach are encouraging.

In summary, recent developments in international responses to homelessness have centred around progressing an integrated approach to service provision across various levels of government. The United States emphasis on the provision of a continuum of care encapsulates ideals regarding 'good practice' in meeting the various needs of the homeless. Such a strategy also recognises the temporality of homelessness and the need to provide varying support across time. (Commonwealth Dept. of Family and Community Services 1999)

Policies to End Homelessness in the United States

Philip Mangano of ¡ENDING HOMELESSNESS! The Roundtable on the Abolition of Homelessness is an emerging national voice in the advocacy discussion of how to address the problem in the United States. The following speech is edited from remarks he made in Rochester, New York, in 1998, in which he draws on the abolition of slavery to present his thoughts on homelessness.

Updating Abolitionism

Frederick Douglass. Born a slave. Escaped. New Bedford. Nantucket. Boston. Orator. Accused of not being a slave. Autobiography. Escapes to England (Fugitive Slave Law). Bought out of slavery. Member of Abolitionist movement. William Lloyd Garrison. Wendell Phillips. Harriet Tubman. Moves to Rochester to start his own newspaper called the "North Star." Friend of John Brown. Friend of Lincoln. Republican. Office holder. Did you watch "Africans in America" on PBS?

He was an Abolitionist—an advocate against slavery and he understood the government and the odds against him well. Here is, perhaps, one of the best summaries of the struggle against social evils:

If there is no struggle there is no progress. Those who profess to favor freedom, and yet depreciate agitation, are men who want crops without plowing up the ground. They want rain without thunder and lightning. They want the ocean without the awful roar of its many waters. This struggle may be a moral one; or it may be a physical one; or it may be both physical and moral; but it must be a struggle. Power concedes nothing without a demand. It never did and it never will. (Frederick Douglass)

The abolitionists faced an impossible task. They wanted to abolish a social institution that was 6,000 years old, accepted by every element of society—business, media, public opinion, legal, religious, political. Especially political.

21 of 27 Speakers of House owned slaves. 16 of 18 Supreme Court justices. 13 of 15 Presidents owned slaves.

How would that effect the legal, political, and moral positions of the country?

Obvious. It was an intractable part of the social landscape. Those abolitionists were just a bunch of troublemakers agitating in the face of history. Slavery was here to stay. Accommodate your world view to its existence. These agitators will come and go, but slavery will remain. Make your peace with slavery. Relax. Even if you don't like it, don't exhaust yourself. Maybe there are some small things you can do. This is what society said to the abolitionist. No wonder William Lloyd Garrison, Douglass' first mentor, said:

I am aware, that many object to the severity of my language; but is there not cause for severity? I will be harsh as truth, and as uncompromising as justice. On this subject, I do not wish to think, or speak, or write, with moderation . . . urge me not to use moderation in a cause like the present. I am in earnest in a cause like the present. I am in earnest—I will not equivocate—I will not excuse—I will not retreat a single inch—AND I WILL BE HEARD. (William Lloyd Garrison)

Doctors, lawyers, Supreme Court justices, lawmen, politicians, corporate executives all lent their support to the institution of slavery. Against this societal accommodation and abetting of slavery, the abolitionists demanded immediate emancipation. They were thought to be fringe people who didn't understand political realities.

The abolitionist movement in the United States had its real start in the 1770's. Despite 6,000 years of history and societal acceptance within 3 generations, the abolitionists had achieved their hope. Slavery was ended in the United States. That which had seemed utterly impossible, and all efforts so futile and foolish, was eradicated from this country. And never reestablished.

A social evil so pernicious that it had rendered comatose the moral compass of most of the country, was abolished. The abolitionists had prevailed.

What can we learn from the abolitionists in our efforts confronting a new social evil?

An evil whose invidiousness has demoralized many policy makers and most of the public. An evil which afflicts the poor and threatens women, children, and the vulnerable. An evil that some say is intractable. A part of our social landscape.

An unresolvable dilemma. The abolitionists do have help for us in seeking a new abolitionism—the ending of homelessness.

Let's model our new abolitionism, our efforts to end homelessness on something that worked. Not an empty rhetoric, but on what works.

First, we are in a marathon, not a sprint. While the abolitionists called for immediate emancipation, it took 3 generations to realize.

Exhibit on the history of homelessness in museum of City of New York a few years ago . . . The exhibit began in 1692. Homelessness has come and gone throughout U.S. history. Just 25 years ago, little of what we would call homelessness. As recently as the early part of this decade, homelessness around the country leveled off and dropped slightly. We thought all our rolled up sleeves and hard work had turned the tide. But the economy got better, and the numbers soared. For the marathon you need stamina. How do you get it? We now know that stamina is linked to ancestry. If your ancestors had stamina, persistence, stick-to-itness, you will too. So, who are our ancestors? Well, Cornel West says that we should place ourselves, our efforts in a larger story, a legacy. So, in Boston, we choose to adopt as our ancestors the abolitionists. You should make the same claim in Rochester. And, let the stamina of the abolitionists, especially Frederick Douglass, fuel your efforts in the new abolitionism.

Second, the abolitionists teach us that there is no correlation between affluence and right action. The South and the Nation grew rich off of the work of the slaves. And when economic times got worse in the late 1850's threatening the wealth, times got worse for slaves—Fugitive Slave Law, the Dred Scott decision. We've got our own modern case of that morally crippling disease. It's the new sickness sweeping through our land. It cripples people's autonomous value system. Its victims become incapable of performing spontaneous acts of justice. It's getting worse nearly every day. The fever climbs—7500—8000—8500. It's a late 20th Century outbreak of Affluenza. Without help, it's addictive and those in its clutches become resource abusers. Most are in denial. They swear they can pick up and put down whenever they want. When, in reality, they're constantly talking to their suppliers—the brokers, getting tips on new fixes. Meanwhile, the impact of this Affluenza hits poor people even harder.

What we've learned in the last 15 years is that when the economy is bullish, poor people get gored. The better the economy, the more homeless people. It's counterintuitive, but true. Whether you look at the 1980's when the greatest economic expansion, some say, in the history of the world pumped a trillion dollars into the economy and the number of homeless people increased faster than the Dow-Jones. Or, the mid-90's when the booming economy correlates with unprecedented demand in homeless services and unprecedented numbers of homeless people. The better the economy, the higher the numbers. Why? Housing is the key to the analysis. More about that later. They tell us poverty is down, income is up. And so is homelessness. The government surpluses, state and federal are at record levels. But how can the government have surplus, if some have nothing. The contradictions parallel each other. In the land of freedom, slavery. In the economic boom, homelessness. And there is even more sad news out there. In the recent downturn, Bill Gates' worth plummeted from $38 billion to $34 billion. I'm personally saddened. We'll pass the hat for him later. There are a record number of millionaires—they say that now 1 in every 750 households has a worth of $1 million or more. And, a record number of homeless people. What's Government's role in all this? The abolitionists understood that government abetted slavery. They reserved their strongest agitation for the Constitution. As new abolitionists, we see an Affluenza in which the private sector takes care of the many.

So it is government's responsibility to take care of the few. The first call on government resources should be for the poorest of the poor. Instead of its role in mediating resources for the most in need, Wendell Berry tells us that government takes on the role of the justice of the peace in marrying wealth and power. And, Walker Percy reminds us that there is no correlation between wealth and character.

Third, the abolitionists teach us that social injustice can be faced realistically and simply.

In their analysis of the southern system, its economic underpinnings, and the financial benefit to northern interests, the abolitionists understood the realistic terms of the issues they faced. But they also approached the issue simply—no man should own another.

We can do analyses on the causes of homelessness—and they are being done, winning tenure for some and book contracts for others. We've learned the complexities of the issues which impact on homelessness and the complexities of each life. We accept all that. Yet know that ultimately it is all about housing. Homelessness is about housing. It's the national emergence.

It is no mystery why 750,000 people across this nation will sleep in shelters or outside tonight. Simply: In 1970 there were 5.3 million low income households. There were 5.8 million affordable units—25% of income. 100 units for every 93 households. In 1995 there were 7.8 million low income households. 4.8 million affordable units. 100 units for every 163 households.

During the late 70s 275,000 units were created each year by the federal government. Currently 77,000 units are created each year. Housing has dried up for the poorest in the age of affluenza. Simply, there are more poor, less housing. The booming economy causes rents to increase, vacancies to decrease. Poor and homeless people are priced out.

With all the complications attributed to its victims, the housing shortage remains at the root of homelessness. The national emergency is unremedied.

The abolitionists taught us that we can have multiple short term responses, but only one long term goal. And that goal is immediate abolition.

The irony of what we do is that we make progress and fall further behind. Are there any fewer homeless people now than when we first started working on the issue 2, 5, 10 years ago?

Yes and no. Yes some have moved beyond and stayed out.
No. Our beds are as filled as ever. Around the country more
filled. Up in Massachusetts we've moved more than 5000 people
out of homelessness to housing and jobs in the last five years.
And our shelters are still filled to capacity. For every six people
going out the back door of shelters, seven are coming in the front
door. We've established a range of programs to end people's
homelessness, just as the abolitionists did for slaves.

The antislavery societies didn't just meet and talk. They
developed strategy after strategy: Mutual aid societies.
Purchased slaves. Called for voluntary freedom. Some wanted
colonization in West. Some infiltrated the South—Harriet
Tubman. Some called for secession from South. Boycotts of
southern goods. Violence. Organizing freed slaves. Publishing
newspapers. And, of course, all the efforts of the underground
railway.

We do the same. We create all manner of programs.
Outreach. Inreach. Mental health. Substance abuse. Recovery.
Transitional programs. Job training. Job retention. Job search.
Housing programs. Subsidies. Section 8. Housing search. Health
care programs. Emergency shelters. Relapse prevention.

And just as the abolitionists did, we end homelessness one
person at a time. And our cumulative small gestures are
substantial over time. We are on the banks of the river (in your
case, the lake) rescuing those coming down stream. And we're
sophisticated and dedicated and creative and successful. We are
schooled in intervention strategies.

But the abolitionists teach us that while all these efforts
must go on, we can never be content with them. We seek a larger
vision. We must go up the river (across the lake) to find out
where all these people are coming from. So that RATHER than
simply intervening in their lives with the Continuum of Care
resources after people become homeless, we are preventing at
risk lives from falling BEFORE they become homeless.

Research into emerging populations coming in the front
door of homelessness refutes the notion that homeless people are
anonymous street people wandering into our shelters.

Who are the new people refilling the beds we've emptied?
They are hardly unknown or anonymous. Quite the contrary
they are often well known—well known to systems of care
funded by the government. They come from youth services,
foster care, state hospitals, managed care hospitals, state and

county correctional facilities, substance abuse programs, from SSI rolls. Sometimes tens of thousands of dollars have been spent on their care. Our tax money invested in vulnerable lives with a performance outcome of homelessness! It's scandalous. If homeless programs had a record of performance, they'd be investigated, humiliated, and shut down. State systems of care are often immune to such scrutiny.

We are told to "mainstream" homeless people. Our research tells us that often homeless people come from the mainstream.

So homeless people are not unknown. They are known. And are victims of systems of neglect. Especially systems which are devoid of appropriate discharge and aftercare planning. Discharge planning is a tangible expression of prevention. Good discharge planning prevents homelessness.

We've made it an issue for a variety of systems in Massachusetts—corrections, mental health facilities, youth and foster care, substance abuse programs, and most recently, the managed care system.

It's a front door prevention strategy just as housing is the back door intervention solution. Even with all these intervention and prevention efforts at the back and the front doors of the homeless system—the intervention/prevention paradigm which as a strategy needs to replace the solely intervention oriented continuum of care strategy so that we're responding to the whole problem, not simply reacting after the fact.

Simply, we know that people don't go out the back door because there is inadequate housing. They come in the front door because there is inadequate discharge planning.

At the same time, we are doing that analysis and creating programs that respond, we are focused on the ultimate goal of all our labors—the abolition of homelessness. So we've created a Special Initiative to House the Homeless Mentally Ill. 1000 units in the past 7 years; increased detox and recovery home beds; recovery home beds targeted to ex-offenders; housing search that has placed hundreds in the past few years; job search that has placed over 1,000 in jobs averaging $7.85 an hour; increased discharge planners and discharge protocols that have zero tolerance for discharge to homelessness; managed care outreach and discharge initiatives; corrections increase in discharge planners; creation of thousands of units across the state. And more.

All good work. All making a difference. But more homeless people now than ever. That irony grips us—we make progress, and fall further behind.

That's why we keep our eyes on the promise of abolition. Though we get positive conditioning from our successes—and feel good—like the abolitionists our only satisfaction will come with complete and immediate abolitionism.

The abolitionists taught us that there are no throwaway populations in America. Slaves were property. They could be whipped, mistreated, sold, hung.

There are some public policy makers who act as if there are currently populations who are expendable:

Young people who are out of services and often thought to be "beyond help." Our research shows that 900 will fall into emergency shelters this year.

Substance abusers we are told have brought on their own troubles. 700 whose SSI was cut off will fall into shelters this year in Massachusetts.

We hear that elderly homeless people aren't worth the investment. Their numbers have climbed to 1000 across the state.

We are told that those in prison should be relegated to breaking rocks and experience some Dantesque vision of hell. 95% will be eventually released. This year over 1200 will fall directly from a prison bed one night to a shelter cot the next.

In honoring each life of a freed slave and ensuring that freed slaves were well represented in the ranks, abolitionists, both black and white taught us that the dignity of each life, and the promise of each life.

The abolitionists taught us that you can't depend on an undependable government.

Every time one step of progress was made, soon two steps were taken backward. Government strategies are often inadequate, inappropriate, and politicized. Our conversations with HHS are a prime example.

Many homeless people and poor people have learned this lesson better than the rest of us. Resources and programs available one day, are gone the next. Housing, income. The instability is too chaotic. We all want about the same things – housing income, a chance and some privacy. Government officials should applaud and welcome these efforts, rather than requiring the proverbial boot strap pulling from those who have no boots.

The abolitionists never trusted the Government. Monitored and coerced it to do the right thing. Remember Frederick Douglass' words: "Power concedes nothing without a demand. It never did and never will."

The abolitionists were opportunistic for the sake of the oppressed.

There were many different groups. Many different approaches. Different philosophies. They all worked separately and sometimes together. But when the great opportunity came to actually end slavery—even though it was through means they detested, with partners they didn't trust, with those who had been enemies—they acted almost in unison. And saw a war as a way to accomplish the mission. They were for the most part pacifists. Some had called for the North to secede from the South. They mistrusted the power structure that had given them the fugitive slave laws and the Dred Scott Decision.

Yet they engaged the war and, ultimately, through their efforts converted a war that was focused on saving the Union to a war to free the slaves.

They were opportunistic. Some sacrificed their efforts and long developed positions to join the effort.

The abolitionists challenge us in this opportunism to think about our own positions, ideologies, and programs. As in the case of the abolitionists, what if the cure seemed to be coming from an unexpected quarter that we were inimical to—would we be knee jerk and reject? Would we object on a variety of grounds? Would we be willing to offer a truce? Support? Could we lay down our own ideas and finely fashioned principles for an opportunistic chance?

What if the for profit world suddenly figured out that they could profit by housing homeless people—how would we react? What if the Republicans stepped forward, claiming to respond to their earliest legacy as abolitionists and offered a plan that included corporations, developers, and their support. Would we offer them a partnership with us? Or would we kvetch and be cynical in our corner?

Don't forget Frederick Douglass was a Republican office holder. Could we move beyond our own prejudices? Would we seize the opportunistic moment?

Are we able to understand that our patient waiting in expectation and anticipation and action is a good deal of our work? That through our efforts we keep alive the moral call to end homelessness? That we give visibility to a tragedy that could sink below public and private consciousness? That our work is to keep a sacramental light burning for our poorest neighbors? That we might not accomplish the goal? It took three generations before the abolitionists ended slavery.

The abolitionists enlisted those who are impacted by the social evil in the cause of abolishing it.

The efforts of Douglass and Garrison to create a place in the Union Army for blacks led to the formation of the 54th Regiment. Glory. In the same way our responsibility is to provide resources and the access for homeless people to be engaged in the work of abolishing homelessness . . .

But by holding the goal and making it visible, we accomplish the means by which the end will come. We hold up a vision that a series of unforeseen political, social, and spiritual events will someday fulfill.

The promise of the last 10 years should be enough to inspire us. While we've been holding up this light, other events deemed impossible have occurred.

The prisoner is released from his cell and becomes President and a country awaiting a transition of bloodshed converts in peace. The years ago who would have believed that Nelson Mandela, a prisoner for 27 years would become President of South Africa in free elections without racial uprisings and bloodshed.

I was in South Africa earlier this year and visited Robben Island, the prison where Mandela spent 11 years. Robben Island was the symbol of racial hatred, torture, injustice, and irresolvable social conflict. That prison is now a museum. The prisoner, the President. And the transition without civil war. No one would have predicted the end of such barbarism in that way. No one could have predicted it would end so swiftly.

What else has happened in the last 10 years.

We've come up out of our fall out shelters. The Berlin Wall and Soviet totalitarian communism have toppled. Talk about intractable social evils. No one gave hope for the freedom of Eastern Europe or the Soviet Republics. We were told to live with it. To accommodate it. And we abetted it. Within 10 years it was gone. Who would have guessed the confluence of events and personalities that would merge to that end. Now those fall out shelters and the Berlin Wall are museums.

And, of course, reaching back 130 years, slavery is vanquished.

All of these seemingly intractable social evils, rigid on the social landscape, accommodated either by us, our institutions, our beliefs, our government. If these be gone – issues far out of our control and power—if Robben Island and the Berlin Wall can be overcome and brought down, what does that mean for us, the new abolitionists.

We don't have the right to believe that homelessness cannot be overcome.

We don't have the right to believe that homelessness can't be ended.

We don't even have the right to doubt that homelessness will be ended.

What we do have is the responsibility to end this social evil. To keep alive that hope.

The abolitionists tell us that the status quo does not have to be the future. And recent events teach us the same . . .

We have a promise to keep and a price to pay for our dream. We promise to keep the light burning. We will find a way.

Our promise is a sacred trust that we dare not violate. We are the new abolitionists. That's our commitment. (Mangano 1998)

A Plan to End Homelessness

In July 2000, the National Alliance to End Homelessness released *A Plan: Not a Dream—How to End Homelessness in Ten Years,* a plan to address U.S. homelessness in the next decade. Following is the Executive Summary from that plan.

Twenty years ago there was not wide-spread homelessness in America. Tonight nearly a million people will be homeless, despite a two billion dollar a year infrastructure designed to deal with the problem. Can homelessness be ended?

While the seeds of homelessness were planted in the 1960s and 1970s with deinstitutionalization of mentally ill people and loss of affordable housing stock, wide-spread homelessness did not emerge until the 1980s. Several factors have affected its growth over the last two decades. Housing has become scarcer for those with little money. Earnings from employment and from benefits have not kept pace with the cost of housing for low income and poor people. Services that every family needs for support and stability have become harder for very poor people to afford or find.

In addition to these systemic causes, social changes have exacerbated the personal problems of many poor Americans, leading them to be more vulnerable to homelessness. These social trends have included new kinds of illegal drugs, more single parent and teen-headed households with low earning power, and thinning support networks.

These causes of homelessness must be addressed. People who are homeless must be helped, and the current system does this reasonably well for many of those who become homeless. But the homeless assistance system can neither prevent people from becoming homeless nor change the overall availability of housing, income and services that will truly end homelessness.

Mainstream social programs, on the other hand, do have the ability to prevent and end homelessness. These are programs like welfare, health care, mental health care, substance abuse treatment, veterans assistance and so on. These programs, however, are oversubscribed. Perversely, the very existence of the homeless assistance system encourages these mainstream systems to shift the cost and responsibility for helping the most vulnerable people to the homeless assistance system. This dysfunctional situation is becoming more and more institutionalized. Can nothing be done?

Ending Homelessness in Ten Years

The Board of Directors of the National Alliance to End Homelessness believes that, in fact, ending homelessness is well within the nation's grasp. We can reverse the incentives in mainstream systems so that rather than causing homelessness, they are preventing it. And we can make the homeless assistance system more outcome-driven by tailoring solution-oriented approaches more directly to the needs of the various sub-populations of the homeless population. In this way, homelessness can be ended within ten years.

To end homelessness in ten years, the following four steps should be taken, simultaneously.

Plan for outcomes

Today most American communities plan how to manage homelessness—not how to end it. In fact, new data has shown that most localities could help homeless people much more effectively by changing the mix of assistance they provide. A first step in accomplishing this is to collect much better data at the local level. A second step is to create a planning process that focuses on the outcome of ending homelessness—and then brings to the table not just the homeless assistance providers, but the mainstream state and local agencies and organizations whose clients are homeless.

Close the front door

The homeless assistance system ends homelessness for thousands of people every day, but they are quickly replaced by others. People who become homeless are almost always clients of public systems of care and assistance. These include the mental health system, the public health system, the welfare system, and the veterans system, as well as the criminal justice and the child protective service systems (including foster care). The more effective the homeless assistance system is in caring for people, the less incentive these other systems have to deal with the most troubled people—and the more incentive they have to shift the cost of serving them to the homeless assistance system.

This situation must be reversed. The flow of incentives can favor helping the people with the most complex problems. As in many other social areas, investment in prevention holds the promise of saving money on expensive systems of remedial care.

Open the back door

Most people who become homeless enter and exit homelessness relatively quickly. Although there is a housing shortage, they accommodate this shortage and find housing. There is a much smaller group of people which spends more time in the system. The latter group—the majority of whom are chronically homeless and chronically ill—virtually lives in the shelter system and is a heavy user of other expensive public systems such as hospitals and jails.

People should be helped to exit homelessness as quickly as possible through a housing first approach. For the chronically homeless, this means permanent supportive housing (housing with services)—a solution that will save money as it reduces the use of other public systems. For families and less disabled single adults it means getting people very quickly into permanent housing and linking them with services. People should not spend years in homeless systems, either in shelter or in transitional housing.

Build the infrastructure

While the systems can be changed to prevent homelessness and shorten the experience of homelessness, ultimately people will continue to be threatened with instability until the supply of affordable housing is increased; incomes of the poor are adequate to pay for necessities such as food, shelter and health care; and disadvantaged people can receive the services they need. Attempts to change the homeless assistance system must take place with the context of larger efforts to help very poor people (National Alliance to End Homelessness 2000).

References

Commonwealth Department of Family and Community Services. Supported Accomodation Assistance Program. Australian Commonwealth, 1999.

Czerwinski, Stanley J. Testimony Before the Committee on Government Reform, House of Representatives. Washington, DC: 23 March 1999.

Department of the Environment, Transport, and the Regions. *Rough Sleeping: The Government's Strategy.* United Kingdom: Department of the Environment, Transport, and the Regions, 16 December 1999.

European Federation of National Organisations Working with the Homeless (FEANTSA). *Europe Against Exclusion: HOUSING FOR ALL.* FEANTSA, 1998

Hombs, Mary Ellen, and Mitch Snyder. *Homelessness in America: A Forced March to Nowhere.* Washington, DC: The Community for Creative Non-Violence, 1983. pp. xvi–xviii.

Interagency Council on the Homeless. *Priority: Home! The Federal Plan to Break the Cycle of Homelessness.* Washington, DC: U.S. Department of Housing and Urban Development, 1994.

Mangano, Philip. "The 'North Star' Revisited: Updating Abolitionism." Speech presented at the Homeless Symposium, October 23, 1998.

National Alliance to End Homelessness. *A Plan—Not a Dream: How to End Homelessness in Ten Years.* Washington, DC: National Alliance to End Homelessness, 2000.

Taking Responsibility for Homelessness: An Action Plan for Toronto. Report of the Mayor's Homelessness Action Task Force, 1999.

Notes

1. No one can say with certainty how many people in this nation are homeless. Not until they come inside will we know for certain how many there are. However, in 1980, we prepared a report, for a congressional committee, on the national dimensions of the problem. At that time, we concluded that approximately 1 percent of the population, or 2.2. million people, lacked shelter. We arrived at that conclusion on the basis of information received from more than 100 agencies and organizations in twenty-five cities and states. That figure has since been widely used by the media, politicos, and organizers. It is as accurate an estimate as anyone in the country could offer, yet it lacks absolute statistical certainty.

In gathering information for this book, we have learned nothing that would cause us to lower our original estimate. In fact, we would increase it, since we are convinced that the number of homeless people in the United States could reach 3 million or more during 1983.

2. Supportive services include those that provide day care, education, employment and training, legal assistance, health care, mental health care, and substance abuse treatment.

3. The Supportive Housing Program was originally established as a demonstration program; Congress made the program permanent in 1992.

6

Legislation on Homeless Assistance

This chapter provides an overview of legislation on homeless assistance in several countries. It begins with legislation in the United States, where the Stewart B. McKinney Homeless Assistance Act in 1987 marked the first federal response to the growing homelessness and created homeless assistance programs across several federal agencies. The chapter includes key details about McKinney programs and their recent funding levels. The chapter goes on to give examples of laws from Europe and the United Kingdom on the provision of assistance for homeless people. While legislative actions are a form of lawmaking, issues concerning legal action on homelessness are covered in Chapter 7, "Homelessness and the Law."

Federal Legislation in the United States

The Stewart B. McKinney Homeless Assistance Act (P.L. 100-77)

Originally this act was introduced as the Urgent Relief for the Homeless Act and was passed quickly by the U.S. Congress to show its concern about the growing problem of homelessness. The act was passed by overwhelming bipartisan majorities in both houses and signed by President Ronald Reagan on July 22, 1987.

The Stewart B. McKinney Homeless Assistance Act (P.L. 100-77) is codified in the U.S. Code at Title 42, Chapter 119—

Homeless Assistance. While the original act created programs in a number of federal agencies, the current version of the programs provides a smaller number of programs exclusively for homeless people in the following federal agencies: Department of Housing and Urban Development; Department of Health and Human Services; Department of Education; Department of Veterans Affairs; and the Federal Emergency Management Agency. Funding levels for these programs are summarized in Table 6.1.

The McKinney Act programs at the U.S. Department of Housing and Urban Development (HUD) are funded annually through a national application process. In recent years, the Congress has commissioned several research reports on these programs, in an effort to determine whether HUD's programs are coordinated effectively or should be reorganized. The report was prepared by the U.S. General Accounting Office (GAO), the official research branch of the government.

The following excerpt from one of these research reports explains some of the key issues.

Pursuant to a congressional request, GAO discussed the potential need to consolidate homeless assistance programs administered by the Department of Housing and Urban Development (HUD), focusing on the: (1) different program requirements for HUD's four Stewart B. McKinney Homeless Assistance Act programs—The Emergency Shelter Grants Program, the Supportive Housing Program, the Shelter Plus Care Program, and the Section 8 Single-Room Occupancy Program; (2) coordination and administrative challenges that the four programs pose; and (3) actions that HUD has taken to overcome these challenges.

GAO noted that: (1) each of HUD's four McKinney programs addresses a distinct need of a specific segment of the homeless population; (2) each of the four programs has its own set of eligibility and funding requirements that are established by the authorizing legislation; (3) these varying requirements have resulted in challenges for HUD in ensuring that adequate coordination occurs among the programs and that they are delivered efficiently without creating undue administrative burdens for the states and communities; (4) HUD has taken actions to overcome the coordination and administrative challenges that these separate programs with varying requirements pose; (5) to improve coordination, HUD developed

TABLE 6.1
2000 HHS Poverty Guidelines

	FY 2001*	FY 2000	FY 1999	FY 1998	FY 1997	FY 1996	FY 1995
(HUD) Homeless Assistance Grants	$1.025 billion	$1.02 billion	$975 million	$823 million	$823 million	$823 million	$1.12 billion
Emergency Food & Shelter Program (FEMA)	$140 million	$110 million	$100 million	$100 million	$100 million	$100 million	$130 million
Health Care for the Homeless (DHHS)	$100.5 million	$88 million	$79.6 million	$71 million	$69 million	$65.4 million	$65.4 million
Projects for Assistance in Transition from Homelessness (PATH) (DHHS)	$37 million	$31 million	$26 million	$23 million	$20 million	$20 million	$29 million
Education for Homeless Children and Youth (USED)	$35 million	$28.8 million	$28.8 million	$28.8 million	$25 million	$23 million	$28.8 million
Runaway and Homeless Youth Programs (DHHS)	$84.14 million	$79 million	$73.6 million	$73.6 million	$66.6 million	$64.16 million	$68.57 million
Homeless Veterans Reintegration Project (DVA)	$15 million	$10 million	$3.0 million	$2.5 million	0	0	$5.0 million

*For FY 2001, Congress also approved an additional $100 million to renew existing permanent housing programs for homeless people with disabilities. Congress also approved $10 million for a new initiative for treatment for homeless people with substance abuse problems.

Source: Compiled from data collected from the House and Senate Appropriations Committees.

a Continuum of Care model for homeless assistance that requires communities to implement a coordinated process for identifying the diverse needs of the homeless population in their area and developing systems to respond these needs; (6) to address the needs identified in their Continuum of Care plans, communities can receive funds from all four of HUD's McKinney programs; (7) to help reduce the administrative burden of applying for three separate competitive grant programs, HUD streamlined the application process for the three programs and combined them into a single national competition, with a single application process, and similar timeframes and rating criteria; (8) HUD's actions have improved the coordination of homeless assistance programs within communities and have helped reduce some of the administrative burdens that separate programs cause; (9) however, additional efficiencies can only be achieved if the underlying differences between these programs are addressed; and (10) consolidation of HUD's McKinney programs can help further reduce the administrative burdens on communities if program eligibility and funding requirements are also streamlined and simplified.

In 1987, the Congress passed the Stewart B. McKinney Homeless Assistance Act (P.L. 100-77) to provide a comprehensive federal response to address the multiple needs of homeless people. HUD is responsible for administering a number of key McKinney Act programs, including the Emergency Shelter Grants program, the Supportive Housing Program, the Shelter Plus Care program, and the Section 8 Single-Room Occupancy program. For these four programs, HUD provides federal funds to state and local organizations through either formula or competitive grants so that communities can develop housing and services for homeless people. Our comments today will focus on the (1) different program requirements for these four programs and the coordination and administrative challenges that they pose and (2) actions that HUD has taken to overcome these challenges.

In summary: Each of the four programs has its own set of eligibility and funding requirements that are established by the authorizing legislation. For example, Emergency Shelter Grants are awarded to state and local governments through a formula, while the other three programs are competitive project-based grants that have different eligibility criteria. These varying requirements have resulted in challenges for HUD in ensuring that adequate coordination occurs among the programs and that they are delivered efficiently without creating undue administrative burdens for the states and communities.

HUD has taken actions to overcome the coordination and administrative challenges that these separate programs with varying requirements pose. To improve coordination, HUD developed a Continuum of Care model for homeless assistance that requires communities to implement a coordinated process for identifying the diverse needs of the homeless population in their area and developing systems to respond to these needs. To address the needs identified in their Continuum of Care plans, communities can receive funds from all four of HUD's McKinney programs. To help reduce the administrative burden of applying for the three separate competitive grant programs, HUD streamlined the application process for the three programs and combined them into a single national competition, with a single application process, and similar time frames and rating criteria.

Background

HUD has responsibility for administering four key homeless assistance programs created by the McKinney Act that are discussed below.

Emergency Shelter Grants program

This program improves the quality of existing emergency shelters for homeless people and makes additional shelters available for this population. In addition, the program is designed to help grantees meet the costs of operating shelters, provide essential social services to homeless people, and prevent homelessness. This program provides formula grants to states, metropolitan cities, urban counties, and territories in accordance with the distribution formula used for HUD's Community Development Block Grant program. According to HUD, grantees are generally notified of their annual Emergency Shelter Grant allocation before the start of each calendar year.

Supportive Housing Program

This program promotes the development of supportive housing and services, including innovative approaches to help homeless people transition from homelessness and enable them to live as independently as possible. States, local governments, other governmental entities (such as public housing authorities), private nonprofit organizations, and community mental health associations that are public nonprofit organizations can annually compete for supportive housing grants through a national competition. These grants may be used to provide (1) transitional housing for up to 24 months and up to 6 months of follow-up services for residents who move to permanent housing; (2) permanent housing with appropriate supportive services for homeless people with disabilities to enable them to live as independently as possible; (3) supportive services only, with no housing; (4) safe havens for homeless individuals with serious mental illness; and (5) innovative approaches to help develop supportive housing that will meet the long-term needs of homeless people. The term for initial grants made under this program is up to 3 years.

Shelter Plus Care program

This program provides rental assistance for hard-to-serve homeless people with disabilities along with supportive services that are funded from other sources. States, units of general government, and public housing authorities are eligible to apply for project grants through a national competition. Grants can be used to provide rental assistance payments for either 5 or 10 years depending on the type of rental assistance requested and the grantee's meeting other program requirements.

Section 8 Single-Room Occupancy Moderate Rehabilitation program

The Single Room Occupancy program brings more standard single-room occupancy units into the local housing supply and makes them available to homeless individuals. These housing units are intended for occupancy by a single person and may or may not contain food preparation or sanitary facilities or both. Under this program, HUD enters into annual contracts with public housing authorities for the moderate rehabilitation of residential properties, so that when the work is done the properties will contain multiple single-room units. The public housing authority is responsible for selecting properties that are suitable for rehabilitation, and for identifying landlords who would like to participate in the program. Under this program, public housing authorities and private nonprofit organizations are eligible to compete for rental subsidies through an annual national competition. Rental assistance payments are provided for a period of 10 years.

Programs' Differing Requirements Cause Coordination and Administrative Challenges

Collectively, HUD's McKinney programs provide a wide variety of housing and services that meet the diverse needs of several segments of the homeless population. However, while the differences in these programs help ensure that the diverse needs of a broad spectrum of homeless people are met, they also create coordination and administrative challenges because each program must be implemented according to differing legislative requirements . . .

Some of the differences between HUD's McKinney programs are essential for providing the various services that the diverse subgroups within the homeless population need. For example, differences in eligible activities for each program result in the Emergency Shelter Grants program providing funds for homelessness prevention activities and emergency shelters, the Supportive Housing Program funding transitional housing and services, and the Single-Room Occupancy and Shelter Plus Care programs funding permanent housing. Similarly, differences among eligible populations for each program help ensure that the needs of different homeless subgroups are met. For example, special preference is given to homeless families through the Supportive Housing Program; the housing needs of homeless individuals are met through the Single-Room Occupancy program; and homeless people with disabilities, especially those with severe mental illness, chronic substance abuse, and/or AIDS are served through the Shelter Plus Care program.

At the same time, some of these program differences can cause coordination difficulties. Coordinating services within communities can become difficult when organizations are eligible to apply for some McKinney programs but not others. For example, state governments can receive Emergency Shelter, Supportive Housing Program, and Shelter Plus Care grants but not Single-Room Occupancy grants. Similarly, private nonprofit organizations can apply for Supportive Housing Program and Single-Room Occupancy grants but not Emergency Shelter and Shelter Plus Care grants. Coordination can be further complicated by the differences in eligible activities. For example, while Emergency Shelter and Supportive Housing Program grants can be used to provide supportive services, Shelter Plus Care and Single-Room Occupancy grants cannot be used for supportive services. Our past work on homelessness shows that coordination of federal programs is essential to ensuring that the wide variety of federally funded programs are made available to the different homeless sub-populations as cost-effectively as possible. In addition, most experts on homelessness widely agree that, without well coordinated and integrated programs, the multiple and diverse needs of the homeless population cannot be effectively addressed.

Moreover, differences in McKinney program requirements can also cause administrative difficulties. For example, while grants from the Emergency Shelter Grant program are formula-based and funds are provided as block grants to communities, the other three programs are competitively awarded and communities have to prepare and submit separate applications to HUD for each project. Moreover, each program's different set of matching fund requirements can cause additional administrative difficulties. For example, states that receive Emergency Shelter grants do not have to match the first $100,000, but they have to provide a dollar-for-dollar match for the remaining funds. If these states also receive Supportive Housing Program grants, they have to match dollar-for-dollar all Supportive Housing Program funds used for acquisition, rehabilitation, and new construction, but they only have to provide a 25 percent match for Supportive Housing Program funds used for supportive services. Our 1999 survey of applicants for Supportive Housing Program funds found that many applicants felt that applying for these grants was not easy. Currently, we are reviewing the administrative difficulties that communities face in completing the application requirements for the three competitive grants administered by HUD. The results of our study will be available by the end of July 2000 and will identify any changes that are needed to improve HUD's grant-making process.

In a January 1995 report to the Congress, HUD concluded that, while the McKinney programs had enabled many types of assistance providers to offer a wide variety of housing and services to a broad spectrum of the homeless population, the number of programs and the differences among them created barriers to their efficient use. In particular, HUD's report found that the differences in target populations, eligible activities, application requirements, and selection criteria made these federal funds difficult to obtain and coordinate for communities. Furthermore, the report found that overlapping regulations and reporting requirements, as well as the unpredictability of the competitive grants, appropriation levels, and varying lengths of the grant awards made it difficult to administer these programs and develop long-term comprehensive strategies for eliminating homelessness. HUD's report echoed the recommendation made by the Interagency Council on the Homeless, in its March 1994 Federal Plan to Break the Cycle of Homelessness, for the need to reorganize, consolidate, and simplify the McKinney programs.

For several years, HUD proposed legislation to consolidate its McKinney programs into a single homeless assistance grant program and deliver these funds to communities through block grants. HUD requested this legislation because it believed that consolidation would create a simpler, less paper-intensive system through which localities could develop coordinated community-based efforts to address and prevent homelessness. Although subsequent congressional action resulted in a single appropriation for HUD's four McKinney homeless assistance programs, consolidating legislation has not yet been enacted.

HUD's Actions to Address Coordination and Administrative Challenges

In the absence of consolidating legislation, HUD has taken steps to improve coordination among its McKinney programs and reduce the administrative burden caused by different program requirements. First, HUD implemented a process called the "Continuum of Care" to encourage and enable localities to develop a coordinated and comprehensive community-based approach for program and service delivery for homeless people. The Continuum of Care process is designed to build partnerships among localities, states, nonprofit organizations and the federal government. Funding for the housing and service needs identified by communities within their Continuum of Care plans are available through HUD's McKinney programs.

HUD also requires that the planning and implementation of the Continuum of Care process take place within the broader context of the community's 5-year Consolidated Plan. The Consolidated Plan describes how resources from HUD's key community development programs, such as the Community Development Block Grant, will be used to create long-term development within a community. A 1996 evaluation of the Continuum of Care process, completed at HUD's request, concluded, that overall this process has had a positive effect on communities across the nation.

Second, to support the coordination and planning inherent in the Continuum of Care process and streamline and simplify the administration of the McKinney competitive grant programs, HUD combined the separate competitions for the Supportive Housing Program, Shelter Plus Care, and Single-Room Occupancy programs into one competitive process. Before HUD combined the application process, these three competitive grant programs had different time frames, application processes, and selection criteria. Under the current application process, communities are required to provide a Continuum of Care plan and an individual application for each project in that plan that is requesting funds from any of the three programs. In addition, HUD now uses the same core rating criteria for making award decisions for all three programs. By streamlining the application process, HUD's goal was to lower the costs and problems of program administration for service and housing providers, with the expectation that this would enable providers to spend more of their resources on implementing the programs.

In conclusion . . . although the wide array of assistance provided by HUD's McKinney Act programs is critical to meeting the diverse needs of homeless people, their complex and differing eligibility and funding requirements cause coordination and administrative challenges for HUD and the communities that rely on these funds. HUD has made a commendable effort in trying to improve coordination and streamline the administrative burden within the existing legislative framework for these programs. However, we believe that the Department will be hard pressed to make additional improvements unless modifications to the McKinney Act are made that would help streamline and simplify these programs. To the extent that further streamlining and simplification can be achieved by consolidating the McKinney programs, it will not only help HUD more efficiently administer these programs but will also help reduce the administrative burden placed on communities that are applying for these funds (GAO/T-RCED 2000).

HUD's Supportive Housing Program

The Supportive Housing Program (SHP) at HUD, described above, is the largest of the federal programs. HUD receives several thousand applications for SHP funding each year during its annual funding competition; the majority of the funds support service programs. The U.S. General Accounting Office (GAO) examined some of the key characteristics of SHP. The GAO report is summarized below and data on states' use of the program is presented in Table 6.2.

Pursuant to a congressional request, GAO provided information on the Department of Housing and Urban Development's Supportive Housing Program, focusing on the: (1) characteristics of Supportive Housing Program applicants; (2) types of programs and services for homeless people that this program supports; (3) importance of Supportive Housing Program grants to applicants' programs for the homeless; and (4) various funding sources, in addition to Supportive Housing Program grants, that applicants rely on for their programs and services for homeless people.

GAO noted that: (1) about 90 percent of the applicants for Supportive Housing Program grants in 1997 are nonprofit organizations; (2) almost 70 percent of the applicants have been in existence for between 10 and 50 years; (3) however, most of the applicants have generally offered services to the homeless only during the last 20 years; (4) about 64 percent of the applicants serve fewer than 500 homeless people each year, and the types of homeless people they most often serve include adults with dependent children, individuals with physical and mental disabilities, and persons with substance abuse problems; (5) the majority of the Supportive Housing Program grants support programs that provide transitional housing with supportive services or supportive services only; (6) on the basis of applicants' responses, GAO estimates that about 59 percent of the requests for Supportive Housing Program grants in 1997 were for programs that provide transitional housing with supportive

TABLE 6.2

State by State Comparison of HUD McKinney Applications and Funding

	Number of Continuum of Care Applications Submitted to HUD	Number of Continuum of Care Applications Receiving Funds	Number of Projects Receiving Funds	Number of Projects Funded	Total Funds Awarded to State
Alabama	6	5	22	8	$5,429,022
Alaska	3	3	6	6	$1,995,160
American Samoa	1	0	1	0	0
Arizona	3	2	32	12	$11,872,922
Arkansas	8	4	14	4	$2,138,795
California	37	32	349	182	$125,348,523
Colorado	8	7	36	17	$7,397,329
Connecticut	7	5	19	8	$5,066,787
Delaware	1	1	21	10	$2,419,729
District of Columbia	2	1	44	21	$8,829,470
Florida	22	16	138	57	$30,023,872
Georgia	10	10	68	31	$14,434,821
Hawaii	2	2	6	4	$2,509,013
Idaho	3	2	9	3	$1,261,617
Illinois	19	15	101	67	$40,641,076
Indiana	8	7	69	45	$10,613,775
Iowa	3	2	16	8	$5,167,099
Kansas	3	0	5	0	0
Kentucky	4	4	30	14	$10,174,431
Louisiana	12	8	59	42	$11,562,347
Maine	2	1	12	6	$956,126

(continues)

TABLE 6.2 (continued)

	Number of Continuum of Care Applications Submitted to HUD	Number of Continuum of Care Applications Receiving Funds	Number of Projects Receiving Funds	Number of Projects Funded	Total Funds Awarded to State
Maryland	7	7	61	44	$15,185,895
Massachusetts	21	21	118	73	$31,536,074
Michigan	18	13	107	61	$28,612,011
Minnesota	11	11	55	36	$12,140,670
Mississippi	4	3	10	4	$,645,478
Missouri	8	7	27	13	$25,176,073
Montana	1	1	8	6	$1,012,233
Nebraska	4	3	22	9	$4,048,915
Nevada	2	2	10	6	$3,163,610
New Hampshire	3	3	32	23	$2,704,078
New Jersey	15	11	70	38	$18,568,338
New Mexico	5	4	21	11	$3,815,909
New York	27	19	219	167	$84,880,780
North Carolina	22	12	74	28	$4,631,303
North Dakota	1	1	1	1	$112,801
Ohio	9	8	85	65	$31,567,471
Oklahoma	4	1	20	15	$2,637,662
Oregon	12	9	50	16	$6,887,053
Pennsylvania	22	18	117	80	$46,890,495
Puerto Rico	10	3	27	9	$5,078,527
Rhode Island	1	1	25	11	$3,832,835
South Carolina	5	5	18	16	$4,738,717

(continues)

TABLE 6.2 (continued)

	Number of Continuum of Care Applications Submitted to HUD	Number of Continuum of Care Applications Receiving Funds	Number of Projects Receiving Funds	Number of Projects Funded	Total Funds Awarded to State
South Dakota	2	1	2	1	$222,325
Tennessee	6	5	39	20	$9,066,283
Texas	17	11	118	61	$31,006,849
Utah	6	3	22	10	$1,961,340
Vermont	2	2	13	6	$1,637,819
Virgin Islands	1	0	3	0	0
Virginia	16	14	79	32	$11,444,012
Washington	9	8	68	52	$19,751,199
West Virginia	8	4	14	5	$1,644,908
Wisconsin	4	4	45	24	$12,393,892
Wyoming	2	1	7	1	$64,765
National Total	448	342	2644	1489	$725,902,234

Source: GAO 1999.

services and 30 percent were for programs that provide supportive services only; (7) the remaining 11 percent were requests for programs that provide permanent housing for persons with disabilities and innovative supportive housing projects; (8) the types of supportive services that applicants most often provide to homeless people include case management, instruction in life skills; (9) Supportive Housing Program grants provide a significant portion of the funding available for some applicants' homeless assistance programs, and applicants generally believe that these grants are an important source of funding for their programs; (10) on the basis of applicants' responses, GAO estimates that Supportive Housing Program grants represent about 45 percent of the resources that applicants receive from all sources to support their programs for the homeless; (11) the importance of the Supportive Housing Program is evident from the negative consequences that applicants often faced when they did not receive an award; (12) GAO's survey results indicate a widespread belief among applicants that the Supportive Housing Program is an important and unique source of funding for homeless assistance programs and that receiving an award from the program confers legitimacy on the applicants' efforts; and (13) in addition to Supportive Housing Program Grants, applicants request and receive funds from a variety of other federal and nonfederal sources to support their homeless assistance programs. (GAO/RCED 1999)

New Legislation on Youth Homelessness

In 1999, Congress approved legislation to provide additional supports to young people who were released from foster care due to having reached the age of eighteen. This group has been documented as increasing in numbers among the adult homeless. The new legislation was named for its chief supporter, the late Senator John Chafee (R-RI). The John H. Chafee Foster Care Independence Program has the following provisions:

Increases funds to states to assist youths to make the transition from foster care to independent living

- Doubles federal funding for the Independent Living Program from $70 million to $140 million a year.

- Allows funds to be used to help youths make the transition from foster care to self-sufficiency by offering them the education, vocational, and employment training necessary to obtain employment and/or prepare for post secondary education, training in daily living skills, substance abuse prevention, pregnancy prevention, and preventive health activities.
- States must contribute a 20 percent state match for Independent Living Program funds.
- States must use federal training funds (authorized by Title IV-E of the Social Security Act) to help foster parents, adoptive parents, group home workers, and case managers to address issues confronting adolescents preparing for independent living.

Recognizes the need for additional assistance for youths ages 18 to 21 who have left foster care

- States must use some portion of their funds for assistance and services for older youths who have left foster care but have not reached age 21.
- States can use up to 30 percent of their Independent Living Program funds for room and board for youths ages 18 to 21 who have left foster care.
- States may extend Medicaid to 18-, 19-, and 20-year-olds who have been emancipated from foster care.

Offers states greater flexibility in designing their independent living programs

- States can serve children of various ages who need help preparing for self-sufficiency (not just those ages 16 and over as in a previous law), children at various stages of achieving independence and children in different parts of the state differently; they also can use a variety of providers to deliver independent living services.
- The asset limit for the federal foster care program is changed to allow youths to have $10,000 in savings (rather than the current $1,000 limit) and still be eligible for foster care payments.

Establishes greater accountability for states in implementing the independent living programs

- The Secretary of Health and Human Services (HHS) must, in consultation with federal, state, and local officials, advocates, youth service providers, and researchers, develop outcome measures to assess state performance. Outcomes include educational attainment, employment, avoidance of dependency, homelessness, non-marital childbirth, high-risk behaviors, and incarceration.
- HHS must collect data to track how many children are receiving services, services received and provided, and implement a plan for collecting needed information. HHS must also report to Congress and propose state accountability procedures and penalties for non-compliance.
- States must coordinate the independent living funds with other funding sources for similar services.
- $2.1 million is set aside for a national evaluation and for technical assistance to states in assisting youths transitioning from foster care.

Other Federal Assistance Programs

The U.S. Congress also asked the U.S. General Accounting Office to examine the availability of targeted and nontargeted assistance for homeless people. To do this, the GAO looked at the availability of programs in all the federal agencies to serve general low-income populations and the extent, if known, that these programs serve homeless people. A summary of the GAO report appears below and data about federal programs is presented in Table 6.3.

Pursuant to a congressional request, GAO reviewed the federal approach to meeting the needs of the homeless, focusing on: (1) identifying and describing characteristics of the federal programs specifically targeted, or reserved, for the homeless, and key nontargeted programs available to assist low-income people generally; (2) identifying the amounts and types of funding for these programs in fiscal year (FY) 1997; and (3)

TABLE 6.3
Number of Targeted and Key Nontargeted Programs Administered by Each Agency

Agency	Number of Programs Targeted to Homeless People	Number of Nontargeted Programs That Could Provide Services to Homeless People	Total
Agriculture	1	9	10
Education	1	1	2
FEMA	1	0	1
HHS	5	12	17
HUD	4	7	11
Labor	1	4	5
SSA	0	1	1
VA	3	0	3
Total	16	34	50

Source: *Homelessness: Coordination and Evaluation of Programs Are Essential.* (Letter Report, 02/26/99, GAO/RCED-99-49).

determining if federal agencies have coordinated their efforts to assist homeless people and developed outcome measures for their targeted programs.

GAO noted that: (1) 50 federal programs administered by eight federal agencies can provide services to homeless people; (2) of the 50 programs, 16 are targeted, or reserved for the homeless, and 34 are nontargeted, or available to low-income people generally; (3) while all of the nontargeted programs GAO identified may serve homeless people, the extent to which they do so is generally unknown; (4) both targeted and nontargeted programs provide an array of services, such as housing, health care, job training, and transportation; (5) in some cases, programs operated by more than one agency offer the same type of service; (6) 26 programs administered by six agencies offer food and nutrition services, including food stamps, school lunch subsidies, and supplements for food banks; (7) in fiscal year (FY) 1997, over $1.2 billion in obligations was reported for programs targeted to the homeless, and about +$215 billion in obligations was reported for nontargeted programs that serve people with low incomes, which can include the homeless; (8) over three fourths of the funding for the targeted programs is provided through project grants, which are allocated to service providers and state and local governments through formula grants; (9) information is not available on how much of the funding for nontargeted programs is used to assist homeless people; (10) however, a significant portion of the funding for nontargeted programs is not used to serve the homeless; (11) about 20 percent of the funding for nontargeted programs provided through formula grants; (12) the remainder of the funding for nontargeted programs consists of direct payments and project grants; (13) federal efforts to assist the homeless are being coordinated in several ways, and many agencies have established performance measures for their efforts; (14) some departments administer specific programs jointly; (15) although some coordination is occurring through the use of these mechanisms and most agencies that administer targeted programs for the homeless have identified crosscutting responsibilities related to homelessness under the Government Performance and Results Act, the agencies have not yet described how they will coordinate or consolidate their efforts at the strategic level; and (16) most agencies have established process or output measures for the services they provide to the homeless through their targeted programs, but they have not consistently incorporated results-oriented goals and outcome measures related to homelessness in their plans.

European Legislation on Homelessness

In May 1997, the European Parliament adopted the following resolution on the social aspects of housing.

Resolution on the Social Aspects of Housing, Committee on Social Affairs and Employment, European Parliament

Contents

1. Motion for a resolution
2. Explanatory statement

By letter of 7 December 1994 the Committee on Social Affairs and Employment requested authorization to draw up a report on the social aspects of housing.

At the sitting of 5 September 1996 the President of Parliament announced that the Conference of Presidents had authorized the committee to report on this subject.

At its meeting of 25 January 1995 the Committee on Social Affairs and Employment appointed Mr. Brian Crowley rapporteur.

It considered the draft report at its meetings of 6 and 27 February and 11 March 1997.

At the last meeting it adopted the motion for a resolution by 17 votes to 12, with 2 abstentions . . .

A Motion For A Resolution On The Social Aspect Of Housing

The European Parliament,

- having regard to Articles 2, 3, 117 and 130a of the Treaty establishing the European Community,
- having regard to Article 1 of the Agreement on social policy concluded between the Member States of the European Community with the exception of the United Kingdom of Great Britain and Northern Ireland,
- having regard to the report by the Committee of the Wise: 'For a Europe of civic and social rights',
- having regard to its resolution of 23 May 1996 on the final report from the Commission on the implementation of the Community programme concerning the economic and social integration of the economically and socially less privileged groups in society 'Poverty 3' (1989–1994),
- having regard to its resolution of 24 May 1996 on the UN Habitat II conference,
- having regard to its resolution of 15 November 1996 on the incorporation of the ECSC into the budget,
- having regard to the Cork Declaration on a Living Countryside of 9 November 1996,
- having regard to the report of the Committee on Employment and Social Affairs. (A40088/97)

A. whereas up to 18 million people within the European Union can now be considered as being either homeless or very badly housed in substandard or overcrowded conditions;

B. whereas in the Union there is a general trend among the governments of the Member States towards the abandonment of their responsibilities in terms of housing policy;

C. whereas the lack of decent housing represents an affront to human dignity and an obstacle to participation in political, economic, social and cultural life for the individuals and families concerned;

D. whereas the problem of homelessness and poor housing has worsened as a result of property speculation and inadequate financial resources devoted to housing and the growth in number of the long-term unemployed, those in atypical or precarious employment and those falling through social security safety nets;

E. whereas there is no policy on the prevention of homelessness, and whereas, if a person loses his or her housing and does not receive prompt and appropriate welfare assistance, the temporary problems he or she faces tend to become permanent handicaps;

F. whereas homelessness and poor housing are both a cause and a consequence of social exclusion, the increase in which is undermining both the fabric and welfare of European societies;

G. whereas, without effective social corrective measures, the housing market is becoming less and less accessible for persons who do not have secure employment, and whereas, in most Member States, the lack of housing assistance constitutes a serious shortcoming in the social protection system;

H. whereas homelessness and poor housing hit particularly the most vulnerable groups in society, such as the disabled, the elderly, single-parent families, immigrants, ethnic minorities and the long-term unemployed; whereas these problems are at their most acute during winter;

I. whereas readily available, good quality housing is an essential factor in attracting investment and business relocation and so is, therefore, important in bringing about social and economic cohesion;

J. whereas, despite the differences between Member States in the area of housing policy, the increasing difficulties of access to adequate housing, affordable on the basis of individual and family incomes, are problems common to all of them and would be tackled more effectively by common action by the Member States at European level; whereas any projects financed at the European level would be those selected on the basis of proposals from the Member States; whereas this would be in accordance with the principle of subsidiarity;

K. whereas a housing policy developed at the European level following this report should be an integrated one in which housing is integrated with education, training, employment, social security and financial assistance, social, health counselling and other services and access to these services ensured, an approach which is much more effective in helping to combat poverty and social exclusion and in contributing to the reintegration of the unemployed into the labour market and of the homeless particularly during the "crisis period" of becoming homeless when access to such services is most difficult;

L. whereas the development of such a housing policy at European level should be based on efforts to provide adequate housing for all;

M. whereas such a policy should not be problematic since all Member States have recognised the right to adequate housing for all as a principle by ratifying the 1966 United Nations International Covenant on Economic, Social and Cultural Rights;

N. whereas the establishment of a European housing policy would not be a radical departure given that structural intervention and European instruments already have an indirect impact on national housing programmes and that since 1955 housing programmes and assistance have been run for coal and steel workers on the basis of the ECSC Treaty;

O. whereas inaction to tackle homelessness and poor housing exacerbates the social and economic problems of the Member States of the Union and places ultimately a greater burden on European economies than a well-constructed and financed policy aimed at eliminating homelessness and poor housing;

Calls on the Member States at the InterGovernmental Conference to include within the Treaty provisions which lead to the progressive realisation of the fundamental social rights of people living in Europe, those rights to include the right to decent and affordable housing for all.

Insists that the right to decent and affordable housing for all be given operational reality by concrete policies and measures carried out at the appropriate administrate and institutional level.

3. Calls on the Member States to shoulder their responsibilities and develop a housing policy: a sufficient supply

of housing; high-quality housing of appropriate sizes; a sufficient supply of affordable housing; a high degree of housing security;

4. Calls on the Member States to take preventive measures, including in the context of the general welfare and housing protection system, to guarantee a minimum level of security for persons facing serious social exclusion problems;

5. Proposes that the Member States should take measures to combat urban property speculation, not least in the form of deterrents designed to prevent owners from leaving housing unoccupied, whether deliberately or through negligence;

6. Believes that housing must be seen as an area of general interest, underpinning all other fundamental social rights, to be taken into consideration at all levels of decision-making in the Union.

7. Suggests that a European housing policy be directed to:

- the collection, exchange and analysis of information on housing policy in the Member States
- the evaluation, exchange and promotion of examples of good practice in Member States with respect to housing projects and housing services, particularly those aimed at helping the homeless and those whose economic situation means that they remained trapped in poor quality housing
- the establishment, with Member States, of minimum objectives for alignment with regard to ensuring access to housing for all and the establishment of terms of reference aimed at achieving these objectives
- the permanent monitoring, for example by a Task Force of relevant Directorates General in the Commission, of the impact of EU policies on the housing sector, to take into account the possible effects on vulnerable and disadvantaged groups and to lead to the development of integrated strategies and coordination of Community resources to achieve maximum effect
- the establishment of a European Housing Forum to act as a consultative body formed from representatives of European organizations active in the field of housing policies including social housing providers, researchers, emergency and transitory housing providers, housing developers and funding bodies,

associations bringing together and representing less-favoured groups, tenants' organizations and local and regional authorities.

8. Proposes that the Commission launch a Community initiative in the form of a Community pilot programme, to be called IGLOO, aimed at funding integrated housing related projects which address at the same time urban development, housing, education, training, employment, social services and health issues, with the participation of the population groups concerned; expects such projects to be selected in the light of proposals put forward by the Member States and concern not only the building of new housing, but also moves to salvage and restore the existing housing stock.

9. Believes that Ministers of Housing of the 15 Member States should meet more regularly to give a European housing policy the necessary political impetus and direction, as well as to oversee the actions foreseen in paragraphs 7 and 8.

10. Believes that, as part of a European housing policy, the European Union should act as a coordinator and facilitator in the question of housing by granting loans or other measures; notes in this context that the ECSC Treaty has, since 1954, permitted European low-cost loans for the housing of coal and steel workers with very positive benefits both for the workers themselves and for the housing areas where loans are granted; believes that this can serve as a model for intervention by the European Union in the question of housing in other sectors, where such intervention may be financed from the Structural Funds post-1999 reform or from ECSC reserves once the Treaty of Paris lapses in 2002; urges the Commission to investigate the feasibility of such an extension; believes that the EU should also look at the utilisation of ESF funding to train the unemployed and homeless, both men and women, in building skills and to build their own homes.

11. Points out that the development of an integrated European housing policy, especially one which promoted both private and public sector housing investment, would have a beneficial impact on employment, and employment insertion for the socially excluded, across the Union not just in the construction sector but also with respect to the kinds of accompanying services, counselling, advice, training, which would flow from such an integrated housing policy.

12. Believes that an integrated housing policy is one that takes into account urban and environmental concerns, in particular the implementation of a proper land-use policy, as well as the prerogatives of social and economic cohesion so thereby contributing to sustainable development; believes that the EU should increase funding for the S.A.V.E. programme to aid energy efficient housing.

13. Stresses, in the context of economic and social cohesion, that properly targeted and integrated housing policies can play a major role in sustaining the economic and social viability of rural, peripheral and ultra-peripheral regions.

14. Points out that the particular housing needs of the disabled and the elderly and women and children at risk must be taken into consideration to ensure not only that decent living conditions are maintained but that they retain a dignified life in the community.

15. Believes that with the present situation regarding rural depopulation and the explosion of urban areas that a policy of rural resettlement should be encouraged and fostered.

16. Believes that all developments must be sustainable and take account of the protection of the environment, conservation of energy and best building practices.

17. Calls on the Member States, when introducing new legislative instruments, to prohibit all forms of discrimination in access to public or private housing, and the implementation of housing policies at all administrative levels.

18. Instructs its President to forward this resolution to the Council, the Commission, the Committee of the Regions, the Economic and Social Committee, the social partners and NGOs involved in the fight against homelessness and social exclusion.

B. Explanatory Statement
1. Introduction

Housing is something of the Cinderella of European social policy. While the Union acts, more or less explicitly, in most areas that traditionally make up social policy it is virtually silent when it comes to the question of housing (although it does have an indirect influence and in the case of the ECSC directly assists with housing provision—see below). Yet housing was one of the earliest areas of social policy in which public authorities began to intervene; the provision of adequate and affordable housing, it is well understood, is an essential element to social policy and integral to policies on social security, social exclusion, employment as well as the urban environment; housing impacts on economic and social cohesion and differences between Member States in their national housing markets and traditions must affect cross-border labour mobility. It is true that the differences in housing tenure structures (broken down into private ownership, the rental sector and social or subsidised housing) of national housing markets are very great indeed, which might at first glance obviate the utility of any European action in this area. But this is the case with other areas of social policy, for example social security, which has not stopped the Union from carrying out actions in these areas. Above all, Member States each face in their different ways the same problems, namely increasing pressure on housing resources, the quality of their housing stock and growth in the numbers without shelter, which is argument enough that these problems be tackled jointly. Such joint action, however it might be organised, would not of course in any way undermine Member States' prerogatives in this field. The ways in which the Union might act are outlined in section 3. In the next section we look at the common challenges facing Member States and some of the trends in national policy responses to these challenges.

2. Challenges and responses

Housing represents for most households, regardless of socio-economic distinctions, proportionately their most important item of expenditure. This is really not surprising. Housing provides shelter, it is the basic infrastructure underpinning people's social and community existence and it directly affects their economic lives. Given this social and economic importance it is also not surprising there has been state intervention in this sector in Western Europe in some cases going back over a hundred years. In its study for the European Parliament the University of Glasgow usefully summarizes housing policy as being in broad terms concerned with: accessibility, that is access to adequate housing, and management and maintenance services, for lower income households

- affordability, involving restricting the burden of housing payments for lower income households

- quality, including raising the standards of new construction or promoting maintenance and rehabilitation to ensure adequate homes for poorer households.

Any analysis of the challenges facing Member States in the field of housing must, therefore, bear these concerns in mind.

Following the Glasgow study these challenges can be discussed under three headings.

First, there is the question of accessibility. Improvements in accessibility have been somewhat mixed over the last 15 years or so depending on the part of the housing market under discussion. In the owner/occupier sector there has been improved access caused by the more widespread availability of mortgage finance and government policies aimed at shifting social housing into the private sector as part of more general urban regeneration strategies, a development particularly exemplified by the United Kingdom. The private rental sector has traditionally been in short supply in many European countries, although there are exceptions, and access appears still to be difficult for immigrants, ethnic minorities and single parents although deregulation of this sector during the 1980s has helped to increase the supply of private accommodation. Pressure, however, appears to have been greatest on the social housing sector, although once the again the Glasgow study emphasizes that there are great geographical differences between Member States, within the same Member State and even within the same city. Their evidence suggests that waiting times increased during the 1980s as a result of demographic change, the growth in the numbers of households, and economic developments, notably the rise in unemployment. Other phenomena, like immigration from Central and Eastern Europe, have also been factors for certain Member States. Against this must be cited actions undertaken in several Member States to assist access for groups with special needs, such as the elderly and disabled.

However, the group with the greatest special need, the homeless, have undoubtedly grown in numbers across the Union, a fact which is perhaps the most obvious manifestation of the existence of an accessibility crisis in housing policy. Determining the extent of homelessness in the European Union is not helped by problems of definition. If within the definition one includes those living in illegal shanty towns, caravans and tents, squatters, those in temporary accommodation (hotels and bed and breakfast) as well as those being put up by friends or relatives then a figure of 3.5 million has been suggested as the total number of homeless in the Union. While figures of the period pre1993 are fairly rudimentary, there is enough anecdotal evidence to point to a rise in homelessness during the 1980s and early 1990s, certainly this is a point on which FEANTSA and the Glasgow study both concur, the latter listing some of the factors which have brought about this increase. These include:

- increased rates of household formation
- family breakdown
- rising unemployment
- reductions in welfare benefits
- deinstitutionalisation of psychiatric patients.

As the Glasgow study points out the homeless more often than not suffer a variety of other social problems (unemployment, poor health, drug addiction etc.), the implication being that simply providing them with housing is not a sufficient response to their predicament but that what is necessary is an integrated approach in which housing is combined with social and health services, education, training, job counselling and so on, a point which your rapporteur stresses repeatedly in his draft resolution.

Affordability is the relationship between housing costs and household income. It appears that affordability has not been generally a problem for those in receipt of subsidised housing or housing benefits. However, within this broad picture certain population groups are experiencing affordability problems. These include those:

- on incomes low enough to have felt in a serious financial way rises in housing rents but high enough to mean that they fall outside qualifying for housing allowances
- who have no access to housing allowances or social housing

- home-owners on low incomes hit by interest rate rises
  or unemployment.

The second of these groups are typically found in southern
Europe while the other two are more prevalent in Northern
Europe.

The quality of Europe's housing stock has improved over
the past 30 years at least when measured against a range of
standard amenities (baths, showers, inside toilets, central
heating, etc.). However, these figures do indicate variations
across the Union with the Cohesion Member States generally
having poorer quality housing. Variations also occur across
income groups (with those on higher incomes not unnaturally
enjoying better quality housing), age (the elderly tending to live
in lower quality housing) and between different housing tenures
(older private rental housing being of poorer quality). It is
therefore not difficult to conclude that many Europeans still live
in housing which falls below generally accepted quality
thresholds. However, reliance on certain qualitative criteria may
hide the true state of housing standards in the European
Community and that integrated approaches to housing policy
which take into account local crime, vandalism and other
problems would give a better overall picture of housing quality
at least from the point of views of residents.

How have Member States responded to the challenge
posed by accessibility, affordability and quality? The Glasgow
study lists 6 trends in national housing policies. These are:

- encouraging growth in the private rental sector by
  means of fiscal incentives and deregulation
- reducing tax incentives for owner-occupiers, a reversal
  of what has historically been national policy in this
  area
- investing less in social housing and gearing policy in
  this area to encouraging tenant participation and to
  adapting housing to meet the needs of particular
  groups (elderly, disabled etc.)
- switching state financial support away from rental
  subsidies to housing allowances
- developing integrated approaches to housing policy
  where housing is treated as only one element in a

package of policies aimed at economic and social regeneration.

3. The role of the European community

In this section we look at the ways in which the Community might assist Member States in tackling the problems outlined in the previous section. However, although many are quick to point that the Community has no competence in this area it would be wrong to assume that it is even now totally inactive in this area. First, one must recognise that for over 40 years European Coal and Steel Community has provided low cost loans, on basis of Articles 2, 3 and 52 of the ECSC Treaty, to help with the individual and collective housing needs of coal and steel workers. These loans have been used to construct and buy new housing as well as to purchase and modernize existing housing. Normally the ECSC loan represents between 10–15% of the total cost of the project which means an important reduction in the financial burden for the workers concerned such that in most cases it is the ECSC loan which make the difference in whether or not the worker gets the house or flat he wants.

The origins of ECSC housing policy were to improve the competitiveness of coal and steel undertakings by reducing the costs of associated with the housing needs of their workers. Aside from such economic considerations it was always seen that ECSC intervention in this area had important social benefits not least in improving living conditions and softening the impact of restructuring. This latter aspect has seen ECSC policy take on more of an "integrated approach" by stressing the social and economic needs of people living on housing estates, improving the local environment of housing estates and using housing intervention as part of a policy of fostering economic recovery and regeneration.

The other way in which the Community has intervened in the housing area has been in the operation of projects financed either by the Structural Funds or from Community programmes. This can be means of:

- projects without an explicit housing component, but targeted on areas of housing deprivation

- projects where housing organisations have diversified their work into activities which are eligible for EU funding
- projects with non-housing objectives where funds 'leak' into housing.
- projects where European funds are used to lever in additional funding into housing investment.

The authors of the Glasgow study give examples of these kinds of projects citing *inter alia* projects from the Poverty 3 programme, Objective 1 and Objective 2 regions in the UK and the URBAN Community Initiative.

The facts about how the Community has acted, and continues to act, in the field of housing policy is not an academic point but designed is slow that opposition to having an explicit Community policy in this area amounts to a self-denying ordinance. It is not clear, at least to your rapporteur, why the idea of a Community housing policy should cause such opposition. The Community after all has had programmes in other areas of social policy, with respect to the elderly, disabled or the socially excluded, without there being any specific reference for these in the Treaty.

It is clear from this report that your rapporteur believes that housing policy should be a legitimate concern for the European Community. But in what ways could it act? Three such ways are put forward.

First, the Community can act as a guarantor of affordable and decent housing by explicitly recognizing in its Treaty a right to housing. To expect this now would of course be quixotic but the proposal put forward by the Pintasilgo Group, in which housing would one of a range of "second generation" social rights to be brought into the Treaty at a subsequent Intergovernmental Conference, is one worth supporting.

Second, there is the model provided by the ECSC which is due to be wound up in 2002 when the Treaty of Paris expires. Your rapporteur would make no secret of his view that the low cost housing loans that have been financed by the ECSC for coal and steel workers should be extended to other sectors to be financed either from existing ECSC reserves or the Structural Funds post-1999 reform. At least the feasibility and cost-benefits of such an extension should be investigated by the Commission.

Third, and perhaps most important, there should be a Community Programme devoted to housing policy. Your rapporteur propose that this should consist of the following elements:

- the collection, exchange and analysis of information on housing policy in the Member States
- the evaluation, exchange and promotion of examples of good practice in Member States with respect to housing projects and housing services, particularly those aimed at treating housing as part of an integrated policy of social economic regeneration
- the establishment, with Member States, of minimum objectives with respect to ensuring access to housing for all
- the permanent monitoring of the impact of EU policies on the housing sector
- the establishment of a European Housing Forum to act as a consultative body formed from representatives of European organizations active in the field of housing policies.

This is a minimalist approach. It would not infringe on Member States overriding competence in this area but it would assist them in the development and improvement of their housing policies. Above all, it would demonstrate the Community's commitment to decent housing for all, the absence of which is a serious gap in the construction and edifice of social Europe. (*European Parliament* 1997)

Legislation in the United Kingdom

The European Observatory on Homelessness, established by the European Federation of National Organizations Working with the Homeless (FEANTSA) in 1991, is a network of national contacts in fifteen countries. These contacts provide information on the issues affecting homeless people in their countries. The excerpt that follows is from the report of the United Kingdom for 1997, *Meeting the needs of homeless people with multiple problems.* It describes the legislation that affects England, Scotland, Northern Ireland, and Wales.

This excerpt examines the roles of both legal and informal organizations in providing the framework for reintegration and resettlement of homeless people.

In describing the complex framework of services provided for homeless people this section will begin by describing the legislative framework, which imposes duties on certain statutory bodies. it will then describe powers of statutory bodies and attempt to describe the non statutory sector in similar terms, distinguishing between duties which organisations are obliged to carry out and powers which they can choose to implement.

The most significant legislation is the Housing (Homeless Persons) Act 1977 which was incorporated into the Housing Act 1985 in England and Wales, the Housing (Scotland) Act 1987 in Scotland and, with some slight differences, into the Northern Ireland Housing Order 1988. In England and Wales this has since been superseded by the Housing Act 1996 which diluted the duties of certain statutory agencies. There has been no significant change in either Scotland or Northern Ireland.

Local Authorities

The Housing (Homeless Persons) Act 1977 (the '77 Act) imposed duties on local authorities in Scotland, England and Wales to provide services for homeless people in certain circumstances. The duties were different depending on the circumstances of the homeless person. In Northern Ireland this duty lies with the province wide Northern Ireland Housing Executive.

If a person is considered to be 'potentially homeless' the local authority has a duty to try to prevent homelessness either by offering advice and assistance or by providing accommodation.

If a person is in the following circumstances they must be housed:

a. is homeless (or threatened with homelessness within 28 days), and
b. is 'in priority need', and
c. is not intentionally homeless, and
d. does not have a local connection with another area

The local authority has a legal duty to provide people in such circumstances with accommodation. Up until 1996 this had always been interpreted as meaning a duty to provide a permanent tenancy, although if a permanent tenancy was not immediately available the person could be housed initially in temporary accommodation, such as a bed and breakfast hotel. In 1995 a court case to the House of Lords (the Supreme Court) (London Borough of Brent v ex parte Awua, known as the Awua case) resulted in a different interpretation. Their interpretation, in summary, was that the duty was simply to house—not to house in permanent accommodation—but that the duty to house was 'indefinite'. This means that a council could choose to house a homeless person in temporary accommodation. However, if the person becomes homeless again from temporary accommodation the council continues to have a duty to house them.

Legislation for England and Wales followed this judgement. The Housing Act 1996 (the 1996 Act) stated that local authorities did not have to provide unintentionally homeless people in priority need with permanent accommodation.

However, since the general election in 1997 the new government has further amended the legislation to ensure that in England and Wales the obligation for local authorities to house homeless people permanently has been restored . . . In Scotland, the original legislation was not changed. However the Awua judgement still applies. A new code of guidance was published by the Scottish Office in September 1997. All local authorities in Scotland must 'have regard to it' in formulating their policies. It states that councils should try to find long term solutions to homelessness including the provision of permanent accommodation. The government has announced its intention to legislate at an early opportunity to ensure the duty for councils to provide permanent rehousing for homeless people is restored.

The law further states that, if a person is homeless, in priority need, not intentionally homeless, but has a local connection with another area, the local authority can refer the application for help to that other area.

If a-person is homeless and in priority need but became homeless intentionally, the local authority is obliged to provide temporary accommodation only. To be intentionally homeless a person must have deliberately done (or failed to do) something which led to their homelessness and they must have been aware of all the relevant facts (e.g., the implications) of what they did.

If the person is homeless but not in priority need, the local authority must provide advice and assistance, but is not obliged to provide accommodation.

In 1993 the NHS and Community Care Act gave local authorities particular duties towards certain 'priority groups' of people. These are not identical to the definition of 'priority need' in the 77 Act. Homeless people per se are not a priority group, but if a homeless person has additional needs, for example due to old age, disability, mental health problems, learning disability, HIV positive status, or drug or alcohol problems, the social work or social services department of the local authority may have a duty to provide financial or physical support (or ensure that it is provided by another agency). They will have a duty to undertake a 'community care assessment' and, depending on the result of the assessment, may have a duty to ensure services are provided for the individual. These can either be provided directly by the local authority, or by the voluntary or private sectors. This is a manifestation of the policy trend of basing funding for care around an assessment of an individual's needs rather than a set amount for a client group.

There is in addition general social work legislation which imposes a duty to assist people in need. it also gives a general power to assist people in need either financially or in kind. Because local government budgets have been severely restricted in recent years, the power is not very widely used.

Children's legislation applies in all parts of the UK. Although the statutes are different in all the various constituent parts of the UK, the separate statutes impose a similar duty on local authorities to assist young people in need, and in certain cases to provide them with accommodation. There are particular duties towards young people who have been 'looked after' by a local authority. In these cases the local authority has a duty to ensure accommodation is provided, and assistance given up until the young person's 19th birthday. There is a power to assist them up until their 22nd birthday. In some cases even if a local authority does not have a duty to house a homeless young person, perhaps because he or she is intentionally homeless, it might still have to house them under the provisions of the children's legislation. Again, councils must undertake an individual assessment of a young person's needs and apply a package of care which suits their individual needs.

Asylum Seekers and Refugees

The 77 Act applied to anyone who fulfilled the criteria described above until legislation in 1995 which applied across the United Kingdom. The Asylum and Immigration Appeals Act 1995 represented the first weakening of the 77 Act. It specifically excluded asylum seekers, or people appealing against a decision denying they were refugees, from the provisions of the 77 Act. Not only were local authorities released from a duty to house them, but they were prevented by law from doing so. The exceptions are people who are granted political asylum or those who apply for political asylum immediately on entry into the UK. If an asylum seeker is granted refugee status he or she—can be housed under the law, but the time spent awaiting the decision on their status cannot be taken into account.

Welfare Benefits

The welfare benefits system is crucial to the resettlement of homeless people in permanent accommodation. Benefits policy is decided by a central government department—the Department of Social Security (the Department of Health and Social Security in Northern Ireland). The benefits are delivered by a number of different agencies. The most significant is the Benefits Agency which provides basic income support, but also administers the Social Fund—an umbrella term covering three different funds. One is a grant—the community care grant which is awarded to people either leaving institutions or to prevent them being institutionalised. It can provide funding for basic furniture, for example, and be used to assist homeless people. However the fund is cash limited and homeless people are not usually the highest priority for such grants. The other two funding mechanisms are repayable loans, which are also delivered from a cash limited budget. Claims are prioritised by different needs groups. Awards are up to the discretion of local offices which may have different priorities in different areas of the country, although there is national guidance provided to the offices. Simply being homeless is usually not enough to be a priority to receive such a loan.

There is a distinction in the funding of residential and nursing care and 'ordinary' housing with support. The former is paid for by a fixed sum 'residential allowance' to meet housing costs paid for by the DSS. Care costs are met through the council's social work or social services department. The latter is paid largely through housing benefit, and varies according to the rent charged for the accommodation.

Housing benefit, which helps to pay rent and certain service charges, is administered by local authorities, though the policy is determined by central government. The scope for flexibility in interpreting the policy is steadily becoming more limited. However, housing benefit is an extremely important tool in resettlement. It is a means tested benefit, awarded on the basis of the income of the claimant and the rent charged for a property.

Local authorities must provide a 24 hour emergency service for homeless people. They assess homeless people and assess people with additional needs (through the social work/social services department). They also have a landlord function, providing housing for rent, sometimes with an option of furnished accommodation, or with other support services. The accommodation is mainly permanent accommodation with secure tenancies, but may include emergency short stay accommodation as well. Support services can range from sheltered housing wardens to people who help with homemaking skills, or sometimes simply a follow up visit to ensure a new tenant has settled in.

Some local authorities also provide hostel accommodation. This too can be variable in quality. Some are old fashioned traditional shelters, but, increasingly, hostels are modern where residents have their own room and counselling or support services may be on hand. The amount of assistance available to help residents move on to permanent accommodation is also extremely variable.

Health Services

The UK has a National Health Service which provides health care for all free of charge on the basis of need. In theory homeless people should be entitled to the same service as every other member of the community. In practice the services to homeless people are variable. In the event of a serious illness or accident there is no doubt that homeless people will be treated in hospital on the same basis as any other patient. However, evidence has shown that homeless people often are not registered with a general practitioner and receive very little preventative care. It may also be that the chances of them following through a course of treatment, or for problems to be identified at an early stage are less likely than in the wider community.

Homeless people are more at risk of certain illnesses, including respiratory illness. Although services should be provided, they are extremely patchy across the country. There is evidence of good practice (e.g., a specialist homeless persons' GP service in Edinburgh, or for example visiting psychiatric services in a number of Day Centres). There is also evidence of bad practice. For example certain doctors refusing to accept homeless people on their list of patients.

Mental Health Services

Mental health services are generally provided through the national health service. They may also be provided by voluntary organisations, who may fund specialised services for particular target groups . . .

The Non Statutory Sector

This sector is very large and extremely varied. its services cover a broad range from offering free soup to people sleeping rough to offering professional counselling services on sexual abuse. Some voluntary organisations build houses or are significant landlords providing or managing accommodation, sometimes with support. Some offer specialist individual services, others offer a broad holistic service.

The non statutory sector normally plays a complementary role to the statutory sector, though it may, on occasion be in competition, particularly in the landlord role. Increasingly, as councils become less direct service providers and more the purchasers of services, the non statutory sector is taking on the services which councils used to provide directly themselves.

The most significant players in the non statutory sector are housing associations. The term housing association encompasses a wide range of housing providers. Some provide general needs housing for rent, at rents below market levels. This is housing for the general community. Others were set up to provide accommodation for particular groups, for example single people, people with learning disabilities, people with physical disabilities etc. Others were set up to regenerate a community.

Some use or rehabilitate existing properties, others build new housing, whilst others provide a mix.

During the 1980s and 1990s housing policy in the UK included a strong political drive to make local authorities adopt a greater 'enabling' role, rather than their traditional role as direct service providers. This extended to their traditional role as the biggest social housing landlords. Housing associations inherited this role and became the main providers of newly built social rented housing. In addition local authorities were encouraged to transfer their housing stock to housing associations. This trend is still in its early stages, but housing associations play an increasingly important role in the resettlement of homeless people into permanent tenancies.

Local authorities have nomination rights to housing associations. They can nominate (Usually) around 50% of the lets for housing associations. In some cases the proportion is even higher. The proportion of these who are homeless or formerly homeless is largely a matter for the individual nominating local authority in negotiation with the receiving housing association. Nomination agreements are extremely variable in their operation.

The non statutory sector is so diverse that it is best illustrated by using the example of one city. This will only give the flavour of the range of services on offer, but to give a comprehensive overview would be too complex a task. Glasgow Council for Single Homeless has produced a directory of services for homeless people in the city. The City has a population of around 750,000. The local authority has one of the largest stocks of council housing in the UK at over 120,000 units.

in addition there are 43 housing associations which operate, each of which provides a different service. Some lease flats to other voluntary sector organisations (e.g., to assist women from ethnic minorities fleeing domestic violence, or to house people with mental health problems), others have flats specifically allocated to house homeless people referred from the local authority.

In addition to the housing associations there is a vast range of voluntary organisations. The resource pack lists 24 organisations which provide accommodation with support. These vary from national church based organisations and very large national charities to, for example a small project offering three bedspaces to young women who have been sexually abused. The total number of bedspaces offered by the voluntary sector is around 1,500 in around 40 projects.

Other voluntary organisations offer advice and information. Some give general housing advice or provide advocates on behalf of homeless people. Others are more specialised, for example offering advice to refugees and asylum seekers. Five voluntary organisations offer this service, although in addition there are more general advice services, such as the Citizens Advice Bureau and the council-run welfare rights service.

Another area of service is support. Some are daytime services, and others operate in the evening. Apart from the organisations which offer some form of support along with accommodation (mentioned above) four services offer specialist support directly to homeless people on alcohol, mental health problems, personal housing plans and recreational support to young homeless people.

One organisation offers an outreach service to young homeless people, and in particular those who are on the streets. It is a multi-agency project composed of a combination of statutory services (social services and community education) as well as the voluntary sector (YMCA and Barnardo's).

There are also a broad range of organisations offering day and night centres as well as basic practical help to homeless people. Seven organisations are identified, offering everything from a comprehensive service of subsidised meals, laundry, counselling, TV, health care and welfare and housing advice, to a drop in clothes centre and a basic soup run.

The voluntary sector embraces large national charities with multi million pound budgets and well paid professional staff, to professionally run local organisations, churches and small groups run by volunteers.

The private or commercial sector has a role in addressing the needs of homeless people. In Glasgow two hostels are privately run supplying almost 250 bed spaces. In addition there are bed and breakfast hotels which are sometimes used for temporary accommodation of homeless people. Private flats, some of them multiply occupied, are often the easiest accommodation for homeless people to access immediately, though restrictions in housing benefit have added new obstacles to single people, particularly those under 25 gaining access to this sector.

Summary

The roles of the statutory and non statutory sectors are largely complementary. The scope of the services offered is so diverse that it is difficult to give a true global picture. The range of services available in Glasgow will be different from those in another city. The voluntary sector provision is likely to reflect a mixture of local needs, gaps in services provided by the statutory services and the interests of individuals or groups who set up voluntary organisations. Voluntary organisations themselves will range from multi million pound operations with professional staff to small groups of volunteers. (FEANTSA 1997)

References

Committee on Social Affairs and Employment, European Parliament. *Resolution on the Social Aspects of Housing.* European Parliament, 1994.

European Observatory National Report 1997, United Kingdom. *Emergency and Transitory Housing for Homeless People: Needs and Best Practices.* European Federation of National Organizations Working with the Homeless (FEANTSA), 1997.

U.S. General Accounting Office. *Homelessness: Consolidating HUD's McKinney Programs.* Testimony, 23 May 2000, GAO/T-RCED-00-187.

U.S. General Accounting Office. *Homelessness: Grant Applicants' Characteristics and Views on the Supportive Housing Program.* Letter Report, 12 August 1999, GAO/RCED-99-239.

7

Homelessness and the Law

This chapter covers several significant efforts to address homelessness through the use of law, including litigation. Litigation on behalf of homeless people in the United States was a key advocacy tool as the homeless population grew in the 1980s, and legal strategies have multiplied as homelessness has continued to raise new issues in communities. Cases have examined issues as diverse as the right to access emergency shelter, the appropriateness of eligibility or intake procedures, the policing of public spaces, the right of homeless people to register and vote, the access of homeless children to education, and the right to permanent housing as a component of treatment or discharge. The institutionalization of federal and state programs for homeless assistance has also created responses from communities concerned about specialized housing and services in their neighborhoods.

This chapter concludes by examining some aspects of international law in relation to homelessness, including United Nations and other international efforts.

Litigation Issues in the United States

The summaries that follow offer an overview of the kinds of issues litigated in the United States in regard to core characteristics of homelessness. Key organizational contacts are listed following the summary section.

Discharge and Aftercare Policies and Practices

A portion of the homeless population has been shown to be recently discharged from one of several publicly funded systems of care, treatment, or custody. These include inpatient mental health facilities, substance abuse treatment programs, primary care hospitals, foster care, and prisons and jails. Legal cases have been filed to establish the obligation of state or local government to ensure the continuation of treatment upon discharge, to secure and place the individual in an appropriate and stable residential setting, and to decrease the length of stay in a institution if placements are inadequate in number.

Policing of Public Spaces and the Criminalization of Homeless People

According to a 1999 report issued by the National Law Center on Homelessness and Poverty, many U.S. cities are continuing to enact and enforce restrictions on homeless people's use of public spaces for necessary activities such as sleeping or sitting and begging and to target homeless people for selective enforcement of general laws. Enforcement includes conducting police "sweeps" designed to remove homeless people from specific areas. *Out of Sight—Out of Mind?*, a report, investigated the growth of anti-homeless ordinances, as well as the selective enforcement of laws, in cities in twenty-seven U.S. states and the District of Columbia. Examples from the report include:

In San Francisco, from January to November of 1998, the police issued over 16,000 "quality of life" violation tickets, the majority of which were issued to homeless people; police are taking pictures of homeless people that they claim are "habitual drinkers," putting the photos together and distributing them to liquor stores (NLCHP 1999).

In Tucson, the police are aggressive in sweeping camps of homeless people, and the city council, at one point, proposed consideration of a plan to privatize the sidewalks and lease them for $1 to businesses, which would have allowed business owners to keep homeless people off the sidewalks.

An example of a long-running federal lawsuit is the case, *Pottinger* v. *Miami,* settled in December 1997. The lawsuit was filed in 1988 by homeless plaintiffs against the City of Miami and challenged Miami's policy of arresting homeless people for conduct such as sleeping, eating, and congregating in public. The city also confiscated and destroyed personal belongings.

Miami must train Miami police officers about the plight of homeless people and ensure that police do not violate homeless people's legal rights. Notably, among other provisions, if a police officer observes a homeless person engaging in an act that violates a city law classified as a "life sustaining conduct" misdemeanor (such as sleeping on a public bench), the homeless person must first be informed of available shelter and offered transportation to the shelter before an arrest may take place. An officer may only arrest a homeless individual in this circumstance if there is available shelter and that individual has refused it.

In addition, the agreement prohibits police from destroying homeless people's property except in very limited circumstances. An advisory committee composed of members selected by both homeless people and city representatives was created to monitor police contacts with homeless people and issue a report every six months for three years following the signing of the agreement. The city will create a compensation fund to provide monetary compensation to homeless plaintiffs who are affected.

Education of Homeless Children

According to the National Law Center on Homelessness and Poverty in Washington, D.C., homeless children and youth are often denied their right to attend public schools. NLCHP's report, *Separate and Unequal: Barriers to the Education of Homeless Children,* documents violations of the McKinney Act and other federal laws guaranteeing homeless children's right of equal access to public schools. NLCHP's report is based on a survey of eighty homeless service providers in thirty-three states. The report finds that homeless children face several barriers to access: transportation, residency requirements, difficulties obtaining needed documentation, and immunization requirements.

In one key case, the court ordered the school board to comply with a settlement agreement on the rights of homeless children. *Salazar* v. *Edwards,* a Chicago case, found widespread noncompliance with the McKinney Homeless Assistance Act, the Illinois Education for Homeless Children Act, and the involved parties' prior settlement agreement. The court ordered the school board to cease discouraging homeless parents from choosing to have their children remain in their school of origin by encouraging them to transfer their children to schools closer to their shelters. The court ordered the school board to (1) begin a "massive" information campaign on the children's rights; (2) warn all school personnel that they must comply; (3) train personnel on compliance and on sensitivity to homeless children's needs; (4) designate school liaisons for identifying, assisting, and enrolling homeless children; (5) provide bus passes for homeless children to attend their school of origin; (6) inform homeless parents about the dispute resolution process; and (7) comply with reporting and information production requirements or be subject to a sanction of up to $1,000 per day.

Further Resources for Research

For current information on cases, contact the following organizations: Bazelon Center for Mental Health Law, National Center for Poverty Law, National Housing Law Project, and National Law Center on Homelessness & Poverty. Complete information on these organizations can be found in Chapter 8.

International Law and Homelessness

The following is information from initiatives and documents of the United Nations on the international aspects of a right to shelter. The first material is drawn from the U.N. Fact Sheet #21, The Human Right to Adequate Housing.

The International Bill of Rights

Introduction

At the core of United Nations action to protect and promote human rights and fundamental freedoms is the International Bill of Rights. The Bill consists of three instruments:

The Universal Declaration of Human Rights (1948);

The International Covenant on Economic, Social and Cultural Rights (1966);

The International Covenant on Civil and Political Rights (1966).

These three documents define and establish human rights and fundamental freedoms. They form the foundation for the more than 50 additional United Nations human rights conventions, declarations, sets of rules and principles.

The Covenants are international legal instruments. This means that members of the United Nations, when they become parties to a Covenant or other conventions by ratifying or acceding to them, accept major obligations grounded in law.

States parties voluntarily bind themselves to bring national legislation, policy and practice into line with their existing international legal obligations.

By ratifying these and other binding texts, States become accountable to their citizens, other States parties to the same instrument and to the international community at large by solemnly committing themselves to respect and ensure the rights and freedoms found in these documents. Many of the major international human rights treaties also require States' parties to report regularly on the steps they have taken to guarantee the realization of these rights, as well as on the progress they have made toward this end.

This Fact Sheet addresses the foundations, implications and content of one particular right found in many international legal texts, including the Covenant on Economic, Social and Cultural Rights and the Universal Declaration: the human right to adequate housing. A series of important developments concerning this right have taken place during the past several years within various United Nations human rights bodies. These and other issues will be outlined below.

Achieving economic, social and cultural rights

Despite the fact that there are two Covenants, each guaranteeing a separate set of human rights, the interdependence and indivisibility of all rights are a long-accepted and consistently reaffirmed principle. In reality, this means that respect for civil and political rights cannot be separated from the enjoyment of economic, social and cultural rights and, on the other hand, that genuine economic and social development requires the political and civil freedoms to participate in this process. It is these underlying principles, of interdependence and indivisibility, which guide the vision of human rights and fundamental freedoms advocated by the United Nations.

Nevertheless, the mutually reinforcing nature of human rights implying that all human rights should be treated equally under law and in fact has proven difficult to translate into practice. While the implementation of all human rights is problematic, the difficulties encountered in realizing economic, social and cultural rights have proved particularly intractable. In response to these challenges and in recognition of the direct link between human rights and development, the United Nations is paying an increasing degree of attention to economic, social and cultural rights and to ways in which the international community can work together to ensure their realization.

A number of specific steps towards the effective implementation of economic, social and cultural rights have been taken by various United Nations human rights bodies in recent years. These include the establishment in 1987 of the Committee on Economic, Social and Cultural Rights (see Fact Sheet No. 16); the appointment by the Sub-Commission on Prevention of Discrimination and Protection of Minorities of Special Rapporteurs on issues such as the right to food, the realization of economic, social and cultural rights, extreme poverty and promoting the realization of the right to adequate housing.

Human rights permeate all areas of United Nations activity and several of the specialized agencies, such as the International Labour Organisation (ILO) and the United Nations Educational, Scientific and Cultural Organization (UNESCO), have maintained human rights portfolios for decades. An increasing number of additional United Nations agencies have begun incorporating human rights concerns into their respective programmes of work. This is particularly true of the United Nations Children's Fund (UNICEF), the United Nations Development Programme (UNDP) and the World Health Organization (WHO).

Each of the above-mentioned developments have facilitated and strengthened United Nations attention to these rights. The right to adequate housing is one of the economic, social and cultural rights to have gained increasing attention and promotion, not only from the human rights bodies but also from the United Nations Centre for Human Settlements (Habitat). This began with the implementation of the Vancouver

Declaration on Human Settlements issued in 1976, followed by
the proclamation of the International Year of Shelter for the
Homeless (1987) and the adoption of the Global Strategy for
Shelter to the Year 2000, by the United Nations General
Assembly in 1988.

What does housing have to do with human rights?

At first glance, it might seem unusual that a subject such as
housing would constitute an issue of human rights. However, a
closer look at international and national laws, as well as at the
significance of a secure place to live for human dignity, physical
and mental health and overall quality of life, begins to reveal
some of the human rights implications of housing. Adequate
housing is universally viewed as one of the most basic human
needs.

Yet as important as adequate housing is to everyone, the
United Nations Centre for Human Settlements estimates that
throughout the world over 1 billion people live in inadequate
housing, with in excess of 100 million people living in conditions
classified as homelessness.

Access to drinking water and adequate sanitation facilities
are additional basic needs directly associated with housing.
According to figures released by the World Health Organization,
1.2 billion people in developing countries do not have access to
drinking water and 1.8 billion people live without access to
adequate sanitation (*WHO Decade Assessment Report*, 1990). These
figures serve to illustrate the enormous scale of the global
struggle to fulfil the right to adequate housing.

The International Year of Shelter for the Homeless in
1987 facilitated the raising of public awareness about the
housing and related problems still prevalent throughout the
world. The follow-up to the Year, the Global Strategy for
Shelter to the Year 2000 has propelled housing issues forward,
and has resulted in housing rights being placed more
prominently than ever before on the human rights agenda of
the United Nations.

The right to adequate housing forms a cornerstone of the
Global Shelter Strategy:

The right to adequate housing is universally recognized by
the community of nations . . . All nations without exception,
have some form of obligation in the shelter sector, as exemplified

by their creation of housing ministries or housing agencies, by their allocation of funds to the housing sector, and by their policies, programmes and projects.

. . . All citizens of all States, poor as they may be, have a right to expect their Governments to be concerned about their shelter needs, and to accept a fundamental obligation to protect and improve houses and neighbourhoods, rather than damage or destroy them. Adequate housing is defined within the Global Strategy as meaning: adequate privacy, adequate space, adequate security, adequate lighting and ventilation, adequate basic infrastructure and adequate location with regard to work and basic facilities—all at a reasonable cost.

How, then, has international human rights law sought to translate this vision of adequate housing into practical legal formulations?

The legal status of housing rights

With the adoption of the Universal Declaration of Human Rights in 1948, the right to adequate housing joined the body of international, universally applicable and universally accepted human rights law. Since that time this right has been reaffirmed in a wide range of additional human rights instruments, each of which is relevant to distinct groups within society. No less than 12 different texts adopted and proclaimed by the United Nations explicitly recognize the right to adequate housing (Annex I).

The housing rights of everyone

Many of the instruments that recognize the right to adequate housing phrase this right as one to which everybody is entitled. This is important, because although other texts mention entitlement to adequate housing in the context of certain groups (thus providing such groups added legal protection), ultimately, adequate housing is the right of every child, woman and man— everywhere. Article 25.1 of the Universal Declaration of Human Rights thus proclaims that:

Everyone has the right to a standard of living adequate for the health and well-being of himself and of his family, including food, clothing, housing and medical care and necessary social services, and the right to security in the event of unemployment, sickness, disability, widowhood, old age or other lack of livelihood in circumstances beyond his control.

The International Covenant on Economic, Social and Cultural Rights has been ratified or acceded to by 108 States. This text contains perhaps the most significant foundation of the right to housing found in the entire body of legal principles which comprise international human rights law. Article 11.1 of the Covenant declares that:

The States Parties to the present Covenant recognize the right of everyone to an adequate standard of living for himself and his family, including adequate food, clothing and housing, and to the continuous improvement of living conditions. The States Parties will take appropriate steps to ensure the realization of this right, recognizing to this effect the essential importance of international co-operation based on free consent.

In addition to these two sources, both the United Nations Declaration on Social Progress and Development (1969) and the United Nations Vancouver Declaration on Human Settlements (1976) recognize the rights of everyone to adequate housing . . .

Housing and other rights: an often unrecognized link

The indivisibility and interdependence of all human rights find clear expression through the right to housing. As recognized by several human rights bodies of the United Nations, the full enjoyment of such rights as the right to human dignity, the principle of non-discrimination, the right to an adequate standard of living, the right to freedom to choose one's residence, the right to freedom of association and expression (such as for tenants and other community-based groups), the right to security of person (in the case of forced or arbitrary evictions or other forms of harassment) and the right not to be subjected to arbitrary interference with one's privacy, family, home or correspondence is indispensable for the right to adequate housing to be realized, possessed and maintained by all groups in society.

At the same time, having access to adequate, safe and secure housing substantially strengthens the likelihood of people being able to enjoy certain additional rights. Housing is a foundation from which other legal entitlements can be achieved. For example: the adequacy of one's housing and living conditions is closely linked to the degree to which the right to environmental hygiene and the right to the highest attainable level of mental and physical health can be enjoyed. The World Health Organization has asserted that housing is the single most important environmental factor associated with disease conditions and higher mortality and morbidity rates.

This relationship or "permeability" between certain human rights and the right to adequate housing show clearly how central are the notions of indivisibility and interdependence to the full enjoyment of *all* rights.

Clarifying Governmental Obligations

The widespread legal recognition of the right to adequate housing is of the utmost importance. In practical terms, however, it is necessary to spell out the specific steps which Governments should take to turn these legal rights into concrete realities for the people who are entitled to them. It is sometimes mistakenly thought that rights such as the right to housing simply require Governments to provide sufficient public funds towards this end and that the subsequent allocation of monetary resources is all that is needed for obligations surrounding this right to be satisfied. However, the right to housing and, indeed, all economic, social and cultural rights confer a much more lengthy and complex series of obligations on States.

The Committee on Economic, Social and Cultural Rights has helped to clarify the various governmental obligations arising from recognition of the right to adequate housing. It has done this through a number of initiatives. These include: (*a*) holding a "general discussion" on this right; (*b*) comprehensively revising the guidelines for States' reports under articles 16 and 17 of the Covenant on Economic, Social and Cultural Rights (Annex II); (*c*) adopting its General Comment No. 4 on the Right to Adequate Housing (Annex III); and (*d*) including in its concluding observations on some States parties' reports remarks to the effect that the State in question was infringing the right to adequate housing owing to the practice of forced eviction.

These steps, and of course the norms of the Covenant and other legal sources of the right to housing outlined above, give rise to various levels of governmental obligations towards the realization of this right.

The legal obligations of Governments concerning the right to housing consist of (i) the duties found in article 2.1 of the Covenant; and (ii) the more specific obligations to recognize, respect, protect and fulfil this and other rights.

Article 2.1 of the Covenant is of central importance for determining what Governments must do and what they should refrain from doing in the process leading to the society-wide enjoyment of the rights found in the Covenant. This article reads as follows:

Each State Party to the present Covenant undertakes to take steps, individually and through international assistance and co-operation, especially economic and technical, to the maximum of its available resources, with a view to achieving progressively the full realization of the rights recognized in the present Covenant by all appropriate means, including particularly the adoption of legislative measures.

Three phrases in this article are particularly important for understanding the obligations of Governments to realize fully the rights recognized in the Covenant, including the right to adequate housing: (*a*) "undertakes to take steps . . . by all appropriate means"; (*b*) "to the maximum of its available resources"; and (*c*) "to achieve progressively."

(a) "undertakes to take steps . . . by all appropriate means"

This obligation is immediate. Steps must be undertaken by States directly upon ratification of the Covenant. One of the first of these appropriate steps should be for the State party to undertake a comprehensive review of all relevant legislation with a view to making national laws fully compatible with international legal obligations.

The Committee on Economic, Social and Cultural Rights has recognized that in many instances legislation is highly desirable, and in some cases, indispensable, for the fulfilment of each of the rights found in the Covenant. At the same time, however, the Committee has emphasized that the adoption of legislative measures alone, or the existence of legislative compatibility is not enough for a State party to fulfil its obligations under the Covenant.

The term "by all appropriate means" has been broadly interpreted. In addition to legislative measures, administrative, judicial, economic, social and educational steps must also be taken.

In general terms, Governments must also take steps which are deliberate, concrete and targeted as clearly as possible towards meeting the obligations recognized in the Covenant. Consequently, rapid steps are required to diagnose the existing situation of the rights found in the Covenant.

States parties are also obliged to develop policies and set priorities consistent with the Covenant, based upon the prevailing status of the rights in question. They are also required to evaluate the progress of such measures and to provide effective legal or other remedies for violations.

With specific reference to the right to adequate housing, States parties are required to adopt a national housing strategy. This strategy should define the objectives for the development of shelter conditions, identify the resources available to meet these goals, as well as the most cost-effective way of using them, and set out the responsibilities and time-frame for the implementation of the necessary measures.

Such strategies should reflect extensive genuine consultation with, and participation by, all social sectors, including the homeless and the inadequately housed and their representatives and organizations.

Additional steps are required to ensure effective coordination between relevant national ministries and regional and local authorities in order to reconcile related policies (economic, agriculture, environment, energy and so forth) with the obligations arising from article II of the Covenant.

(b) "to the maximum of its available resources"

This means that both the resources within a State and those provided by other States or the international community must be utilized for the fulfilment of each of the rights found in the Covenant. Even when "available resources" are demonstrably inadequate, States parties must still strive to ensure the widest possible enjoyment of the relevant rights under the prevailing circumstances.

Importantly, this principle requires an equitable and effective use of and access to the resources available. Although the alleged lack of resources is often used to justify non-fulfilment of certain rights, the Committee on Economic, Social and Cultural Rights has emphasized that even in times of severe economic contraction and the undertaking of measures of structural adjustment within a State, vulnerable members of society can and indeed must be protected by the adoption of relatively low-cost targeted programmes.

If a State claims that it is unable to meet even its minimum obligations because of a lack of resources, it must at least be able to demonstrate that every effort has been made to use all resources that are at its disposal in an effort to satisfy, as a matter of priority, those minimum obligations. However, lack of resources can never be used to justify failure of a State to fulfil its obligation to monitor non-enjoyment of the rights found in the Covenant.

In essence, the obligation of States is to demonstrate that, in aggregate, the measures being taken are sufficient to realize the right to adequate housing for every individual in the shortest possible time using the maximum available resources.

(c) "to achieve progressively"

This imposes an obligation on States to move as quickly and effectively as possible towards the goal of realizing fully each of the rights found in the Covenant. Put simply, States cannot indefinitely postpone efforts to ensure their full realization. However, not all rights under this text are subject to progressive implementation. Both the adoption of legislation relating to the non-discrimination clauses of the Covenant and monitoring of the status of realization of the rights in question must occur *immediately* following ratification.

This obligation "to achieve progressively" must be read in the light of article 11.1I of the Covenant, in particular the reference to the right to the "continuous improvement of living conditions." Any deliberately retrogressive measures in that regard would require the most careful consideration and would need to be fully justified by reference to the totality of the rights provided for in the Covenant and in the context of the full use of the maximum available resources.

The obligation of progressive realization, moreover, exists independently of any increase in resources. Above all, it requires effective use of resources available.

"A minimum core obligation"

Under the Covenant on Economic, Social and Cultural Rights, each State party, notwithstanding its level of economic development, is under a minimum core obligation to ensure the satisfaction of, at the very least, minimum essential levels of each of the rights found in this instrument. Under the same Covenants, a State party in which any significant number of individuals is deprived of basic shelter and housing is, prima facie, failing to perform its obligations under the Covenant. Beyond this core requirement are four levels of additional governmental obligations relating to the right to adequate housing.

"To recognize"

The obligation of States to recognize the right to housing manifests itself in several key areas. First, all countries must recognize the human rights dimensions of housing, and ensure that no measures of any kind are taken with the intention of eroding the legal status of this right.

Second, legislative measures, coupled with appropriate policies geared towards the progressive realization of housing rights, form part of the obligation "to recognize." Any existing legislation or policy which clearly detracts from the legal entitlement to adequate housing would require repeal or amendment. Policies and legislation should not be designed to benefit already advantaged social groups at the expense of those in greater need.

Another dimension of the duty to recognize this right can be expressed in terms of policy. Specifically, housing rights issues should be incorporated into the overall development objectives of States. In addition, a national strategy aimed at progressively realizing the right to housing for all through the establishment of specific targets should be adopted.

Third, the recognition of the right to housing means that measures must be undertaken by States to assess the degree to which this right is already enjoyed by the population at the time of ratification. Even more importantly, a genuine attempt must be made by States to determine the degree to which this right is not in place, and to target housing policies and laws towards attaining this right for everyone in the shortest possible time. In this respect, States must give due priority to those social groups living in unfavourable conditions by according them particular consideration.

"To respect"

The duty to respect the right to adequate housing means that Governments should refrain from any action which prevents people from satisfying this right themselves when they are able to do so. Respecting this right will often only require abstention by the Government from certain practices and a commitment to facilitate the "self-help" initiatives of affected groups. In this context, States should desist from restricting the full enjoyment of the right to popular participation by the beneficiaries of housing, rights, and respect the fundamental right to organize and assemble.

In particular, the responsibility of respecting the right to adequate housing means that States must abstain from carrying out or otherwise advocating the forced or arbitrary eviction of persons and groups. States must respect people's rights to build their own dwellings and order their environments in a manner which most effectively suits their culture, skills, needs and wishes. Honouring the right to equality of treatment, the right to privacy of the home and other relevant rights also form part of the State's duty to respect housing rights.

"To protect"

To protect effectively the housing rights of a population, Governments must ensure that any possible violations of these rights by "third parties" such as landlords or property developers are prevented. Where such infringements do occur, the relevant public authorities should act to prevent any further deprivations and guarantee to affected persons access to legal remedies of redress for any infringement caused.

In order to protect the rights of citizens from acts such as forced evictions, Governments should take immediate measures aimed at conferring legal security of tenure upon all persons and households in society who currently lack such protection. In addition, residents should be protected, by legislation and other effective measures, from discrimination, harassment, withdrawal of services or other threats.

Steps should be taken by States to ensure that housing-related costs for individuals, families and households are commensurate with income levels. A system of housing subsidies should be established for sectors of society unable to afford adequate housing, as well as for the protection of tenants against unreasonable or sporadic rent increases.

States should ensure the creation of judicial, quasi-judicial, administrative or political enforcement mechanisms capable of providing redress to alleged victims of any infringement of the right to adequate housing.

"To fulfil"

In comparison with the duties to recognize, to respect and to protect, the obligation of a State to *fulfil* the right to adequate housing is both positive and interventionary. It is in this category, in particular, that issues of public expenditure, government regulation of the economy and land market, the provision of public services and related infrastructure, the redistribution of income and other positive obligations emerge.

The Committee on Economic, Social and Cultural Rights has asserted that identifiable governmental strategies aimed at securing the right of all persons to live in peace and dignity should be developed. Access to land as an entitlement should be included in such strategies. The Committee has stated further that many of the measures required to satisfy the right to housing will involve resource allocations and that, in some cases, public funds allocated to housing might most usefully be spent on direct construction of new housing.

Generally, on the issue of housing finance, States must establish forms and levels of expenditure which adequately reflect society's housing needs, and which are consistent with the obligations arising from the Covenant and other legal sources.

As proclaimed in the Limburg Principles on the Implementation of the Covenant on Economic, Social and Cultural Rights, and reiterated subsequently by the Committee, due priority shall be given, in the use of all available resources, to the realization of rights recognized in the Covenant, mindful of the need to assure to everyone the satisfaction of subsistence requirements, as well as the provision of essential services.

Other initiatives

In his 1990 report to the Sub-Commission on Prevention of Discrimination and Protection of Minorities, the Special Rapporteur on the realization of economic, social and cultural rights initiated a process of elaborating the content of housing rights within the framework of possible areas of future standard-setting by the United Nations.

In 1992, a working paper entitled "The right to adequate housing" prepared by the Special Rapporteur was considered by the Sub-Commission. A key element of this paper was the effort further to elucidate the obligations of States *vis-à-vis* this right. The study also explored the question of whether the United Nations should eventually adopt a specific convention on housing rights.

The Obligations of the International Community

The obligations of the international community (a term which encompasses all States and international agencies) towards the realization of the right to adequate housing are more extensive than is generally assumed.

For example, under Articles 55 and 56 of the Charter of the United Nations and in accordance with well-established principles of international law, international cooperation for the realization of economic, social and cultural rights is an obligation of *all* States. This responsibility is particularly incumbent upon those States which are in a position to assist others in this regard.

Similarly, the 1986 Declaration on the Right to Development emphasizes that in the absence of an active programme of international, technical and financial assistance and cooperation, the full realization of economic, social and cultural rights will remain an unfulfilled aspiration in many countries.

In more specific terms, related to the right to adequate housing, the international community as a whole is legally obligated to ensure protection of this right through a number of measures, such as:

Refraining from coercive measures designed to force a State to abrogate or infringe its housing rights obligations;

Providing financial or other assistance to States affected by natural, ecological or other disasters, resulting in, *inter alia*, the destruction of homes and settlements;

Ensuring the provision of shelter and/or housing to displaced persons and international refugees fleeing persecution, civil strife, armed conflict, droughts, famine, etc.;

Responding to abject violations of housing rights carried out in any State; and

Diligently reaffirming the importance of the right to adequate housing, at regular intervals, and ensuring that newly adopted legal texts do not in any way detract from existing levels of recognition accorded to this right.

The Entitlements of Housing Rights

One of the barriers to achieving housing rights has been the absence of a universally recognized definition of the set of entitlements comprising this norm. This hurdle was perhaps more the result of perception than genuine legal analysis. In recent times, a number of steps have been taken to refine legal approaches to this matter. Most notably, General Comment No. 4, of the Committee on Economic, Social and Cultural Rights, on the Right to Adequate Housing defines this right as being comprised of a variety of specific concerns. Viewed in their entirety, these entitlements form the core guarantees which, under international law, are legally vested in all persons.

1. Legal security of tenure

All persons should possess a degree of security of tenure which guarantees legal protection against forced eviction, harassment and other threats. Governments should consequently take immediate measures aimed at conferring legal security of tenure upon those households currently lacking such protection. Such steps should be taken in genuine consultation with affected persons and groups.

2. Availability of services, materials and infrastructure

All beneficiaries of the right to adequate housing should have sustainable access to natural and common resources, clean drinking water, energy for cooking, heating and lighting, sanitation and washing facilities, food storage facilities, refuse disposal, site drainage and emergency services.

3. Affordable housing

Personal or household costs associated with housing should be at such a level that the attainment and satisfaction of other basic needs are not threatened or compromised. Housing subsidies should be available for those unable to obtain affordable housing, and tenants should be protected from unreasonable rent levels or rent increases. In societies where natural materials constitute the chief sources of building materials for housing, steps should be taken by States to ensure the availability of such materials.

4. Habitable housing

Adequate housing must be habitable. In other words, it must provide the inhabitants with adequate space and protect them from cold, damp, heat, rain, wind or other threats to health, structural hazards and disease vectors. The physical safety of occupants must also be guaranteed.

5. Accessible housing

Adequate housing must be accessible to those entitled to it. Disadvantaged groups must be accorded full and sustainable access to adequate housing resources. Thus, such disadvantaged groups as the elderly, children, the physically disabled, the terminally ill, HIV-positive individuals, persons with persistent medical problems, the mentally ill, victims of natural disasters, people living in disaster-prone areas and other vulnerable groups should be ensured some degree of priority consideration in the housing sphere. Both housing law and policy should take fully into account the special housing needs of these groups.

6. Location

Adequate housing, must be in a location which allows access to employment options, health care services, schools, child care centres and other social facilities. Housing should not be built on polluted sites nor in immediate proximity to pollution sources that threaten the right to health of the inhabitants.

7. Culturally adequate housing

The way housing is constructed, the building materials used and the policies underlying these must appropriately enable the expression of cultural identity and diversity. Activities geared towards development or modernization in the housing sphere should ensure that the cultural dimensions of housing are not sacrificed.

These extensive entitlements reveal some of the complexities associated with the right to adequate housing. They also show the many areas which must be fully considered by States with legal obligations to satisfy the housing rights of their population. Any person, family, household, group or community living in conditions in which these entitlements are not fully satisfied, could reasonably claim that they do not enjoy the right to adequate housing as enshrined in international human rights law.

Monitoring the Right to Adequate Housing

The wide range of issues arising from the right to adequate housing requires the United Nations to undertake a variety of monitoring activities.

Monitoring by habitat

Many of the more technical issues associated with this right are monitored by the United Nations Centre for Human Settlements (Habitat) in accordance with the Global Strategy for Shelter to the Year 2000.

Habitat has worked out a set of key indicators designed to capture the essential elements of shelter sector performance in all countries. These indicators emphasize the availability of basic services as an integral component of shelter adequacy. Other relevant factors include price, quantity, quality, supply and demand. Reports from Governments based on these indicators are to be prepared every two years for consideration by the Commission on Human Settlements.

Related monitoring of the implementation of the Global Strategy for Shelter to the Year 2000 is also coordinated by Habitat. This process is designed to indicate action taken and progress made, not just by States Members of the United

Nations but also by agencies of the United Nations system as well as regional, bilateral and non-governmental organizations.

On 5 May 1993, the Commission on Human Settlements adopted a resolution on the human right to adequate housing (see excerpt reproduced in Annex I). The Resolution recommends, *inter alia,* that the Preparatory Committee for the planned 1996 United Nations Conference on Human Settlements (Habitat II), consider the question of the human right to adequate housing

Monitoring by the United Nations human rights system

Under the Covenant on Economic, Social and Cultural Rights, States parties are required to submit reports once every five years, outlining, *inter alia,* the legislative and other measures they have taken to realize for all people under their jurisdiction the right to adequate housing.

The Committee on Economic, Social and Cultural Rights issues guidelines to assist States parties in compiling their reports. These guidelines were completely revised in 1990. The guidelines on the right to adequate housing are contained in Annex II.

States parties to the Covenant are encouraged under the new guidelines to report on such developments and measures as: the number of homeless individuals and families; the number of people currently inadequately housed; the number of persons evicted during the previous five-year period; the number of people lacking legal protection against arbitrary or forced evictions; the existence of legislation affecting the realization of the right to adequate housing; measures taken to release unutilized land for the purposes of housing; and measures taken to ensure that international assistance for housing and human settlements is used to fulfil the needs of the most disadvantaged groups.

The Committee on Economic, Social and Cultural Rights examines these reports very carefully along with any other available information. It also engages in discussions with the representative of the State party presenting his or her country's report. Through this process, the Committee is in a position to monitor the degree to which the rights set forth in the Covenant have been realized by and in each State party.

With respect to the right to adequate housing, the Committee and other United Nations human rights bodies have recognized that comprehensively monitoring the extent to which this right is respected and enjoyed is a difficult task.

Part of the difficulty stems from the fact that very few States systematically collect housing statistics or indicators which are directly relevant to the concerns expressed in the Covenant.

However, the Committee in its General Comment No. 4 makes it clear that the obligation to monitor effectively the situation with respect to housing is a positive one. States parties are therefore required to take whatever steps are necessary, either alone or on the basis of international cooperation, to ascertain the full extent of homelessness and inadequate housing within their jurisdiction.

States parties must, in particular, provide detailed information to the Committee about those groups within society that are vulnerable and disadvantaged with regard to housing.

Reports from each of the States parties to the Covenant are public. Copies are available from the United Nations Centre for Human Rights in Geneva.

Towards the Justiciability of Housing Rights

The question of whether the legal principle of justiciability or the provision of domestic legal remedies are applicable to economic, social and cultural rights, in particular the right to adequate housing, has been answered affirmatively by the Committee on Economic, Social and Cultural Rights. According to the Committee, areas where such provisions would apply, include:

(a) Legal appeals aimed at preventing planned evictions or demolitions through the issuance of court-ordered injunctions;
(b) Legal procedures seeking compensation following an illegal eviction;
(c) Complaints against illegal actions carried out or supported by landlords (whether public or private) in

relation to rent levels, dwelling maintenance and racial or other forms of discrimination;

(*d*) Allegations of any form of discrimination in the allocation and availability of access to housing;

(*e*) Complaints against landlords concerning unhealthy or inadequate housing conditions; and

(*f*) Class action suits in situations involving significantly increased levels of homelessness.

Violations of housing rights

Various United Nations human rights bodies have confirmed that housing rights can be violated by Governments. In one of the first opinions on this issue, the Committee on Economic, Social and Cultural Rights noted at its fourth session (1990) that:

The right to housing can be subject to violation. Acts and omissions constituting violations will need to be explored by the Committee, especially in the context of evictions . . .

Housing rights: is there a right to complain?

The Covenant on Economic, Social and Cultural Rights creates no formal mechanisms by which individuals could submit complaints alleging non-compliance by their Governments with their housing rights. Nevertheless, by working with non-governmental organizations which are active at the annual sessions of the Committee on Economic, Social and Cultural Rights, affected persons and groups can draw the attention of this body to practices and legislation of States parties that are believed to be inconsistent with the obligations of the Covenant . . .

Non-governmental organizations and housing rights

Non-governmental organizations are both local and international, important actors in efforts to promote and enforce the right to adequate housing.

At the local and national levels, non-governmental organizations can carry out a wide range of initiatives designed to promote the realization of the right to adequate housing. With specific regard to the Covenant on Economic, Social and Cultural

Rights, they can publicize and distribute this instrument to vulnerable and disadvantaged groups in society. They can also seek to participate in the reporting process engaged in by governments.

Some non-governmental organizations have consultative status with the United Nations. This allows them certain rights of participation in the United Nations system. Individuals, local groups and other organizations without consultative status can forward their concerns through them to the Committee on Economic, Social and Cultural Rights and other bodies dealing with housing rights issues.

In addition, any person or group, anywhere, can send information about violations by any State party of any of the rights found in the Covenant directly to the secretary of the Committee at the Centre for Human Rights. These communications are placed in the relevant country file for eventual distribution to Committee members.

Non-governmental organizations can provide legal education, training and advice to citizens in States which have ratified the Covenant or other relevant instruments, with a view to informing people of their rights and how to enforce them.

Campaigns for housing rights exist in more than a dozen countries, as well as at the international level. These campaigns seek to monitor the situation as well as to enforce the right to adequate housing through a variety of means including reliance on the international legal standards which have been set out in this Fact Sheet . . .

LEGAL SOURCES OF THE RIGHT TO ADEQUATE HOUSING UNDER INTERNATIONAL HUMAN RIGHTS LAW

International Conventions and Covenants

International Covenant on Economic, Social and Cultural Rights (1966)

adopted by United Nations General Assembly resolution 2200 A (XXI) on 16 December 1966, entered into force on 3 January 1976; 106 States Parties as of June 1992 . . .

International Convention on the Elimination of All Forms of Racial Discrimination (1965)

adopted by General Assembly resolution 2106 A (XX) on 21 December 1965, entered into force on 4 January 1969; 130 States Parties as of January 1992 . . .

Convention on the Elimination of All Forms of Discrimination Against Women (1979)

adopted by General Assembly resolution 34/180 of 18 December 1979, entered into force on 3 September 1981; 99 States Parties as of January 1992 . . .

Convention on the Rights of the Child (1989)

adopted by General Assembly resolution 44/25 on 20 November 1989, entered into force on 2 September 1990; 69 States Parties as of January 1992 . . .

Convention Relating to the Status of Refugees (1951)

adopted on 28 July 1951 by the United Nations Conference of Plenipotentiaries of the Status of Refugees and Stateless Persons, entered into force on 22 April 1954 . . .

International Convention on the Protection of the Rights of All Migrant Workers and Members of their Families (1990)

adopted by General Assembly resolution 45/158 on 16 December 1990; not yet in force . . .

International Declarations and Recommendations

The Universal Declaration of Human Rights (1948)

adopted and proclaimed by United Nations General Assembly resolution 217 A (III) of 10 December 1948. Article 25.1 states:

Everyone has the right to a standard of living adequate for the health and well-being of himself and his family, including food, clothing, *housing* and medical care and necessary social services, and the right to security in the event of unemployment, sickness, disability, widowhood, old age or other lack of livelihood in circumstances beyond his control.

Declaration of the Rights of the Child (1959)
proclaimed by General Assembly resolution 1386 (XIV) on 29 November 1959 . . .

International Labour Organisation (ILO) Recommendation No. 115 on Worker's Housing (1961)
adopted at the forty-fourth session of the ILO Governing Body on 7 June 1961 . . .

Declaration on Social Progress and Development (1969)
proclaimed by General Assembly resolution 2542 (XXIV) on 11 December 1969 . . .

Vancouver Declaration on Human Settlements (1976)
adopted by the United Nations Conference on Human Settlements in 1976.

Declaration on the Right to Development (1986)
adopted by General Assembly resolution 41/128 on 4 December 1986 . . .

REVISED GUIDELINES REGARDING THE FORM AND CONTENTS OF STATES REPORTS TO BE SUBMITTED BY STATES PARTIES UNDER ARTICLES 16 AND 17 OF THE COVENANT ON ECONOMIC, SOCIAL AND CULTURAL RIGHTS

The Right to Adequate Housing

(a) Please furnish detailed statistical information about the housing situation in your country.

(b) Please provide detailed information about those groups within your society that are vulnerable and disadvantaged with regard to housing. Indicate, in particular:

(i) The number of homeless individuals and families;

(ii) The number of individuals and families currently inadequately housed and without ready access to basic amenities such as water, heating (if necessary), waste disposal, sanitation facilities, electricity, postal services, etc. (in so far as you consider these amenities relevant in your country). Include the number of people living in overcrowded, damp, structurally unsafe housing or other conditions which affect health;

(iii) The number of persons currently classified as living in "illegal" settlements or housing;

(iv) The number of persons evicted within the last five years and the number of persons currently lacking legal protection against arbitrary eviction or any other kind of eviction;

(v) The number of persons whose housing expenses are above any government-set limit of affordability, based upon ability to pay or as a ratio of income;

(vi) The number of persons on waiting lists for obtaining accommodation, the average length of waiting time and measures taken to decrease such lists, as well as to assist those on such lists in finding temporary housing;

(vii) The number of persons in different types of housing tenure by: social or public housing; private rental sector; owner-occupiers; "illegal" sector; and others.

(c) Please provide information on the existence of any laws affecting the realization of the right to housing, including:

(i) Legislation which gives substance to the right to housing in terms of defining the content of this right;

(ii) Legislation such as housing acts, homeless person acts, municipal corporation acts, etc.;

(iii) Legislation relevant to land use, land distribution, land allocation, land zoning, land ceilings, expropriations including provisions for compensation, land planning including procedures for community participation;

(iv) Legislation concerning the rights of tenants to security of tenure, to protection from eviction, to housing finance and rent control (or subsidy), housing affordability, etc.;

    (v)   Legislation concerning building codes, building regulations and standards and the provision of infrastructure;

    (vi)   Legislation prohibiting any and all forms of discrimination in the housing sector, including against groups not traditionally protected;

    (vii) Legislation prohibiting any form of eviction;

    (viii) Any legislative appeal or reform of existing laws which detracts from the fulfilment of the right to housing;

    (ix)   Legislation restricting speculation on housing or property, particularly when such speculation has a negative impact on the fulfilment of housing rights for all sectors of society;

    (x)   Legislative measures conferring legal title to those living in the "illegal" sector;

    (xi)   Legislation concerning environmental planning and health in housing and human settlements.

(d) Please provide information on all other measures taken to fulfil the right to housing, including:

    (i)   Measures taken to encourage "enabling strategies" whereby local community-based organizations and the "informal sector" can build housing and related services. Are such organizations free to operate? Do they receive government funding?;

    (ii)   Measures taken by the State to build housing units and to increase other construction of affordable rental housing;

    (iii) Measures taken to release unutilized, underutilized or misutilized land;

    (iv) Financial measures taken by the State, including details of the budget of the Ministry of Housing or other relevant Ministry as a percentage of the national budget;

    (v)   Measures taken to ensure that international assistance for housing and human settlements is used to fulfil the needs of the most disadvantaged groups;

    (vi)   Measures taken to encourage the development of small and intermediate urban centres, especially at the rural level;

(vii) Measures taken during, *inter-alia,* urban renewal programmes, redevelopment projects, site upgrading, preparation for international events (Olympics, World Fairs, conferences, etc.), "beautiful city" campaigns, etc., which guarantee protection from eviction or guarantee rehousing based on mutual agreement, by any persons living on or near to affected sites.

(e) During the reporting period, have there been any changes in the national policies, laws and practices negatively affecting the right to adequate housing? If so, please describe the changes and evaluate their impact.

The United Nations Centre for Human Settlements (Habitat)

The United Nations Centre for Human Settlements (Habitat) was established in 1978, two years after the United Nations Conference on Human Settlements in Vancouver, Canada. Based in Nairobi, Kenya, UNCHS (Habitat) is the lead agency within the UN system for coordinating activities in the field of human settlements.

The Centre was the secretariat for the second United Nations Conference on Human Settlements (Habitat II), held in Istanbul, Turkey, in June 1996. This conference formulated the Habitat Agenda and the Istanbul Declaration in which governments committed themselves to the goals of adequate shelter for all and sustainable urban development. Habitat is the focal point for the implementation of these commitments.

Habitat's operational activities focus on promoting housing for all, improving urban governance, reducing urban poverty, improving the living environment and managing disaster mitigation and post-conflict rehabilitation. The Centre is supporting the implementation of the Habitat Agenda at local, national and regional levels. At the end of 1998 UNCHS (Habitat) had 238 technical programmes and projects under execution in 86 countries, with an annual budget totaling US$70 million.

During the biennium 2000–2001 Habitat will launch two significant global campaigns, one for secure tenure and the other on urban governance. The aim of these campaigns is to reduce urban poverty through policies which emphasize equity, sustainability and social justice. Strategic and operational partnerships with government, local authorities, non-governmental and community based organisations, the private sector and UN agencies are crucial to the success of these campaigns.

Another major activity for the biennium is the preparation and servicing of Istanbul+5, the special session of the UN General Assembly planned in June 2001,which will review and appraise the worldwide implementation of the Habitat Agenda. Key excerpts from the Habitat Agenda follow.

Campaign for Secure Tenure

Security of Tenure is a fundamental requirement for the progressive integration of the urban poor in the city and is one of the most important components of housing rights. Habitat will launch this rights-based Campaign in support of a shelter strategy that is pragmatic, affordable and implementable. This Campaign, undertaken with Habitat's partners, will be backed by a work programme offering assistance in key policy areas including land markets and tenure reform. Access to urban services and infrastructure, particularly water and sanitation, are vital elements of the strategy. Habitat will also provide policy advice and technical support in housing finance, with an emphasis on micro-credit and micro-enterprise, as well as urban transport policy and shelter delivery systems . . .

The Habitat Agenda

Istanbul Declaration on Human Settlements

Government delegations and representatives of non-governmental organizations (NGOs) and not-for-profit organizations from all over the world gathered in Istanbul, Turkey, in June 1995, for Habitat II, the U.N. sponsored conference on human settlements. The right to housing was a key issue at the conference. Many countries and the U.N. consider that the right has been recognized in prior international documents, but the United States led a small number of other countries in opposition.

The document agreed to at the Istanbul Conference follows. Istanbul+5 is scheduled to occur in June 2001 to monitor progress on this agenda.

1. We, the Heads of State or Government and the official delegations of countries assembled at the United Nations Conference on Human Settlements (Habitat II) in Istanbul, Turkey from 3 to 14 June 1996, take this opportunity to endorse the universal goals of ensuring adequate shelter for all and making human settlements safer, healthier and more livable, equitable, sustainable and productive. Our deliberations on the two major themes of the Conference—adequate shelter for all and sustainable human settlements development in an urbanizing world—have been inspired by the Charter of the United Nations and are aimed at reaffirming existing and forging new partnerships for action at the international, national and local levels to improve our living environment. We commit ourselves to the objectives, principles and recommendations contained in the Habitat Agenda and pledge our mutual support for its implementation.

2. We have considered, with a sense of urgency, the continuing deterioration of conditions of shelter and human settlements. At the same time, we recognize cities and towns as centres of civilization, generating economic development and social, cultural, spiritual and scientific advancement. We must take advantage of the opportunities presented by our settlements and preserve their diversity to promote solidarity among all our peoples.

3. We reaffirm our commitment to better standards of living in larger freedom for all humankind. We recall the first United Nations Conference on Human Settlements, held at Vancouver, Canada, the celebration of the International Year of Shelter for the Homeless and the Global Strategy for Shelter to the Year 2000, all of which have contributed to increased global awareness of the problems of human settlements and called for action to achieve adequate shelter for all. Recent United Nations world conferences, including, in particular, the United Nations Conference on Environment and Development, have given us a

comprehensive agenda for the equitable attainment of peace, justice and democracy built on economic development, social development and environmental protection as interdependent and mutually reinforcing components of sustainable development. We have sought to integrate the outcomes of these conferences into the Habitat Agenda.

4. To improve the quality of life within human settlements, we must combat the deterioration of conditions that in most cases, particularly in developing countries, have reached crisis proportions. To this end, we must address comprehensively, inter alia, unsustainable consumption and production patterns, particularly in industrialized countries; unsustainable population changes, including changes in structure and distribution, giving priority consideration to the tendency towards excessive population concentration; homelessness; increasing poverty; unemployment; social exclusion; family instability; inadequate resources; lack of basic infrastructure and services; lack of adequate planning; growing insecurity and violence; environmental degradation; and increased vulnerability to disasters.

5. The challenges of human settlements are global, but countries and regions also face specific problems which need specific solutions. We recognize the need to intensify our efforts and cooperation to improve living conditions in the cities, towns and villages throughout the world, particularly in developing countries, where the situation is especially grave, and in countries with economies in transition. In this connection, we acknowledge that globalization of the world economy presents opportunities and challenges for the development process, as well as risks and uncertainties, and that achievement of the goals of the Habitat Agenda would be facilitated by, inter alia, positive actions on the issues of financing of development, external debt, international trade and transfer of technology. Our cities must be places where human beings lead fulfilling lives in dignity, good health, safety, happiness and hope.

6. Rural and urban development are interdependent. In addition to improving the urban habitat, we must also work to extend adequate infrastructure, public services and employment opportunities to rural areas in order to enhance their attractiveness, develop an integrated network of settlements and minimize rural-to-urban migration. Small- and medium-sized towns need special focus.

7. As human beings are at the centre of our concern for sustainable development, they are the basis for our actions as in implementing the Habitat Agenda. We recognize the particular needs of women, children and youth for safe, healthy and secure living conditions. We shall intensify our efforts to eradicate poverty and discrimination, to promote and protect all human rights and fundamental freedoms for all, and to provide for basic needs, such as education, nutrition and life-span health care services, and, especially, adequate shelter for all. To this end, we commit ourselves to improving the living conditions in human settlements in ways that are consonant with local needs and realities, and we acknowledge the need to address the global, economic, social and environmental trends to ensure the creation of better living environments for all people. We shall also ensure the full and equal participation of all women and men, and the effective participation of youth, in political, economic and social life. We shall promote full accessibility for people with disabilities, as well as gender equality in policies, programmes and projects for shelter and sustainable human settlements development. We make these commitments with particular reference to the more than one billion people living in absolute poverty and to the members of vulnerable and disadvantaged groups identified in the Habitat Agenda.

8. We reaffirm our commitment to the full and progressive realization of the right to adequate housing as provided for in international instruments. To that end, we shall seek the active participation of our public, private and non-governmental partners at all levels to ensure legal security of tenure, protection from discrimination and equal access to affordable, adequate housing for all persons and their families.

9. We shall work to expand the supply of affordable housing by enabling markets to perform efficiently and in a socially and environmentally responsible manner, enhancing access to land and credit and assisting those who are unable to participate in housing markets.

10. In order to sustain our global environment and improve the quality of living in our human settlements, we commit ourselves to sustainable patterns of production, consumption, transportation and settlements development; pollution prevention; respect for the carrying capacity of ecosystems; and the preservation of opportunities for future generations. In this connection, we shall cooperate in a spirit of global partnership to

conserve, protect and restore the health and integrity of the Earth's ecosystem. In view of different contributions to global environmental degradation, we reaffirm the principle that countries have common but differentiated responsibilities. We also recognize that we must take these actions in a manner consistent with the precautionary principle approach, which shall be widely applied according to the capabilities of countries. We shall also promote healthy living environments, especially through the provision of adequate quantities of safe water and effective management of waste.

11. We shall promote the conservation, rehabilitation and maintenance of buildings, monuments, open spaces, landscapes and settlement patterns of historical, cultural, architectural, natural, religious and spiritual value.

12. We adopt the enabling strategy and the principles of partnership and participation as the most democratic and effective approach for the realization of our commitments. Recognizing local authorities as our closest partners, and as essential, in the implementation of the Habitat Agenda, we must, within the legal framework of each country, promote decentralization through democratic local authorities and work to strengthen their financial and institutional capacities in accordance with the conditions of countries, while ensuring their transparency, accountability and responsiveness to the needs of people, which are key requirements for Governments at all levels. We shall also increase our cooperation with parliamentarians, the private sector, labour unions and non-governmental and other civil society organizations with due respect for their autonomy. We shall also enhance the role of women and encourage socially and environmentally responsible corporate investment by the private sector. Local action should be guided and stimulated through local programmes based on Agenda 21, the Habitat Agenda, or any other equivalent programme, as well as drawing upon the experience of worldwide cooperation initiated in Istanbul by the World Assembly of Cities and Local Authorities, without prejudice to national policies, objectives, priorities and programmes. The enabling strategy includes a responsibility for Governments to implement special measures for members of disadvantaged and vulnerable groups when appropriate.

13. As the implementation of the Habitat Agenda will require adequate funding, we must mobilize financial resources

at the national and international levels, including new and additional resources from all sources—multilateral and bilateral, public and private. In this connection, we must facilitate capacity-building and promote the transfer of appropriate technology and know-how. Furthermore, we reiterate the commitments set out in recent United Nations conferences, especially those in Agenda 21 on funding and technology transfer.

14. We believe that the full and effective implementation of the Habitat Agenda will require the strengthening of the role and functions of the United Nations Centre for Human Settlements (Habitat), taking into account the need for the Centre to focus on well-defined and thoroughly developed objectives and strategic issues. To this end, we pledge our support for the successful implementation of the Habitat Agenda and its global plan of action. Regarding the implementation of the Habitat Agenda, we fully recognize the contribution of the regional and national action plans prepared for this Conference.

15. This Conference in Istanbul marks a new era of cooperation, an era of a culture of solidarity. As we move into the twenty-first century, we offer a positive vision of sustainable human settlements, a sense of hope for our common future and an exhortation to join a truly worthwhile and engaging challenge, that of building together a world where everyone can live in a safe home with the promise of a decent life of dignity, good health, safety, happiness and hope.

Chapter I—Preamble

We recognize the imperative need to improve the quality of human settlements, which profoundly affects the daily lives and well-being of our peoples. There is a sense of great opportunity and hope that a new world can be built, in which economic development, social development and environmental protection as interdependent and mutually reinforcing components of sustainable development can be realized through solidarity and cooperation within and between countries and through effective partnerships at all levels. International cooperation and universal solidarity, guided by the purposes and principles of the Charter of the United Nations, and in a spirit of partnership, are crucial to improving the quality of life of the peoples of the world.

The purpose of the second United Nations Conference on Human Settlements (Habitat II) is to address two themes of equal global importance: "Adequate shelter for all" and "Sustainable human settlements development in an urbanizing world." Human beings are at the centre of concerns for sustainable development, including adequate shelter for all and sustainable human settlements, and they are entitled to a healthy and productive life in harmony with nature.

As to the first theme, a large segment of the world's population lacks shelter and sanitation, particularly in developing countries. We recognize that access to safe and healthy shelter and basic services is essential to a person's physical, psychological, social and economic well-being and should be a fundamental part of our urgent actions for the more than one billion people without decent living conditions. Our objective is to achieve adequate shelter for all, especially the deprived urban and rural poor, through an enabling approach to the development and improvement of shelter that is environmentally sound . . .

More people than ever are living in absolute poverty and without adequate shelter. Inadequate shelter and homelessness are growing plights in many countries, threatening standards of health, security and even life itself. Everyone has the right to an adequate standard of living for themselves and their families, including adequate food, clothing, housing, water and sanitation, and to the continuous improvement of living conditions . . .

The needs of children and youth, particularly with regard to their living environment, have to be taken fully into account. Special attention needs to be paid to the participatory processes dealing with the shaping of cities, towns and neighbourhoods; this is in order to secure the living conditions of children and of youth and to make use of their insight, creativity and thoughts on the environment. Special attention must be paid to the shelter needs of vulnerable children, such as street children, refugee children and children who are victims of sexual exploitation. Parents and other persons legally responsible for children have responsibilities, rights and duties, consistent with the Convention on the Rights of the Child, to address these needs . . .

In shelter and urban development and management policies, particular attention should be given to the needs and participation of indigenous people. These policies should fully respect their identity and culture and provide an appropriate environment that enables them to participate in political, social and economic life . . .

Encountering disabilities is a part of normal life. Persons with disabilities have not always had the opportunity to participate fully and equally in human settlements development and management, including decision-making, often owing to social, economic, attitudinal and physical barriers, and discrimination. Such barriers should be removed and the needs and concerns of persons with disabilities should be fully integrated into shelter and sustainable human settlement plans and policies to create access for all.

Older persons are entitled to lead fulfilling and productive lives and should have opportunities for full participation in their communities and society, and in all decision-making regarding their well-being, especially their shelter needs. Their many contributions to the political, social and economic processes of human settlements should be recognized and valued. Special attention should be given to meeting the evolving housing and mobility needs in order to enable them to continue to lead rewarding lives in their communities.

Chapter II—Goals and Principles

The objectives of the Habitat Agenda are in full conformity with the purposes and principles of the Charter of the United Nations and international law.

While the significance of national and regional particularities and various historical, cultural and religious backgrounds must be borne in mind, it is the duty of all States to promote and protect all human rights and fundamental freedoms, including the right to development.

Implementation of the Habitat Agenda, including implementation through national laws and development priorities, programmes and policies, is the sovereign right and responsibility of each State in conformity with all human rights and fundamental freedoms, including the right to development, and taking into account the significance of and with full respect for various religious and ethical values, cultural backgrounds, and philosophical convictions of individuals and their communities, contributing to the full enjoyment by all of their human rights in order to achieve the objectives of adequate shelter for all and sustainable human settlements development.

We, the States participating in the United Nations Conference on Human Settlements (Habitat II), are committed to a political, economic, environmental, ethical and spiritual vision of human settlements based on the principles of equality, solidarity, partnership, human dignity, respect and cooperation. We adopt the goals and principles of adequate shelter for all and sustainable human settlements development in an urbanizing world. We believe that attaining these goals will promote a more stable and equitable world that is free from injustice and conflict and will contribute to a just, comprehensive and lasting peace. Civil, ethnic and religious strife, violations of human rights, alien and colonial domination, foreign occupation, economic imbalances, poverty, organized crime, terrorism in all its forms, and corruption are destructive to human settlements and should therefore be denounced and discouraged by all States, which should cooperate to achieve the elimination of such practices and all unilateral measures impeding social and economic development. At the national level we will reinforce peace by promoting tolerance, non-violence and respect for diversity and by settling disputes by peaceful means. At the local level, the prevention of crime and the promotion of sustainable communities are essential to the attainment of safe and secure societies. Crime prevention through social development is one crucial key to these goals. At the international level, we will promote international peace and security and make and support all efforts to settle international disputes by peaceful means, in accordance with the Charter of the United Nations.

We reaffirm and are guided by the purposes and principles of the Charter of the United Nations and we reaffirm our commitment to ensuring the full realization of the human rights set out in international instruments and in particular, in this context, the right to adequate housing as set forth in the Universal Declaration of Human Rights and provided for in the International Covenant on Economic, Social and Cultural Rights, the International Convention on the Elimination of All Forms of Racial Discrimination, the Convention on the Elimination of All Forms of Discrimination against Women and the Convention on the Rights of the Child, taking into account that the right to adequate housing, as included in the above-mentioned international instruments, shall be realized progressively. We reaffirm that all human rights—civil, cultural, economic, political and social - are universal, indivisible, interdependent and interrelated. We subscribe to the principles and goals set out below to guide us in our actions.

Equitable human settlements are those in which all people, without discrimination of any kind as to race, colour, sex, language, religion, political or other opinion, national or social origin, property, birth or other status, have equal access to housing, infrastructure, health services, adequate food and water, education and open spaces. In addition, such human settlements provide equal opportunity for a productive and freely chosen livelihood; equal access to economic resources, including the right to inheritance, the ownership of land and other property, credit, natural resources and appropriate technologies; equal opportunity for personal, spiritual, religious, cultural and social development; equal opportunity for participation in public decision-making; equal rights and obligations with regard to the conservation and use of natural and cultural resources; and equal access to mechanisms to ensure that rights are not violated. The empowerment of women and their full participation on the basis of equality in all spheres of society, whether rural or urban, are fundamental to sustainable human settlements development.

The eradication of poverty is essential for sustainable human settlements. The principle of poverty eradication is based on the framework adopted by the World Summit for Social Development and on the relevant outcomes of other major United Nations conferences, including the objective of meeting the basic needs of all people, especially those living in poverty and disadvantaged and vulnerable groups, particularly in the developing countries where poverty is acute, as well as the objective of enabling all women and men to attain secure and sustainable livelihoods through freely chosen and productive employment and work.

Sustainable development is essential for human settlements development, and gives full consideration to the needs and necessities of achieving economic growth, social development and environmental protection. Special consideration should be given to the specific situation and needs of developing countries and, as appropriate, of countries with economies in transition. Human settlements shall be planned, developed and improved in a manner that takes full account of sustainable development principles and all their components, as set out in Agenda 21 and related outcomes of the United Nations Conference on Environment and Development. Sustainable human settlements development ensures economic development, employment opportunities and social progress, in harmony with the environment. It incorporates, together with the principles of the Rio Declaration on Environment and Development, which are equally important, and other outcomes of the United Nations Conference on Environment and Development, the principles of the precautionary approach, pollution prevention, respect for the carrying capacity of ecosystems, and preservation of opportunities for future generations. Production, consumption and transport should be managed in ways that protect and conserve the stock of resources while drawing upon them. Science and technology have a crucial role in shaping sustainable human settlements and sustaining the ecosystems they depend upon. Sustainability of human settlements entails their balanced geographical distribution or other appropriate distribution in keeping with national conditions, promotion of economic and social development, human health and education, and the conservation of biological diversity and the sustainable use of its components, and maintenance of cultural diversity as well as air, water, forest, vegetation and soil qualities at standards sufficient to sustain human life and well-being for future generations.

The quality of life of all people depends, among other economic, social, environmental and cultural factors, on the physical conditions and spatial characteristics of our villages, towns and cities. City lay-out and aesthetics, land-use patterns, population and building densities, transportation and ease of access for all to basic goods, services and public amenities have a crucial bearing on the liveability of settlements. This is particularly important to vulnerable and disadvantaged persons, many of whom face barriers in access to shelter and in participating in shaping the future of their settlements. People's need for community and their aspirations for more liveable neighbourhoods and settlements should guide the process of design, management and maintenance of human settlements. Objectives of this endeavour include protecting public health, providing for safety and security, education and social integration, promoting equality and respect for diversity and cultural identities, increased accessibility for persons with disabilities, and preservation of historic, spiritual, religious and culturally significant buildings and districts, respecting local landscapes and treating the local environment with respect and care. The preservation of the natural heritage and historical human settlements, including sites, monuments and buildings, particularly those protected under the UNESCO Convention on World Heritage Sites, should be assisted, including through international cooperation. It is also of crucial importance that spatial diversification and mixed use of housing and services be promoted at the local level in order to meet the diversity of needs and expectations.

The family is the basic unit of society and as such should be strengthened. It is entitled to receive comprehensive protection and support. In different cultural, political and social systems, various forms of the family exist. Marriage must be entered into with the free consent of the intending spouses, and husband and wife should be equal partners. The rights, capabilities and responsibilities of family members must be respected. Human settlements planning should take into account the constructive role of the family in the design, development and management of such settlements. Society should facilitate, as appropriate, all necessary conditions for its integration, reunification, preservation, improvement, and protection within adequate shelter and with access to basic services and a sustainable livelihood.

All people have rights and must also accept their responsibility to respect and protect the rights of others— including future generations—and to contribute actively to the common good. Sustainable human settlements are those that, inter alia, generate a sense of citizenship and identity, cooperation and dialogue for the common good, and a spirit of voluntarism and civic engagement, where all people are encouraged and have an equal opportunity to participate in decision-making and development. Governments at all appropriate levels, including local authorities, have a responsibility to ensure access to education and to protect their population's health, safety and general welfare. This requires, as appropriate, establishing policies, laws and regulations for both public and private activities, encouraging responsible private activities in all fields, facilitating community groups' participation, adopting transparent procedures, encouraging public-spirited leadership and public-private partnerships, and helping people to understand and exercise their rights and responsibilities through open and effective participatory processes, universal education and information dissemination.

Partnerships among countries and among all actors within countries from public, private, voluntary and community-based organizations, the cooperative sector, non-governmental organizations and individuals are essential to the achievement of sustainable human settlements development and the provision of adequate shelter for all and basic services. Partnerships can integrate and mutually support objectives of broad-based participation through, inter alia, forming alliances, pooling resources, sharing knowledge, contributing skills and capitalizing on the comparative advantages of collective actions. The processes can be made more effective by strengthening civil organizations at all levels. Every effort must be made to encourage the collaboration and partnership of all sectors of society and among all actors in decision-making processes, as appropriate.

Solidarity with those belonging to disadvantaged and vulnerable groups, including people living in poverty, as well as tolerance, non-discrimination and cooperation among all people, families and communities are foundations for social cohesion. Solidarity, cooperation and assistance should be enhanced by the international community as well as by States and all other relevant actors in response to the challenges of human settlements development. The international community and Governments at all appropriate levels are called upon to promote sound and effective policies and instruments, thereby strengthening cooperation among Governments and non-governmental organizations, as well as to mobilize complementary resources to meet these challenges.

To safeguard the interests of present and future generations in human settlements is one of the fundamental goals of the international community. The formulation and implementation of strategies for human settlements development are primarily the responsibility of each country at the national and local levels within the legal framework of each country, inter alia, by creating an enabling environment for human settlements development, and should take into account the economic, social and environmental diversity of conditions in each country. New and additional financial resources from various sources are necessary to achieve the goals of adequate shelter for all and sustainable human settlements development in an urbanizing world. The existing resources available to developing countries—public, private, multilateral, bilateral, domestic and external—need to be enhanced through appropriate and flexible mechanisms and economic instruments to support adequate shelter for all and sustainable human settlements development. These should be accompanied by concrete measures for international technical cooperation and information exchange.

Human health and quality of life are at the centre of the effort to develop sustainable human settlements. We therefore commit ourselves to promoting and attaining the goals of universal and equal access to quality education, the highest attainable standard of physical, mental and environmental health, and the equal access of all to primary health care, making particular efforts to rectify inequalities relating to social and economic conditions, including housing, without distinction as to race, national origin, gender, age, or disability, respecting and promoting our common and particular cultures. Good health throughout the life-span of every man and woman, good health for every child, and quality education for all are fundamental to ensuring that people of all ages are able to develop their full capacities in health and dignity and to participate fully in the social, economic and political processes of human settlements, thus contributing, inter alia, to the eradication of poverty. Sustainable human settlements depend on the interactive development of policies and concrete actions to provide access to food and nutrition, safe drinking water, sanitation, and universal access to the widest range of primary health-care services, consistent with the report of the International Conference on Population and Development; to eradicate major diseases that take a heavy toll of human lives, particularly childhood diseases; to create safe places to work and live; and to protect the environment.

Chapter III—Commitments
Introduction
Embracing the foregoing principles as States participating in this Conference, we commit ourselves to implementing the Habitat Agenda, through local, national, subregional and regional plans of action and/or other policies and programmes drafted and

executed in cooperation with interested parties at all levels and supported by the international community, taking into account that human beings are at the centre of concerns for sustainable development, including adequate shelter for all and sustainable human settlements development, and that they are entitled to a healthy and productive life in harmony with nature.

In implementing these commitments, special attention should be given to the circumstances and needs of people living in poverty, people who are homeless, women, older people, indigenous people, refugees, displaced persons, persons with disabilities and those belonging to vulnerable and disadvantaged groups. Special consideration should also be given to the needs of migrants. Furthermore, special attention should be given to the specific needs and circumstances of children, particularly street children.

Adequate shelter for all

We reaffirm our commitment to the full and progressive realization of the right to adequate housing, as provided for in international instruments. In this context, we recognize an obligation by Governments to enable people to obtain shelter and to protect and improve dwellings and neighbourhoods. We commit ourselves to the goal of improving living and working conditions on an equitable and sustainable basis, so that everyone will have adequate shelter that is healthy, safe, secure, accessible and affordable and that includes basic services, facilities and amenities, and will enjoy freedom from discrimination in housing and legal security of tenure. We shall implement and promote this objective in a manner fully consistent with human rights standards.

We further commit ourselves to the objectives of:

(a) Ensuring consistency and coordination of macroeconomic and shelter policies and strategies as a social priority within the framework of national development programmes and urban policies in order to support resource mobilization, employment generation, poverty eradication and social integration;

(b) Providing legal security of tenure and equal access to land to all people, including women and those living in poverty; and undertaking legislative and administrative reforms to give women full and equal access to economic resources, including the right to inheritance and to ownership of land and other property, credit, natural resources and appropriate technologies;

(c) Promoting access for all people to safe drinking water, sanitation and other basic services, facilities and amenities, especially for people living in poverty, women and those belonging to vulnerable and disadvantaged groups;

(d) Ensuring transparent, comprehensive and accessible systems in transferring land rights and legal security of tenure;

(e) Promoting broad, non-discriminatory access to open, efficient, effective and appropriate housing financing for all people, including mobilizing innovative financial and other resources—public and private—for community development;

(f) Promoting locally available, appropriate, affordable, safe, efficient and environmentally sound construction methods and technologies in all countries, particularly in developing countries, at the local, national, regional and subregional levels that emphasize optimal use of local human resources and encourage energy-saving methods and are protective of human health;

(g) Designing and implementing standards that provide accessibility also to persons with disabilities in accordance with the Standard Rules on the Equalization of Opportunities for Persons with Disabilities;

(h) Increasing the supply of affordable housing, including through encouraging and promoting affordable home ownership and increasing the supply of affordable rental, communal, cooperative and other housing through partnerships among public, private and community initiatives, creating and promoting market-based incentives while giving due respect to the rights and obligations of both tenants and owners;

(i) Promoting the upgrading of existing housing stock through rehabilitation and maintenance and the adequate supply of basic services, facilities and amenities;

(j) Eradicating and ensuring legal protection from discrimination in access to shelter and basic services, without distinction of any kind, such as race, colour, sex, language, religion, political or other opinion, national or social origin, property, birth or other status; similar protection should be ensured against discrimination on the grounds of disability or age;

(k) Helping the family, in its supporting, educating and nurturing roles, to recognize its important contribution to social integration, and encouraging social and economic policies that are designed to meet the housing needs of families and their individual members, especially the most disadvantaged and vulnerable members, with particular attention to the care of children;

(l) Promoting shelter and supporting basic services and facilities for education and health for the homeless, displaced persons, indigenous people, women and children who are survivors of family violence, persons with disabilities, older persons, victims of natural and man-made disasters and people belonging to vulnerable and disadvantaged groups, including temporary shelter and basic services for refugees;

(m) Protecting, within the national context, the legal traditional rights of indigenous people to land and other resources, as well as strengthening of land management;

(n) Protecting all people from and providing legal protection and redress for forced evictions that are contrary to the law, taking human rights into consideration; when evictions are unavoidable, ensuring, as appropriate, that alternative suitable solutions are provided.

[We further commit ourselves to] Providing continued international support to refugees in order to meet their needs and to assist in assuring them a just, durable solution in accordance with relevant United Nations resolutions and international law.

References

Centre on Housing Rights and Evictions. *Bibliography on Housing Rights and Evictions.* Utrecht, Netherlands: Centre on Housing Rights and Evictions 1993.

Lekie. *Housing as a Need, Housing as a Right: International Human Rights Law and the Right to Adequate Housing.* London, United Kingdom: International Institute for Environment and Development, 1992.

National Campaign for Housing Rights. *A People's Bill of Housing Rights: Essential Requirements.* Calcutta, India: National Campaign for Housing Rights, 1990.

National Law Center on Homelessness and Poverty. *Out of Sight—Out of Mind?* Washington, DC: 1999.

Ortiz. *The Right to Housing: A Global Challenge.* Mexico City, Mexico: Habitat International Coalition 1990.

Sachar. *Working Paper on The Right to Adequate Housing.* United Nations Document No. E/CN.4/Sub.2/1992/15, 1992.

8

Directory of Organizations, Associations, and Government Agencies

National Organizations

American Bar Association
Commission on Homelessness and Poverty
740 15th Street NW
Washington, DC 20005
(202) 331-2291; (202) 331-2220 FAX
www.abanet.org/homeless
Josephine A. McNeil, Chair

The commission assists local and state bar associations and other legal organizations to create pro bono programs to aid poor people.

PUBLICATIONS: Advocates for Housing, a four-hour video training program and manual with greater emphasis on the creation of permanent housing; *America's Children at Risk,* written by a working group representing over a dozen ABA entities, including the Commission on Homelessness and Poverty, outlining a legal agenda for children, primarily those in poverty; *Small Steps: A Handbook for Lawyers and for Staff in Microenterprise Programs,* prepared specifically for legal organizations seeking to include business and banking law services in their pro bono programs; *Resource Guide to State and Local Bar Association and Law School Homeless Programs,* an overview of over fifty legal projects around the country serving homeless and very poor clients.

American Red Cross
National Headquarters
431 18th Street NW
Washington, DC 20006
(202) 639-3520
www.redcross.org
Enso V. Bighinatti, Emergency Food and
Shelter National Board Member

The Red Cross has traditionally provided services to those made homeless by disasters such as fires or floods. More than 600 local chapters now provide services to homeless people through McKinney Act FEMA funds. Local Red Cross chapters can provide more information.

Bazelon Center for Mental Health Law
1101 15th Street NW, Suite 1212
Washington, DC 20005
(202) 467-5730; (202) 223-0409 FAX
(202) 467-4232 TDD
www.bazelon.org
Robert Bernstein, Executive Director

The Bazelon Center is a legal advocacy organization for the rights of mentally disabled people, including on fair housing issues. The Center focuses its work on reform of public systems for people with mental disabilities, access to housing, health care and support services, and protection against discrimination.

PUBLICATIONS: *Update* published six times a year; *Community Watch*.

Catholic Charities USA
1731 King Street, Suite 200
Alexandria, VA 22314
(703) 549-1390; (703) 549-1656 FAX
www.catholiccharitiesusa.org
Brother Joseph Berg, Emergency Food and
Shelter National Board Member

This nationwide federation of organizations and individuals, including more than 600 agencies, is a traditional service provider to the hungry and homeless.

Center for Law and Social Policy

1616 P Street NW, Suite 150
Washington, DC 20036
(202) 328-5140; (202) 328-5195 FAX
www.clasp.org
Alan Houseman, Executive Director

CLASP is a national nonprofit organization with expertise in both law and policy affecting the poor. Through education, policy research, and advocacy, CLASP seeks to improve the economic security of low-income families with children. CLASP is also a partner in the State Policy Documentation Project (SPDP), a joint project of the Center on Budget and Policy Priorities and CLASP, which tracks state policy choices on Temporary Assistance to Needy Families (TANF) programs and Medicaid in the fifty states and the District of Columbia.

PUBLICATIONS: *CLASP UPDATE* and periodic audio conferences.

Center on Budget and Policy Priorities

820 1st Street NE, Suite 510
Washington, DC 20002
(202) 408-1080; (202) 408-1056 FAX
www.cbpp.org
Robert Greenstein, Executive Director

The Center issues regular reports analyzing federal program data and policy issues affecting poor Americans; reports on poverty among women, minorities, and rural residents; and analysis reports of federal budget issues and programs for the poor.

PUBLICATIONS: *Holes in the Safety Net: Poverty Programs and Policies in the States,* a national overview and fifty state reports; *A Place to Call Home,* a study of the housing crisis and the poor.

Child Welfare League of America (CWLA)

440 1st Street NW, Suite 310
Washington, DC 20001
(202) 638-2952; (202) 638-4004 FAX
www.cwla.org
Shay Bilchik, Executive Director

CWLA is an association of more than 1,000 public and private nonprofit agencies that assist over 2.5 million abused and neglected children and their families each year with a wide range of services. CWLA works on issues of adolescent pregnancy and parenting, chemical dependency, parents in prison, foster care, health care, housing, and homelessness.

PUBLICATIONS: *Child Welfare,* a bimonthly journal; *Washington Social Legislation Bulletin,* a biweekly report; "*Homeless Children and Families*" *The Youngest of the Homeless II,* a report on boarder babies.

Children's Defense Fund (CDF)
25 E Street NW
Washington, DC 20001
(202) 628-8787;
www.childrensdefense.org
Marian Wright Edelman, President

CDF's goal is to educate policy makers about the needs of poor and minority children. It monitors federal and state policy and legislation on health, education, child welfare, mental health, teen pregnancy, and youth employment.

PUBLICATIONS: *CDF Reports* is published monthly as an update on relevant issues. *A Children's Defense Budget* is an annual analysis of federal budget proposals and their effects on children; *The State of America's Children Yearbook 2000,* an annual analysis of the status of children in the U.S.; *Children in the States 2000* ranks each state's standing in population, federal nutrition, education, teen pregnancy, and foster care; *Congressional Workbook,* a guide to the legislative process; *An Advocate's Guide to the Media; An Advocate's Guide to Using Data;* and *An Advocate's Guide to Fund Raising.*

Corporation for Supportive Housing
50 Broadway 17th Floor
New York, NY 10004
(212) 986-2966; (212) 986-6552 FAX
www.csh.org
Carla Javits, President

This national organization promotes the expansion of supportive housing for special needs groups through direct financing for projects. It also provides technical assistance and information about program models.

Council of State Community Development Agencies (COSCDA)
444 North Capitol Street NE, Suite 224
Washington, DC 20001
(202) 624-3630; (202) 624-3639 FAX
www.coscda.org
John M. Sidor, Executive Director

This national network of state-level community development officials monitors federal legislation and state initiatives on affordable housing and economic development and employment issues.

PUBLICATIONS: *States and Housing,* a newsletter; Strategic Alliances for Housing and Community Development; *States, HOME, and Tenant-Based Assistance.*

¡ENDING HOMELESSNESS! Round Table on the Abolition of Homelessness
5 Park Street
Boston, MA 02108
(617) 367-6447; (617) 367-5709 FAX
www.endinghomelessness.com
Philip F. Mangano, Executive Director

This new initiative is an advocacy dialogue group focused on brining about a new national strategy to end homelessness.

Enterprise Foundation
10227 Wincopin Circle, Suite 500
Columbia, MD 21044
(410) 964-1230; (410) 964-1918 FAX
www.enterprisefoundation.org
Bart Harvey, Chairman and CEO

The Enterprise Foundation provides technical assistance and financial aid to community development corporations and low-income housing developers. Enterprise works with partners and a national network of more than 1,500 nonprofit organizations in 550 locations.

PUBLICATIONS: *Beyond Housing: Profiles of Low-Income, Service-Enriched Housing for Special Needs Populations and Property Management Programs, second edition,* profiling twenty-nine service-enriched housing programs that successfully integrated social services and housing.

Fannie Mae Foundation
4000 Wisconsin Avenue NW, North Tower
Washington, DC 20016
(202) 274-8000; (202) 274-8100 FAX
www.fanniemae.com
Stacey Davis, President and CEO

PUBLICATIONS: *Housing Research; Housing Policy Debate; Journal of Housing Research;* and *Housing Facts & Findings.*

Habitat for Humanity
121 Habitat Street
Americus, GA 31709
(800) 422-4828; (912) 924-0641 FAX
www.habitat.org
Kathy Doyle, Manager/Volunteer Support Services

Habitat for Humanity is a Christian housing organization that operates in the United States and thirty-five countries. It builds or renovates simple homes for people without adequate shelter. Habitat for Homeless Humanity is its project for homeless housing. Volunteers and potential residents cooperate in building or renovation.

PUBLICATIONS: *Habitat World,* a newsletter.

Health Care for the Homeless Information Resource Center
262 Delaware Avenue
Delmar, NY 12054-1123
(888) 439-3300 ext. 246; (518) 439-7612 FAX
Nan Brady, Director

This technical assistance center provides both clinical and management information of health issues affecting people who are homeless. Resources include bibliographies, research articles, and practice guidelines.

Housing Assistance Council
1025 Vermont Avenue NW, Suite 606
Washington, DC 20005
(202) 842-8600; (202) 347-3441 FAX
www.ruralhome.org
Jennifer Holt, Executive Director

HAC provides technical assistance, loans, research, and information on rural low-income housing development, especially Farmers Home Administration programs. It publishes regular reports on federal rural programs and trends in rural poverty and development.

PUBLICATIONS: *HAC News* a biweekly newsletter; *State Action Memorandum,* a bimonthly newsletter; HAC *Technical Manuals* on rural housing and community issues.

International Union of Gospel Missions
1045 Swift Street
Kansas City, MO 64116-4127
(816) 471-8020; (816) 471-3718 FAX
www.iugm.org
Phil Rydman, Director of Communications

IUGM is an association of faith-based providers of emergency services, meals, and other services. It publishes data on its clients, their needs, and use of services, as well as public opinion data on homelessness.

Local Initiatives Support Corporation
733 3rd Avenue, 8th Floor
New York, NY 10017
(212) 455-9800; (212) 682-5929 FAX
www.liscnet.org
Michael Rubinger, President and CEO

This project of the Ford Foundation and six corporations offers financing and technical assistance to nonprofit organizations working on community development and low-income housing by channeling private sector resources into community development corporations.

National Alliance for the Mentally Ill
Colonial Place Three
2107 Wilson Blvd., Suite 300
Arlington, VA 22201
(703) 524-7600; (703) 524-9094 FAX
TDD: (703) 516-7227
www.nami.org

This national advocacy and research organization for the mentally ill seeks to create a coordinated system of care.

National Alliance to End Homelessness
1518 K Street NW, Suite 206
Washington, DC 20005
(202) 638-1526; (202) 638-4664 FAX
www.naeh.org
Nan Roman, President

The Alliance is a coalition of corporations, service providers, and individuals, which sponsors conferences and uses research and public education in its efforts to address homelessness.

PUBLICATIONS: *The Alliance* newsletter and *Web of Failure,* a report on foster care and homelessness.

National Center for Homeless Education (NCHE)
1100 West Market Street, Suite 300
Greensboro, NC 27403
(336) 334-3211; (336) 574-3890 FAX
www.serve.org
Dr. Beth Garriss, Director

NCHE is funded by the U.S. Department of Education to provide support to those who seek to remove or overcome barriers to education and to improve educational opportunities and outcomes for homeless children and youth. NCHE acts as a national resource center of research and information, enabling communities to successfully address the needs of homeless youth and families.

PUBLICATIONS: *The Education of Homeless Children and Youth: A Compendium of Research and Information,* which provides an overview of issues such as legislative and policy issues, educational considerations, and community support structures; *Parent Pack: A Resource for Homeless Families,* a folder that assists families in gathering school documentation; *National Symposium on Transportation for Homeless Children and Youth Proceedings,* from the February 2000 gathering for state and local homeless education coordinators and shelter providers.

National Center for Poverty Law
205 W. Monroe, 2nd floor
Chicago IL 60606
(312) 263-3830; (312) 263-3846 FAX
www.povertylaw.org
Rita McLennon, Executive Director

The center banks legal and other documents on a range of poverty-related issues and provides them for free for legal services programs and for a small charge for general distribution.

PUBLICATIONS: *Clearinghouse Review,* a monthly journal of poverty law developments. Legal papers in numerous homelessness-related cases are available.

National Coalition for the Homeless
1012 14th Street, Suite 600
Washington, DC 20005
(202) 737-6444; (202) 737-6445 FAX
www.nationalhomeless.org
Sue Watlov Phillips, Acting Executive Director

NCH is a national advocacy network of homeless persons, activists, service providers, and others committed to addressing homelessness through public education, policy advocacy, grassroots organizing, and technical assistance.

PUBLICATIONS: *Safety Network,* a regular newsletter.

National Coalition for Homeless Veterans
333 ½ Pennsylvania Avenue SE
Washington, DC 20003
(202) 546-1969; (202) 546-2063 FAX; (800) 838-4357;
(888) 233-8582 Help Lines
www.nchv.org
Linda Boone, Executive Director

NCHV serves as a liaison between branches of the federal government and community-based homeless veteran service providers.

National Health Care for the Homeless Council
HCH Clinicians' Network
P.O. Box 60427
Nashville, TN 37206-0427
(615) 226-2292; (615) 226-1656 FAX
www.nhchc.org
John Lozier, Executive Director

Two dozen Health Care for the Homeless projects belong to this council. The projects provide primary health care, mental health services, drug and alcohol services; and the council coordinates their advocacy.

PUBLICATIONS: *Medical Respite Services for Homeless People: Practical Models; Utilization & Costs of Medical Services by Homeless Persons: A Review of the Literature and Implications for the Future; Can Managed Care Work for Homeless People?: Guidance for State Medicaid Programs; Searching for the Right Fit: Homelessness and Medicaid Managed Care;* and *Organizing Health Services for Homeless People: A Practical Guide.*

National Housing Law Project
614 Grand Avenue, Suite 320
Oakland, CA 94610
(510) 251-9400; (510) 451-2300 FAX
www.nhlp.org
NHLP Washington, DC, Office
1629 K Street NW, Suite 600
Washington, DC 20006
(202) 463-9461; (202) 463-9462 FAX
Gideon Anders, Executive Director

NHLP is a national legal services support center that advises and assists local legal services lawyers working on housing and community development issues with training litigation assistance and research.

PUBLICATIONS: *Housing Law Bulletin,* published bimonthly, as well as numerous manuals on federal housing programs.

National Law Center on Homelessness & Poverty
1411 K Street NW, Suite 1400
Washington, DC 20005
(202) 638-2535; (202) 628-2737 FAX
www.nlchp.org
Maria Foscarinis, Executive Director

The Law Center was established in 1989 and monitors federal agency action on McKinney Act programs. It publishes regular reports on the education of homeless children and the growth of local antihomeless ordinances.

PUBLICATIONS: *In Just Times,* a newsletter, and regular reports on local laws and homeless children

National Low Income Housing Coalition
1012 14th Street NW, Suite 610

Washington, DC 20005
(202) 662-1530; (202) 683-8639 FAX
www.nlihc.org
Sheila Crowley, President

NLIHC is a national organization focused on education, advocacy, and organizing for low-income housing. LIHIS emphasizes federal housing programs and policies.

PUBLICATIONS: *Advocate's Resource Book; Low Income Housing Round-up,* published monthly and supplemented with *Special Memorandum,* which focuses on specific housing topics.

National Mental Health Association (NMHA)
1021 Prince Street
Alexandria, VA 22314
(703) 684-7722 (703) 684-5968

NMHA works to improve citizen advocacy on mental health services, to prevent mental illness, and to promote mental health through citizen effort. It has 600 local and state affiliated groups across the country.

PUBLICATIONS: *FOCUS* (newsletter) and *Homeless in America,* a video.

National Network for Youth
1319 F Street NW, Suite 401
Washington, DC 20004
(202) 783-7949; (202) 783-7955 FAX
Della Hughes, Executive Director

More than 1,000 local shelter agencies and state networks are members of this national network that sponsors training, offers information on model programs, and sponsors a national telecommunications system for youth programs.

PUBLICATIONS: *Network News,* a quarterly newsletter; *Policy Report,* published eight times yearly; *Alcohol and Drug Use Among Runaway, Homeless, and Other Youth: To Whom Do They Belong?*

National Resource Center on Homelessness and Mental Illness Policy Research Associates Inc.
262 Delaware Avenue
Delmar, NY 12054

(800) 444-7415 ext.232; (518) 439-7612 FAX
www.prainc.org
Edward DeBerri, Executive Director

This center is under contract to the federal government and provides technical assistance and other information on housing and services needed by homeless, mentally ill people. It maintains a database of published and unpublished work and offers bibliographies, custom searches, and other material.

PUBLICATIONS: *Access,* published quarterly; and a national organizational referral list of groups working in the field of homelessness.

National Student Campaign Against Hunger & Homelessness
11965 Venice Blvd. #408
Los Angeles, CA 90066-3954
(800) 664-8647 x324; (310) 391-0053 FAX
Julie Miles, Director

PUBLICATIONS: *Hunger and Homelessness Action: A Comprehensive Resource Book for Colleges and Universities; Going Places,* a catalog of domestic and international internship, volunteer, travel, and career opportunities in the fields of hunger, housing, homelessness, and grassroots development; *Setting a New Course,* a guide to expanding collegiate curricula to incorporate the study of domestic and international hunger and homelessness; *SPLASH Action Handbook,* a guide to the federal legislative process and how groups can organize grassroots education and action campaigns to impact congressional decisions; *Food Salvage Manual,* a guide to collecting surplus food from campus dining facilities and regularly distributing it to emergency food programs; and *Hunger and Homelessness Week Organizing Guide.*

Salvation Army
615 Slaters Lane Box 269
Alexandria, VA 22314
(703) 684-5521; (703) 684-5538 FAX
Lt. Col. Eugene Slusher, Emergency Food and Shelter National Board Member

This international religious charity is one of the historic providers of shelter and alcohol and drug rehabilitation services with more than 10,000 local chapters.

Travelers Aid International
1612 K Street NW, Suite 506
Washington, DC 20006
(202) 546-1127; (202) 546-9112 FAX
Raymond K. Flynt, President

Travelers Aid is a network of service providers, often located in public transportation terminals, who assist stranded travelers and the homeless with emergency financial aid, food, shelter, and clothing.

United States Conference of Mayors
1620 I Street NW
Washington, DC 20005
(202) 293-7330; (202) 293-2352 FAX
www.usmayors.org
Laura DeKoven Waxman, Assistant Executive Director

The Conference of Mayors is an education and lobbying organization for mayors of cities over 30,000 population providing background information and position statements on vital issues. Its Task Force on Hunger and Homelessness conducts an annual survey of member cities and their services and conditions.

PUBLICATIONS: *The Continued Growth of Hunger, Homelessness and Poverty in America's Cities*, an annual report; *Mentally Ill and Homeless: A City Assessment of the 1990 Shelter and Street County Survey.*

State Homeless and Low-Income Housing Organizations

Most states have at least one organization devoted to issues of homelessness and housing for homeless or low-income people. In addition, most large- and medium-sized cities have at least one of these organizations. State coalitions can provide information on the urban organizations as well as information on specific activities such as state legislative action or advocacy on behalf of homeless people. Most of the organizations, as well as the local coalitions, publish newsletters and actively seek volunteers and other resources. They can also provide referrals to organizations and services operated by homeless people for other homeless people.

A list of state and local organizations can be found at the website of the National Coalition for the Homeless at *www.national homeless.org*.

Federal Agencies

Department of Education (USED)
400 Maryland Avenue SW
Washington, DC 20202
(202) 205-5499
www.ed.gov

National Coordinator for the Education of Homeless Children and Youth

Department of Health and Human Services (HHS)
200 Independence Avenue SW
Washington, DC 20201
(202) 245-6296
www.dhhs.gov

HHS oversees the McKinney Act program to provide primary health care to homeless people through public and private non-profit organizations, as well as research and demonstration efforts at the Substance Abuse and Mental Health Services Administration (SAMHSA).

Department of Housing and Urban Development (HUD)
451 7th Street SW
Washington, DC 20410
(202) 708-1112
www.hud.gov

HUD administers the McKinney homeless programs, as well as a variety of low-income housing programs with components involving housing for homeless people. It publishes a variety of reports and research data on housing and homelessness.

Department of Veterans Affairs
810 Vermont Avenue NW
Washington, DC 20420
(202) 233-2300
www.va.gov

The VA operates veterans' reintegration programs and the McKinney Act domiciliary care program to use surplus space in VA hospitals as shelter beds for homeless veterans. The agency also administers a 1987 program to make single-family homes foreclosed from VA loans available for homeless veterans and their families.

Social Security Administration
Office of Supplemental Security Income
6401 Security Boulevard
Baltimore, MD 21235
(800) 772-1213
www.ssa.gov

SSA provides income-support programs for elderly and disabled people. SSA collaborates in a joint project with the Department of Veterans Affairs to handle claims for homeless veterans.

Government Clearinghouses and Information Hot Lines

CDC National AIDS Clearinghouse
(800) 458-5321

Federal Surplus Real Property Program (Title V)
(800) 927-7588

Food and Nutrition Center (USDA)
(301) 504-5719

HUD Community Connections
(800) 998-9999

HUD User Research Reports
(800) 998-9999

HUD Veterans Resource Center: HUDVET
(800) 998-9999

National Clearinghouse for Alcohol and Drug Information
(800) 729-6686

National Clearinghouse on Child Abuse and Neglect Information
(800) FYI-3366

National Clearinghouse on Families and Youth
(301) 608-8098

National Domestic Violence Hotline
(800) 799-SAFE

National Resource Center on Domestic Violence
(800) 537-2238

National Resource Center on Homelessness and Mental Illness
(800) 444-7415

Veterans Benefits Information Hotline
(800) 827-1000

International Organizations and Institutions

Centre on Housing Rights and Evictions (COHRE)
83 Rue de Montbrillant
1202 Geneva, Switzerland
41 22 734 1028 Phone and FAX
www.cohre.org
Havikstraat 38bis 3514 TR Utrecht
Netherlands
Tel: 31 30 731976

COHRE's chief objective is to promote practical legal and other solutions to problems of homelessness, inadequate housing and living conditions, and forced evictions. COHRE promotes the use of international human rights law. COHRE works with a network of organizations and individuals spanning over eighty countries. COHRE's six primary activity areas are legal advocacy and training, monitoring and preventing forced evictions, research and publications, activities at the United Nations, fact-finding missions, and special projects.

Comité Européen de Coordination de l'Habitat Social (CECODHAS)
Olympia 1, 1213 NS Hilversum
P.O. Box 611
NL-1200 AP Hilversum
31 35 6268 333; 31 35 6268 433 FAX
www.cecodhas.org
Tineke Zuidervaart, Secrétaire Exécutive

CECODHAS is a nonprofit organization that promotes the work of social housing organizations in the European Union. It fosters the exchange of ideas and experience among its members, provides an information service for its members, and promotes good practice through conferences, seminars, reports, and other activities. CECODHAS monitors developments in European Community law, provides its members with improved access to European funding, and campaigns for the right to a decent home for all Europeans. The thirty-seven full members of CECODHAS are national and regional housing organizations from the fifteen EU member states. There are associate members in other European countries.

European Anti Poverty Network
rue du Congrès 37–41-Bte 2
B-1000 Brussels
Belgium
32.2.230.44.55; 32.2.230.97.33 FAX
www.eapn.org

EAPN brings together grassroots organizations representing people affected by social exclusion in all the member states of the European Union.

European Federation of National Organizations
Working with the Homeless
(Fédération Européenne d'Associations Nationales
Travaillant avec les Sans-Abri) (FEANTSA)
1 rue Defacqz
1000 Brussels
Belgium
32 2 538 6669; 32 2 539 4174 FAX
www.feantsa.org

FEANTSA is an international nongovernmental organization that brings together more than sixty charitable and not-for-profit organizations that provide a wide range of vital services to homeless people in all the European Union member states and also in other European countries. Its goal is to promote and support the work of nongovernmental organizations that provide services to meet the needs of homeless people.

FEANTSA aims to raise public awareness about the situation of homeless people and of the need to recognize and realize the right to decent and affordable housing.

PUBLICATIONS: *Homelessness in the European Union: Social and legal context of housing exclusion in the 1990s; The Invisible Hand of the Housing Market: A study of the effects of changes in the housing market on homelessness in the European Union; Youth Homelessness in the European Union; Services for Homeless People: Innovation and change in the European Union; Is the European Union housing its poor? Where to sleep tonight? Where to live tomorrow? Current Trends in Social Welfare and access to Housing in Europe; Europe against Exclusion : HOUSING FOR ALL.*

Habitat International Coalition (HIC)
Cordobanes No. 24, Col. San José Insurgentes
Mexico D.F. 03900
Mexico
52 5 6516807

International Network of Street Newspapers
Fleet House 57
Clerkenwell Road
London EClM 5NP
United Kingdom
44-171-418 0418; 44-171-418 0428 FAX
www.bigissue.co.uk

This street-newspaper organization supports homeless people through the provision of an income source and a media voice on issues affecting them. Members sign a common charter of rules and practices.

SHELTER
88 Old Street
London, EC1V 9HU
United Kingdom
www.shelter.org.uk.

SHELTER is the largest homelessness charity in the United Kingdom and publishes a variety of fact sheets and self-help resources on homelessness. It maintains a national help line that tracks the demand for shelter. It publishes a variety of reports on policy, including *Best Value and Homelessness.*

United Nations Centre for Human Settlements (UNCHS)
P. O. Box 30030
Nairobi, Kenya
(254-2) 623153; (254-2) 624060 FAX
E-mail: habitat@unchs.org
www.unchs.org
UNCHS (Habitat) New York Office
(212) 963-4200; (212) 963-8721 FAX

UNCHS is the lead agency concerned with issues of housing and shelter. It convened the Habitat conference in Istanbul and will convene a follow-up conference in 2001 on progress in achieving a right to housing.

9

Selected Print and Nonprint Resources

Print Resources

This chapter first covers general reference materials on homelessness. Literally thousands of books, research articles, news stories, and dissertations have been written on homelessness in the United States. While some of those included here are more recent, others are important contributions that have stood the test of time and continue to offer insight into the roots of homelessness and the responses to it. The goal of this chapter is to identify key resources that are accessible, non-technical, and, together, offer a variety of views into the problem. Some books are included because they offer a historical perspective, others are included because they are a resource on a specific aspect of homelessness. Entries that are hard to locate or are highly technical have been kept to a minimum. This list does not include the numerous articles published in periodicals and academic journals, or the useful, detailed reports issued by many of the organizations and government agencies listed in Chapter 8. Those organizations often publish listings of the materials they distribute and, increasingly, provide direct access to publications via their web sites. They also publish many newsletters and bulletins that are resources for staying current with new publications. A second section of the listing includes resources specifically on international aspects of homelessness. Again, many informal publications, such as fact sheets and periodic reports are available from international organizations, especially via the Internet.

General Reference Materials

Argerious, Milton, and Dennis McCarty. *Treating Alcoholism and Drug Abuse among Homeless Men and Women.* Binghamton, NY: Haworth Press, 1990. 164 pp. ISBN 0–86656–992–8.

This collection of eleven articles includes examinations of nine community demonstration grants in alcohol and drug treatment among homeless people, funded by the National Institute on Alcohol Abuse and Alcoholism. Two chapters cover the overall thrust of the program and some initial research findings. The projects include ones for dually diagnosed individuals, chronic public inebriates, and women at risk of alcoholism.

Barak, Gregg. *Gimme Shelter: A Social History of Homelessness.* New York: Praeger, 1992. 212 pp. ISBN 0–275–94401–8.

The author is a criminologist who analyzes homelessness as a crime against those who experience it. He also examines the history of advocacy efforts, both in public education and in litigation.

Baumohl, Jim, editor. *Homelessness in America.* Phoenix, AZ: Oryx Press, 1996. 291 pp. ISBN: 0–89774–869–7.

This collection of articles by experts, researchers, providers, and academics focuses on causes, known data, and solutions for contemporary homelessness.

Baxter, Ellen, and Kim Hopper. *Private Lives/Public Spaces: Homeless Adults on the Streets of New York City.* New York: Community Service Society (105 East Twenty-second Street, New York, NY 10010), 1981. 129 pp.

This early study primarily reports on the causes of contemporary homelessness, as they were first revealed in New York and other cities. It describes in detail the procedures and operations of the existing public and private shelters and the ways that homeless people survive on the streets.

Bingham, Richard D., Roy E. Green, and Sammis B. White, editors. *The Homeless in Contemporary Society.* Beverly Hills, California: Sage Publications, 1986. 277 pp. ISBN 0–8039–2889–0.

A brief history of homelessness in the United States is presented in this anthology, with essays on veterans, women and children, and the debate over how to develop an accurate count of homeless people. Attention is then turned to the role of nonprofit and religious organizations, local, state, and federal government roles, and programs in other countries.

Birch, Eugenie Ladner, editor. *The Unsheltered Woman: Women and Housing in the 80's.* New Brunswick, NJ: Rutgers University Center for Urban Policy Research, 1985. 313 pp. ISBN 0–88285–104–7.

Twenty essays on women and their housing needs that were prepared as an overview of necessary shelter and support services for a joint program of the Ford Foundation and Hunter College.

Boxhill, Nancy A., editor. *Homeless Children: The Watchers and the Waiters.* Binghamton, NY: The Haworth Press, 1990. 156 pp. ISBN 0–86656–789–5.

This collection of articles covers a range of issues affecting children in shelters; children in several Atlanta shelters were studied here. Material on mother and child relations, behavior of children, and children's health is included.

Brickner, Philip, M.D., Linda Keen Scharer, Barbara Conanan, Alexander Elvy, and Marianne Savarese, editors. *Health Care of Homeless People.* New York: Springer Publishing Company, 1985. 349 pp. ISBN 0–8261–4990–1.

An overview of health issues for homeless people is presented with special sections on medical disorders, mental health and illness, the organization of health services, and models of health care for homeless, poor people. The offerings are from twenty-four different authors or collaborators, with expertise on subjects ranging from infestations to alcoholism to nutrition.

Burt, Martha R. *Over the Edge: The Growth of Homelessness in the 1980s.* Washington, DC: Urban Institute Press and Russell Sage Foundation, 1991. 267 pp. ISBN 0–87154–177–7.

Persistent homelessness is related to structural changes in the nation, according to the author, who surveyed numerous cities and interviewed homeless people seeking services. She calls for increased low-rent housing production, more housing subsidies, restructured employment (including education and training), and more community-based care.

Burt, Martha, Laudan Aron, Toby Douglas, Jesse Valente, Edgar Lee, and Britta Iwen. *Homelessness: Programs and the People They Serve. Findings of the National Survey of Homeless Assistance Providers and Clients (NSHAPC).* Washington, DC: The Urban Institute, 1999. 176 pp. ISBN: 0–87766–472–2–170.

The authors analyze the results of a 1996 survey of homeless programs and homeless people that was sponsored by twelve federal agencies.

Crane, Maureen. *Understanding Older Homeless People: Their Circumstances, Problems, and Needs.* London: Open University Press, 1999. 192 pp. ISBN: 0335201865.

Although elders have a safety net of social programs available, growing numbers have become homeless. The author examines some of the key causes of this problem.

Culhane, Dennis P., and Steven Hornburg, editors. *Understanding Homelessness: New Policy and Research Perspectives.* Washington, D.C.: Fannie Mae Foundation, 1997. 380 pp. ISBN 0–9662039–0–9. Fannie Mae Foundation, 4000 Wisconsin Avenue NW, North Tower, Washington, DC 20016.

The three sections of this book represent the work of some of the key researchers who have studied the growth of homelessness and its characteristics. Here they examine the means of defining homelessness, of counting and tracking homeless people, as well as the causes and prevention of homelessness and the possible policy and research initiatives.

Currie, Elliott. *Reckoning: Drugs, the Cities, and America's Future.* New York: Hill and Wang, 1993. 405 pp. ISBN 0–8090–8049–4.

The epidemic of urban drug use is already known as a symptom of larger social ills, but the author dissects the documentation on when drug use occurs in poor families, especially immigrants, and how this plague has been increased by the destruction of poor communities through economic policy, housing loss, and other factors. He suggests ways that employment and redirected spending can end or prevent the resulting problems, including homelessness.

Day, Dorothy. *The Long Loneliness: An Autobiography.* New York: Harper and Row, 1981. 286 pp. ISBN 0–06–061751–9.

In the decades preceding the 1980s, there were two significant sources of help for homeless people: the traditional missions and Salvation Army establishments and the Catholic Worker Houses of Hospitality spread around the nation. This book, by the co-founder of the CW and its newspaper editor for over thirty years, tells the story of the Great Depression–era founding of the small shelters and soup lines that still exist today. The book also includes the story of Day's longtime leadership on issues of social justice, peace, and racial equality.

Dear, Michael J., and Jennifer R. Wolch. *Landscapes of Despair: From Deinstitutionalizaton to Homelessness.* Princeton: Princeton University Press, 1987. 220 pp. ISBN 0–691–07754–1.

Early social welfare institutions in the United States are examined here, in an analysis of the development of large-scale treatment settings for the retarded, elderly, mentally disabled, indigents, offenders, and orphans. The significant turn in public policy toward community-based care resulted in massive depopulation of facilities and has been closely linked, by many writers, to homelessness. The book looks in depth at San Jose, California, and attempts to offer some answers for the future development of institutions and land-use tools.

Dolbeare, Cushing N. *Out of Reach: The Growing Gap between Housing Costs and Income of Poor People in the United States.* National Low Income Housing Coalition, September 2000.

Detailed information on the gap between the cost of decent housing and what people can afford to pay is provided on a state-by-state basis. Profiles of the gap faced by people earning a minimum wage in various housing markets, as well as those renters who rely on public assistance for their income are offered.

Fosburg, Linda B., and Deborah L. Dennis, editors. *Practical Lessons: The 1998 National Symposium on Homelessness Research.* Washington, D.C.: Department of Health and Human Services, 1999. 350 pp.

Researchers from across the nation submitted articles and made presentations for this national conference on homelessness research. This volume, subsequently issued by the federal health and human services agency, compiles the papers presented and the commentary on them.

Hirsch, Kathleen. *Songs from the Alley.* New York: Ticknor & Fields, 1989. 420 pp. ISBN 0–89919–488–5.

The lives of two homeless women in Boston—Wendy and Amanda—are traced from their beginnings to the harsh everyday life of homelessness. In an unusual format, this account runs side by side with the history of aid to homeless, poor people during the 200 years of Massachusetts's history, including recent political activism for homeless people.

Hombs, Mary Ellen, and Mitch Snyder. *Homelessness in America: A Forced March to Nowhere.* 2d ed. Washington, D.C.: Community for Creative Non-Violence (425 2nd Street NW, Washington, DC 20001), 1983. 146 pp. ISBN 0–686–39879–3.

This national survey of homelessness and its origins was first released in conjunction with the original 1982 congressional hearings of the same title. When it was subsequently updated the following year, it included the estimates of national homelessness that engendered national controversy.

Interagency Council on Homelessness. *Priority: Home! The Federal Plan to Break the Cycle of Homelessness.* Washington, DC: U.S. Department of Housing and Urban Development, 1994.

This report was produced after a lengthy national process in response to the Executive Order on Homelessness, signed by President Clinton at the beginning of his administration. This report combines data with the insights of providers and policy makers across the nation.

Jencks, Christopher. *The Homeless.* Boston: Harvard University Press, 1995. 175 pp. ISBN: 067440596X.

The author focuses on the "visible homeless" and discusses the size of the population and possible solutions for their homelessness.

Keigher, Sharon M., editor. **Housing Risks and Homelessness among the Urban Elderly.** Binghamton, NY: The Haworth Press, 1991. 156 pp. ISBN 1–56024–165–9.

Gentrification, demolition, and federal cuts in benefits have all contributed to homelessness in the last decade, yet the elderly appear to be underrepresented among homeless people. This collection of articles examines the unique housing problems of the older American, as well as the growing shortage of affordable housing.

Kozol, Jonathan. *Rachel and Her Children: Homeless Families in America.* New York: Ballantine Books, 1989. 261 pp. ISBN 0–449–90339–7.

This vivid account of life in the welfare hotels of New York City demonstrates not only the financial waste of this method for serving homeless families, but also the damage done to young lives and struggling parents. Alongside the personal stories told by mothers, fathers, and children are the chilling statistics that explain how poverty works in daily life.

Liebow, Elliot. *Tell Them Who I Am.* New York: The Free Press, 1993. 339 pp. ISBN 0–02–919095–9.

The author wrote the groundbreaking and widely hailed *Tally's Corner* in 1967 to describe the life of so-called "street corner men" in a black neighborhood of Washington, D.C. After years of volunteering, observing, and interviewing homeless women in shelters in the Maryland suburbs of Washington, D.C, he provides this picture of the women's individual stories as homeless persons, as well as his own views of the broader economic, social, and political forces that cause and continue homelessness.

Miller, William. *Dorothy Day: A Biography.* New York: Harper and Row, 1982. 527 pp. ISBN 0–06–065752–8.

This biography of Catholic Worker co-founder Dorothy Day offers a candid portrait of her work in the social justice movement.

National Academy of Science, Institute of Medicine. *Homelessness, Health and Human Needs.* Washington, D.C.: National Academy Press, 1988. 165 pp. ISBN 0–309–03832–4.

This controversial report had a congressional mandate to assess the provision of health care services to homeless people. The resulting work provides background data and recommendations on housing, income, employment, mental illness, and deinstitutionalization, as these subjects relate to the problem. The document was debated on its release, when ten of the thirteen experts who contributed to it released a dissenting report, calling for national action on housing, wages, and benefits, in order to fight homelessness.

Rader, Victoria. *Signal through the Flames: Mitch Snyder and America's Homeless.* Kansas City, MO: Sheed & Ward, 1986. 272 pp. ISBN 0–934134–24–3.

The work of Washington, D.C.'s Community for Creative Non-Violence is explored here from a campaign viewpoint, with the development of the organization's various public efforts for peace and justice explored from inception to retrospective analysis. Significant insight into the workings of the community result from the availability of community members past and present, as well as the use of the group's extensive archives on its work.

Rossi, Peter. *Without Shelter: Homelessness in the 1980s.* New York: Priority Press Publications, A Twentieth Century Fund paper, 1989. 79 pp. ISBN 0–087078–234–7.

This volume examines some of the recent growth of homelessness, with a focus on research studies that have attempted to assess the problem.

Rowe, Michael. *Crossing the Border: Encounters between Homeless People and Outreach.* Los Angeles: University of California Press, 1999. 208 pp. ISBN 0520218833.

The first lengthy study of outreach work to the mentally ill homeless, this book depicts both a particular group of homeless people and their interactions with those who try to help them. The author was director of the New Haven ACCESS outreach project.

Sheehan, Susan. *Is There No Place on Earth for Me?* New York: Houghton Mifflin, 1982. 320 pp. ISBN 0–395–31871–8.

This carefully detailed account of the repeated hospitalization and treatment of Sylvia Frumkin, a chronically mentally ill woman in New York, paints a careful portrait of the deficiencies of the public mental health system and the toll of mental illness on one family.

Takahashi, Lois M. *Homelessness, AIDS, and Stigmatization: The NIMBY Syndrome in the United States at the End of the Twenti-*

eth Century. London: Oxford University Press, 1999. 296 pp. ISBN 0198233620.

Community opposition to the location of homeless shelters, as well as housing programs and health care facilities, often has been reported. This book looks at changing ways in which people with various characteristics are identified as being unacceptable neighbors and the ways in which governments act in such disputes.

Tidwell, Mike. *In the Shadow of the White House.* Rocklin, CA: Prima Publishing, 1992. 341 pp. ISBN 1–55958–108–5.

Images of homeless single men as users of drugs and alcohol abound; for those who work to pull themselves out of addiction, the road is hard and unwelcoming: a daily struggle with recovery, no transportation, no résumé, few chances at employment that pays enough to acquire housing or reunite a family. The author tells in gritty detail the efforts—frequently unsuccessful—of the men he encountered as a drug counselor in a transitional housing program in Washington, D.C.

Torrey, E. Fuller. *Nowhere to Go: The Tragic Odyssey of the Homeless Mentally Ill.* New York: Harper & Row, Publishers, 1988. 256 pp. ISBN 0–06–015993–6.

The careless depopulation of public mental hospitals resulted in the creation of Community Mental Health Centers and a vast new federal government structure of ready financing. But the seriously mentally ill, whose plight was supposed to be bettered by these developments, instead were displaced by the "worried well" who sought treatment at these facilities, and they found themselves unable to re-enter hospitals that had tightened admissions standards.

Watson, Sophie. *Housing and Homelessness: A Feminist Perspective.* Routledge & Kegan Paul, 1986. 186 pp. ISBN 0–7102–0400–0.

Although written from the point of view of British society, this is a worthwhile study of how Western society, in general, defines housing needs and provides for them, with a particular emphasis on the impact of these policies on women.

Winerip, Michael. *9 Highland Road: Sane Living for the Mentally Ill.* New York: Vintage Books, 1994. 449 pp. ISBN 0–679–76160–8.

The author writes on mental health issues for the *New York Times*. He spent two years getting to know staff and residents at a group home after he began reporting on the story when community opposition arose to the opening of the house. He presents the stories of those in the house over time, their struggles with illness and treatment, and their successes and failures.

International Homelessness

Avramov, Dragana, editor. *Coping with Homelessness: Issues to Be Tackled and Best Practices in Europe.* London: Ashgate Publishing Company, 1999. 85 pp. ISBN 1840149094.

The author is one of the leading analysts of homelessness in Europe and is active in international organizations. She presents some of the critical issues in the European Union and some of the leading initiatives to address homelessness.

Helvie, Carl O., and Wilfried Kunstmann, editors. *Homelessness in the United States, Europe, and Russia: A Comparative Perspective.* Toronto: Bergin & Garvey, 1999. 185 pp. ISBN 0897895010.

The editors of this book have backgrounds in health care and have assembled articles by professionals in seven industrialized nations to examine the prevalence, causes, trends, demographics, and health concerns of homelessness and to evaluate potential solutions. They also report on the resources available to the homeless by the public and private sectors in each of the seven countries studied: the United States, Germany, the Czech Republic, Denmark, England, Russia, and Spain.

Mickelson, Roslyn Arlin, editor. *Children on the Streets of the Americas: Globalization, Homelessness, and Education in the United States, Brazil, and Cuba.* New York: Routledge, 2000. 288 pp. ISBN 0415923220.

The number of street children in developed and developing nations is rising, often in the midst of prosperity. The authors compare the situation of homeless children in the United States, Brazil, and Cuba.

Humphreys, Robert. *No Fixed Abode: A History of Responses to the Roofless and the Rootless in Britain.* London: St. Martins Press, 1999. 240 pp. ISBN 0312225636.

The author examines the history of homelessness and transients in Britain. He considers legal and policy responses aimed at what homelessness represents, as well as the lack of attention to factors such as economic fluctuation, bad harvests, disease, and war.

Nonprint Resources

Materials that are important reference sources of keys to understanding homelessness are increasingly available through nonprint sources. Some of these include traditional media such as videos; others are purely derivatives of the electronic age and include web sites. Some of the primary resources are listed in this chapter.

Films and Videos

Many of the following films and videos have been recognized with awards for their depictions of the realities of homelessness and the stories of people experiencing it. Many of the works have been chosen to ensure a diverse picture of the differing needs and experiences of families and individuals, dimensions of urban, rural, and suburban homelessness, and the array of challenges in being homeless. The list below does not attempt to catalog feature films or made-for-television films that depict homelessness. These are often available as video rentals.

Some of the issues associated with homelessness include addiction, mental illness, street life, family violence, and death. These can be challenging for people of all ages and backgrounds. It is highly recommended that films and videos be screened before use in a group setting. Many distributors have additional printed information about the films, and some productions routinely include discussion guides and advocacy material to assist viewers with understanding the material shown. Librarians can also provide assistance in locating appropriate viewing material for various audiences.

A Call to Care: Stories of Courage, Compassion, and America's Health
57 minutes
Catholic Health Association, St. Louis, MO

Video/Action
1000 Potomac Street NW
Washington, DC 20007
(202) 338-1094
(202) 342-2660 FAX
www.vaf.org

This documentary tells the story of women who built Catholic health care in America. Focusing on several women through history and into the present, this Video/Action production depicts women addressing leprosy, AIDS, cancer, alcoholism, and primary health, through the use of historical photographs, diaries, letters, and witnesses.

A Healing Place
23 minutes
Fanlight Productions
4196 Washington Street, Suite 2
Boston, MA 02131
(800) 937-4113
(617) 469-4999
(617) 469-3379 FAX
www.fanlight.com

A profile of the staff and residents of the Orr Compassionate Care Center. The center is a respite program for homeless and elderly patients who have been released from the hospital, but who are not yet able to manage their own follow-up care on the streets or in their homes.

Almost Home
25 minutes
Fanlight Productions
4196 Washington Street, Suite 2
Boston, MA 02131
(800) 937-4113
(617) 469-4999
(617) 469-3379 FAX
www.fanlight.com

Depicts the lives of children in a homeless shelter in the Bronx. They live in an uncertain world but have valued relationships such as that with a recreation counselor who teaches them friendship, courage, and self-respect. Shows the family's transition to permanent housing. Narrated by the children.

Back Wards to Back Streets—Deinstitutionalization of Mental Patients
55 minutes
Filmakers Library
124 East 40th St., Suite 901
New York, NY 10016
(212) 808-4980
(212) 808-4983 FAX
www.filmakers.com

Efforts to reintegrate former mental patients into the community are largely regarded as unsuccessful, inadequate, and a major contributing cause of 1980s homelessness. This film looks at some successful community projects and some of the failures that affected individuals with mental illness.

Dark Side of the Moon
25 minutes
Fanlight Productions
4196 Washington Street, Suite 2
Boston, MA 02131
(800) 937-4113
(617) 469-4999
(617) 469-3379 FAX
www.fanlight.com

The story of three formerly homeless men with mental illness and how they succeeded in becoming part of their community, their families, and the solution for others in need.

Defending Our Lives
English—42 minutes; dubbed in Spanish—30 minutes
Cambridge Documentary Films
P.O. Box 390385
Cambridge, MA 02139
(617) 484-3993
(617) 484-0754 FAX
www.shore.net/~cdf

Domestic violence is a leading cause of homelessness for women and children. This film shows the scope of the problem and the realities of several women incarcerated for killing their abusers.

Healthcare for the Homeless
33 minutes
Fanlight Productions
4196 Washington Street, Suite 2
Boston, MA 02131
(800) 937-4113
(617) 469-4999
(617) 469-3379 FAX
www.fanlight.com

Basic health problems both cause and result from homelessness. This film depicts the work of those medical professionals who help homeless people and identifies some of the issues raised for the health care system.

Hope for the Future
45 minutes
Fanlight Productions
4196 Washington Street, Suite 2
Boston, MA 02131
(800) 937-4113
(617) 469-4999
(617) 469-3379 FAX
www.fanlight.com

Hope for the Future is a workshop on the education of homeless children and youth in California. This film describes strategies for helping to educate homeless children.

On a Mission
52 minutes
Filmakers Library
124 East 40th St. Suite 901
New York, NY 10016
(212) 808-4980
(212) 808-4983 FAX
www.filmakers.com

Homeless addicts on the streets of New York City talk about their lives, their dependency on drugs or alcohol, and the degradation, ill health, and poverty they experience.

100 Years of Service
9 minutes

Fanlight Productions
4196 Washington Street, Suite 2
Boston, MA 02131
(800) 937-4113
(617) 469-4999
(617) 469-3379 FAX
www.fanlight.com

An introduction to the Travelers Aid Society of Rhode Island and its Travelers Aid Medical Van that visits shelters in the downtown area of Providence, Rhode Island, providing medical care for people in need.

Peter, Donald, Willie, Pat
30 minutes
Fanlight Productions
4196 Washington Street, Suite 2
Boston, MA 02131
(800) 937-4113
(617) 469-4999
(617) 469-3379 FAX
www.fanlight.com

Four homeless men are shown as they go about their everyday lives in Boston, over a period of six months, staying in shelters and living on the streets.

Promises to Keep
57 minutes
Durrin Productions, Washington, DC
4926 Sedgwick Street NW
Washington, DC 20016
(800) 536-6843
(202) 237-6738 FAX
www.durrinproductions.com

This Oscar-nominated documentary tells the story of the four-year struggle by the late activist Mitch Snyder and the Washington-based Community for Creative Non-Violence to hold onto a previously vacant federal building for use as a shelter.

The Rebuilding of Mascot Flats
59 minutes
Filmakers Library
24 East 40th St., Suite 901

New York, NY 10016
(212) 808-4980
(212) 808-4983 FAX
www.filmakers.com

A group of homeless New Yorkers plans to rebuild an abandoned building. With the help of Habitat for Humanity, they fight the odds.

Shelter Stories
14 minutes
Fanlight Productions
4196 Washington Street, Suite 2
Boston, MA 02131
(800) 937-4113
(617) 469-4999
(617) 469-3379 FAX
www.fanlight.com

Young adults are the fastest growing population in shelters. This production looks at the experiences of five formerly homeless teenagers.

Shooting Back
30 minutes
Video/Action
1000 Potomac Street NW
Washington, DC 20007
(202) 338-1094
(202) 342-2660 FAX
www.vaf.org

Through workshops offered by professional news photographers in Washington, D.C., homeless children learn how to create their own powerful black-and-white images. The photographs express the harshness of daily life, but the film also shows their pleasure in the reaction of others to their talent. It also shows the young photographers at a gallery opening exhibiting their work.

Street Life: The Invisible Family
58 minutes
Fanlight Productions
4196 Washington Street, Suite 2

Boston, MA 02131
(800) 937-4113
(617) 469-4999
(617) 469-3379 FAX
www.fanlight.com

A portrait of homeless families in the Rocky Mountain area. The families are in search of work and support from programs where demand is high and resources often slim.

We are Not Who You Think We Are
12 minutes
Video/Action
1000 Potomac Street NW
Washington, DC 20007
(202) 338-1094
(202) 342-2660 FAX
www.vaf.org

Women prisoners tell about the roots and rootlessness of their lives, and, in the telling, relate stories of economic hardship, child abuse, and personal challenges. Filmed at Bedford Hills Corrections Facility in New York State, this is a story of those who are increasingly the next generation of homeless people: the prison population and their children.

What's Wrong With This Picture?
28 minutes
Fanlight Productions
4196 Washington Street, Suite 2
Boston, MA 02131
(800) 937-4113
(617) 469-4999
(617) 469-3379 FAX
www.fanlight.com

Four homeless families in Michigan provide a picture of the working poor whose low wages disallow them entry into the housing market.

Women of Substance
30 minutes
Video/Action

1000 Potomac Street NW
Washington, DC 20007
(202) 338-1094
(202) 342-2660 FAX
www.vaf.org

The impact of substance abuse on three women and their children is shown. It is also a story about their courage and determination to rebuild their lives. It is now known that the best way to help the children is to help the mothers, and the best way to reach the mothers is through their children.

Databases on the Web
Housing Cost Data:
U.S. Department of Housing and Urban Development——HUD User:
www.hud.gov
National Low Income Housing Coalition
www.nlihc.org

National Survey Data
International Union of Gospel Missions (IUGM)
www.iugm.org
Homelessness: Programs and the People They Serve—U.S. Department of Housing and Urban Development
www.urban.org/housing/homeless/homeless.html

Litigation Summaries
National Center for Poverty Law
www.povertylaw.org

Electronic Bibliographies
National Resource Center on Homelessness and Mental Illness, Policy Research Associates Inc.
www.prainc.org

Web Sites
U.S. Legislative and Budget Information:
thomas.loc.gov

**U.S. Benefit and Entitlement Programs
and Spending—"The Green Book":**
waysandmeans.house.gov/publica.htm

**Directories of U.S. Homelessness Advocacy
and Service Organizations:**
www.nationalhomeless.org

**Directories of European Homelessness
Advocacy and Service Organizations:
European Federation of National Organizations
Working with the Homeless**
*(Fédération Européenne d'Associations Nationales Travaillant avec les
Sans-Abri)* (FEANTSA)
www.feantsa.org

Directory of State Government Sites
janus.state.me.us/states.htm

European Union Sites
www.europa.eu.int

United Nations Centre for Human Settlements (UNCHS)
www.unchs.org

Glossary

AFDC   Aid to Families with Dependent Children, the primary cash assistance program for poor people, which became Temporary Assistance to Needy Families (TANF) in 1996.

Affordable housing   Usually the idea that a renter or homeowner will pay no more than 30 percent of income for housing.

Appropriation   The legal provision that establishes budget authority so that a federal agency can incur expenses and make payments for specific purposes. Annual appropriations provide the dollar figure against which an agency may spend.

Appropriations   The amount of funding Congress provides for a program or line item in a given year. Language sometimes sets the terms under which funds may be spent.

Assisted housing   Housing that is subsidized by federal, state, or other funds, so that the resident pays only a portion of the cost of the unit.

Authorization   Legislation that establishes or continues a federal program or agency, specifies its general goals and conduct, and usually sets a ceiling on the amount of money that can be appropriated for it. The original authorization for the federal McKinney Act programs was passed in 1987.

Block grants   Funding allocations to states and some cities that can be used for a variety of purposes. Block grants are funded by annual appropriations from Congress and allocated to states by formula. Block grants usually provide considerable flexibility to governors and mayors for delivering the services outlined in the block grant.

Budget authority   Authority to enter into obligations that will result in immediate or future outlays involving federal funds. Appropriation bills provide budget authority.

Chronically mentally ill   A state of severe and persistent mental illness that interferes with function and requires long-term mental health care.

Community Planning and Development (CPD)   One of the major offices within the U.S. Department of Housing and Urban Development (HUD), and the one with responsibility for the HUD homeless programs.

Consolidated Plan   The Consolidated Plan, or ConPlan, is the key planning document through which cities and states receive formula funding for several federal housing programs: Community Development Block Grants (CDBG), HOME, Emergency Shelter Grants (ESG), Housing Opportunities for People With AIDS (HOPWA), and programs, such as HOME, that require a Comprehensive Housing Affordability Strategy (CHAS).

Continuum of Care   A planning and funding concept of the U.S. Department of Housing and Urban Development, used to define the relation of homeless programs and services in a community. It was adopted under the Clinton Administration.

Creaming   The practice by service providers or program operators of selecting as program participants or tenants those individuals who are likely to achieve success in the program with less difficulty. This practice renders programs more free of challenging participants and gives programs a higher success rate.

Criminalization   The trend toward attaching criminal charges and penalties to common acts of homeless people, such as sleeping in public places (parks, etc.) and begging. Numerous jurisdictions have passed laws of this sort, as well as laws against sleeping or camping for extended periods in parks or on beaches.

Day labor   Usually manual labor jobs that are available to homeless and poor workers on a temporary basis. Workers are paid very low wages, charged for their equipment (such as gloves, brooms, etc.), and are not protected from unsafe conditions or practices. Workers wait at designated corners or go to hiring halls to seek jobs.

Deinstitutionalization   Officially defined by the National Institute of Mental Health (NIMH) as the prevention of inappropriate mental hospital admissions through the provision of community alternatives for treatment, the release to the community of all institutionalized patients who have been given adequate preparation for such discharge, and the establishment and maintenance of community support systems for noninstitutionalized people receiving mental health services in the community.

Discharge planning   The practice of preparing a person in an institution for release and integration into the community.

Doubling up   An accommodation to a housing crisis in which one or more households share housing.

Drop in center   Usually a daytime service for homeless clients that includes meals, clothing and laundry facilities, showers, support groups, and service referrals, but does not provide overnight accommodations.

Dual diagnosis   Also referred to as co-occurring disorders. Usually defined as the presence of both a substance abuse and a mental health problem. Also can refer to multiple diagnoses, such as drug abuse, mental illness, and HIV/AIDS.

EITC   Earned Income Tax Credit, a tax credit available to working poor people. EITC is intended to provide tax relief from the Social Security payroll tax and to increase work incentives.

Emergency Shelter Grant (ESG)   One of the components of the McKinney Act programs of the U.S. Department of Housing and Urban Development. ESG funds are distributed to cities and states by formula and can be used for shelter and services for homeless people. ESG funds are the only HUD McKinney funds that can be used for homelessness prevention.

Emergency shelter   Facilities that provide a place to stay, usually only at night. Some shelters operate on a first-come, first-served basis where shelter residents must leave in the morning and have no guaranteed bed for the next night. Some programs have a definite length of stay and only offer a specific number of nights to each person. Some programs serve only one group (domestic violence, youth, veterans) and some operate only during winter months.

Entitlement   Program mandating the payment of benefits to any person meeting eligibility requirements established by statute. The amount spent is not controlled by annual congressional appropriations. Entitlement programs include Social Security, Medicare, Aid to Families with Dependent Children (AFDC), and Medicaid.

Extremely Low Income   A household income below 30 percent of area median, as defined by HUD.

Fair Market Rents (FMR)   HUD's annual estimate of the market rent for a specific size housing unit in a given area. Fair Market Rents are then used to calculate payments for low income tenants using assisted housing programs, where HUD will pay the difference between 30 percent of the person's income and the FMR.

Family unification   Efforts to return children to their homes through the provision of adequate housing or other measures.

FEMA   The Federal Emergency Management Agency

Fiscal year (FY)   The federal government's annual accounting period, which begins October 1 and ends September 30.

Flophouse   Older hotels in which rooms are generally cheaply rented by the night. Often only a bed is provided, and rooms may actually be cubicles.

Food bank   A nonprofit clearinghouse for surplus or salvaged food that is usually redistributed to soup kitchens, meal programs, and shelters.

Food stamps   A national program to improve the ability of poor families to purchase food by providing monthly coupons for a specific dollar amount. The coupons can be used in most grocery stores.

Formula funding   Some federal funding arrangements are set in law and known as formulas. These are tied to certain factors, such as population, poverty levels, and unemployment.

General assistance   State and county funded programs designed to provide basic benefits to low income people who are not eligible for federally funded cash assistance. Jurisdictions determine general assistance benefit levels, eligibility criteria, and length of eligibility.

Gentrification   The transformation of a neighborhood to a higher income area, through the displacement of lower-rent tenants, renovation of buildings, and the opening of higher-priced businesses.

Homeless person   The McKinney Homeless Assistance Act, first passed in 1987, defines a homeless person as: an individual who lacks a fixed, regular, and adequate nighttime residence that is: a) a supervised publicly or privately operated shelter designed to provide temporary living accommodations (including welfare hotels, congregate shelters, and transitional housing for the mentally ill); b) an institution that provides a temporary residence for individuals intended to be institutionalized; or c) a public or private place not designed for, or ordinarily used as, a regular sleeping accommodation for human beings.

HUD   The U.S. Department of Housing and Urban Development, the key federal agency responsible for housing and homeless programs.

Low income   A household with income below 80 percent of metropolitan area median, as defined by HUD. HUD also uses the terms Extremely low income and Very low income.

McKinney   A general term for the set of federal programs created by the Stewart B. McKinney Homeless Assistance Act in 1987. The majority of existing programs now are HUD programs.

NIMBY   Not In My Back Yard, the resistance of neighborhoods to the siting of any facility or residence identified as undesirable, in this case, programs or housing for people with special needs.

NOFA   Notice of Funding Availability, the means by which the federal government distributes funds through competitive processes.

Outreach programs   Often street-based programs that contact homeless people to offer food, blankets, or other necessities to engage them in medical or other services, and to offer assistance on a regular basis to develop relationships.

Permanent housing   Programs for formerly homeless people that provide long-term housing, sometimes with rental assistance and/or support services for which homelessness is a primary requirement for program eligibility. Examples include the Shelter Plus Care Program, the Section 8 Moderate Rehabilitation Program for Single-Room Occupancy (SRO) Dwellings, and the Permanent Housing for the Handicapped Homeless Program administered by the Department of Housing and Urban Development (HUD). Permanent housing can also include specific set-asides of assisted housing units or housing vouchers for homeless clients by public housing agencies, or ordinary private market rental or other housing.

Poverty line   An official government measure produced by the U.S. Department of Health and Human Services to define the income needed to provide basic necessities.

Project based assistance   Rental assistance that is assigned to a specific housing development or building.

Rental assistance   Financial assistance to a low-income household to help meet housing costs.

Safe haven   A drop-in program intended to help engage mentally ill homeless people who might be wary of traditional shelters or other settings. Safe havens are small in scale, provide a variety of needed services (such as mail, laundry, and food) and have staff who are skilled at developing relationships with hard-to-reach individuals.

Safety net   A general term for the array of benefits and assistance available to meet basic needs, such as food, housing, income, and health care.

Shelter Plus Care   A permanent housing program with services for homeless people with disabilities. This program is a part of the HUD McKinney programs.

Skid Row   A general term for an impoverished urban area where cheap housing, day labor, and other marginal businesses can be found. Many Skid Row areas have been wiped out by gentrification.

Soup kitchen   A food program that includes soup kitchens, food lines, and programs distributing prepared breakfasts, lunches, or dinners.

SRO   Single Room Occupancy units are inexpensive rental units in hotel settings, where tenants share bath and kitchen facilities, if available.

Supplemental Security Income (SSI)   A federally administered means-tested income assistance program authorized by Title XVI of the Social Security Act. SSI was begun in 1974 to provide monthly cash payments in accordance with uniform, nationwide standards of eligibility for the needy aged, blind, and disabled. Disabled persons are those unable to engage in any substantial gainful activity by reason of a serious impairment that will result in death or that has lasted or will last for a continuous period of at least twelve months. Some states provide a state SSI supplement.

Supportive services   Programs providing job training, alcohol or drug treatment services, case management assistance, educational services, and the like. Services may be provided in conjunction with housing or shelter or in a different site.

System kids   Young people who have had multiple contacts with social services, foster care, and juvenile programs.

Temporary Assistance For Needy Families (TANF)   Block grant to states created by federal welfare reform under the Personal Responsibility and Work Opportunity Reconciliation Act of 1996, which established a new welfare system. The TANF block grant replaced Aid to Families with Dependent Children (AFDC).

Tenant based assistance   Rental assistance that is assigned to a specific individual and permits that person to find eligible housing according to the program's rules, rather than in a specific building.

Time limits   In welfare programs, the length of time a recipient will be eligible for benefits without an additional requirement, such as receiving only two years of benefits before having to be employed.

Transitional programs   Residential programs that provide a post shelter placement for persons before moving to permanent housing. Transitional programs funded under the McKinney Act allow a maximum stay of two years and offer support services to promote self-sufficiency and to help obtain permanent housing. A program may have a specific target population, such as persons with mental illnesses, runaway youths, victims of domestic violence, homeless veterans, etc.

Very low income   A level of household income below 50 percent of area median, as defined by HUD.

Working poor   Individuals or families who are employed in low-wage jobs and cannot afford other basic necessities, such as permanent housing, health care, etc. These individuals may not qualify for assistance programs because their income levels are too high. These low-wage workers do not receive direct government support but face economic problems related to the cost of child care, lack of buying power, and need for health insurance.

Index

283

About the Author

Mary Ellen Hombs holds a senior staff position at the Massachusetts Housing and Shelter Alliance. She is the author of *Welfare Reform, American Homelessness,* and *AIDS Crisis in America,* first edition.